D1011552

ROUND THE WORLD NON-STOP

ROUND THE WORLD NON-STOP

JOHN RIDGWAY
and ANDY BRIGGS

Patrick Stephens, Wellingborough

First published 1985

British Library Cataloguing in Publication Data

Ridgway, John
Round the world non-stop.
1. Voyages around the world—1951-
2. Yachts and yachting
I. Title II. Briggs, Andy
910.4'1 G419

ISBN 0-85059-757-9

Patrick Stephens Limited is part of the Thorsons Publishing Group

Photoset in 11 on 12 pt Plantin by Avocet Marketing Services, Aylesbury, Bucks.
Printed in Great Britain on Cream Antique Wove Vol 18 80 grm, and bound, by The Garden City Press, Letchworth, Herts, for the publishers, Patrick Stephens Limited, Denington Estate, Wellingborough, Northants, NN8 2QD, England.

Contents

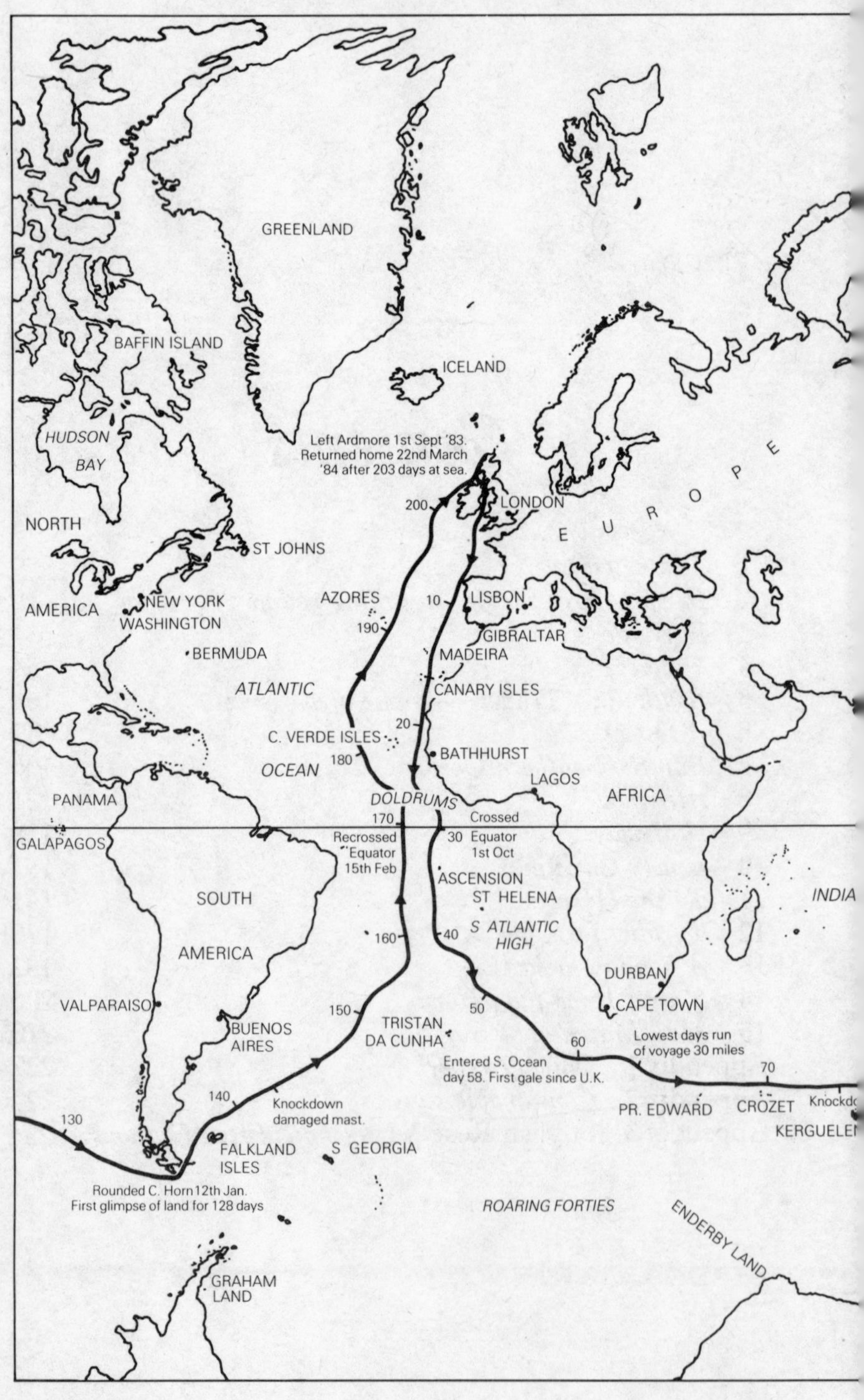
GREENLAND
BAFFIN ISLAND
ICELAND
HUDSON BAY
Left Ardmore 1st Sept '83. Returned home 22nd March '84 after 203 days at sea.
200
LONDON
E U R O P E
NORTH AMERICA
ST JOHNS
NEW YORK
WASHINGTON
AZORES
10
LISBON
190
GIBRALTAR
BERMUDA
MADEIRA
ATLANTIC
CANARY ISLES
20
C. VERDE ISLES
180
BATHHURST
OCEAN
LAGOS
PANAMA
DOLDRUMS
AFRICA
170
Crossed Equator 1st Oct
30
Recrossed Equator 15th Feb
GALAPAGOS
ASCENSION
ST HELENA
INDIA
SOUTH AMERICA
160
40
S ATLANTIC HIGH
DURBAN
VALPARAISO
150
50
CAPE TOWN
BUENOS AIRES
TRISTAN DA CUNHA
60
Lowest days run of voyage 30 miles
Entered S. Ocean day 58. First gale since U.K.
70
140
Knockdown damaged mast.
PR. EDWARD
CROZET
130
FALKLAND ISLES
S GEORGIA
Rounded C. Horn 12th Jan. First glimpse of land for 128 days
ROARING FORTIES
ENDERBY LAND
GRAHAM LAND

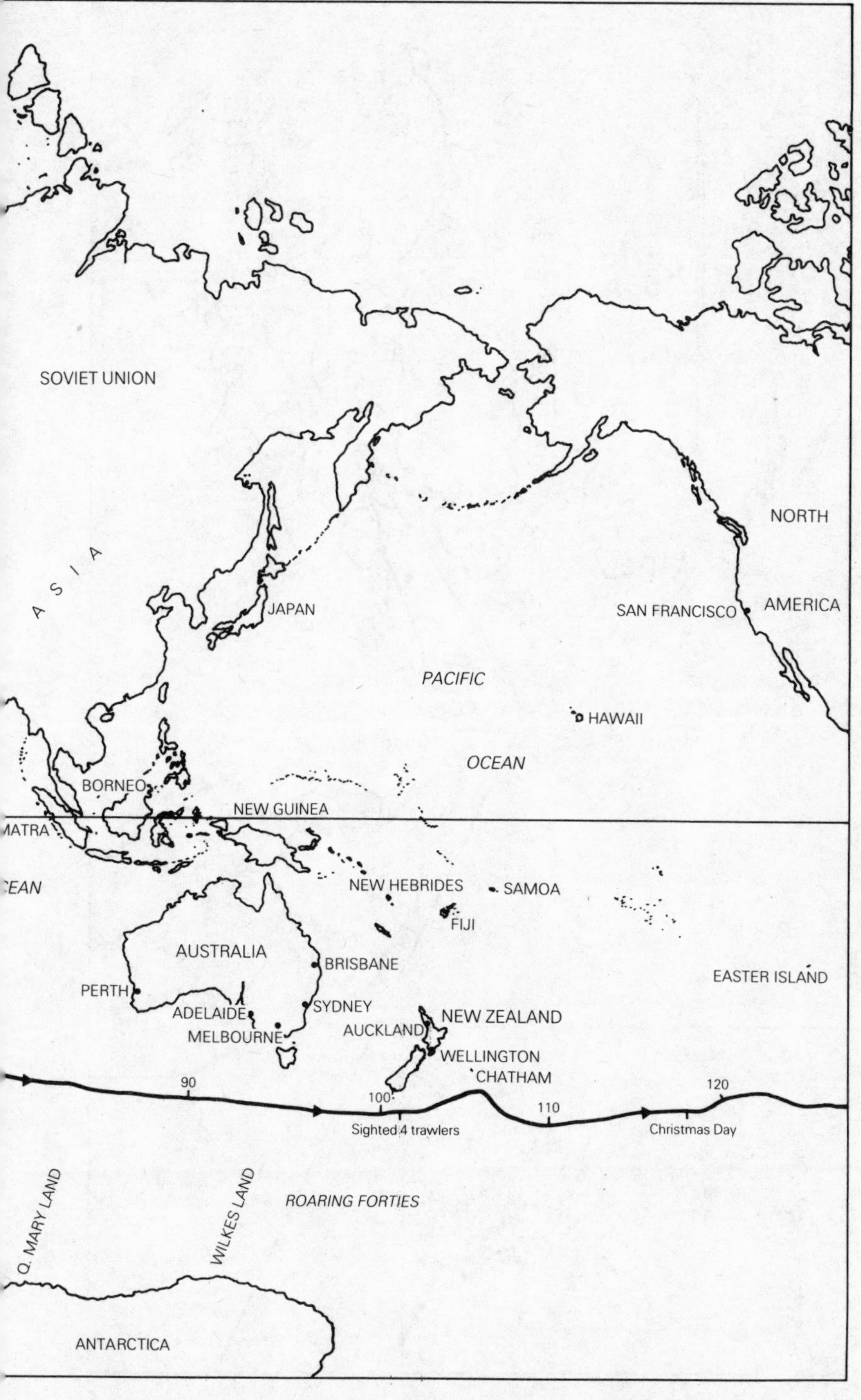
SOVIET UNION
A S I A
JAPAN
NORTH
AMERICA
SAN FRANCISCO
PACIFIC
OCEAN
HAWAII
BORNEO
NEW GUINEA
MATRA
CEAN
NEW HEBRIDES
SAMOA
FIJI
AUSTRALIA
BRISBANE
EASTER ISLAND
PERTH
SYDNEY
ADELAIDE
MELBOURNE
AUCKLAND
NEW ZEALAND
WELLINGTON
CHATHAM
90
100
110
120
Sighted 4 trawlers
Christmas Day
Q. MARY LAND
WILKES LAND
ROARING FORTIES
ANTARCTICA

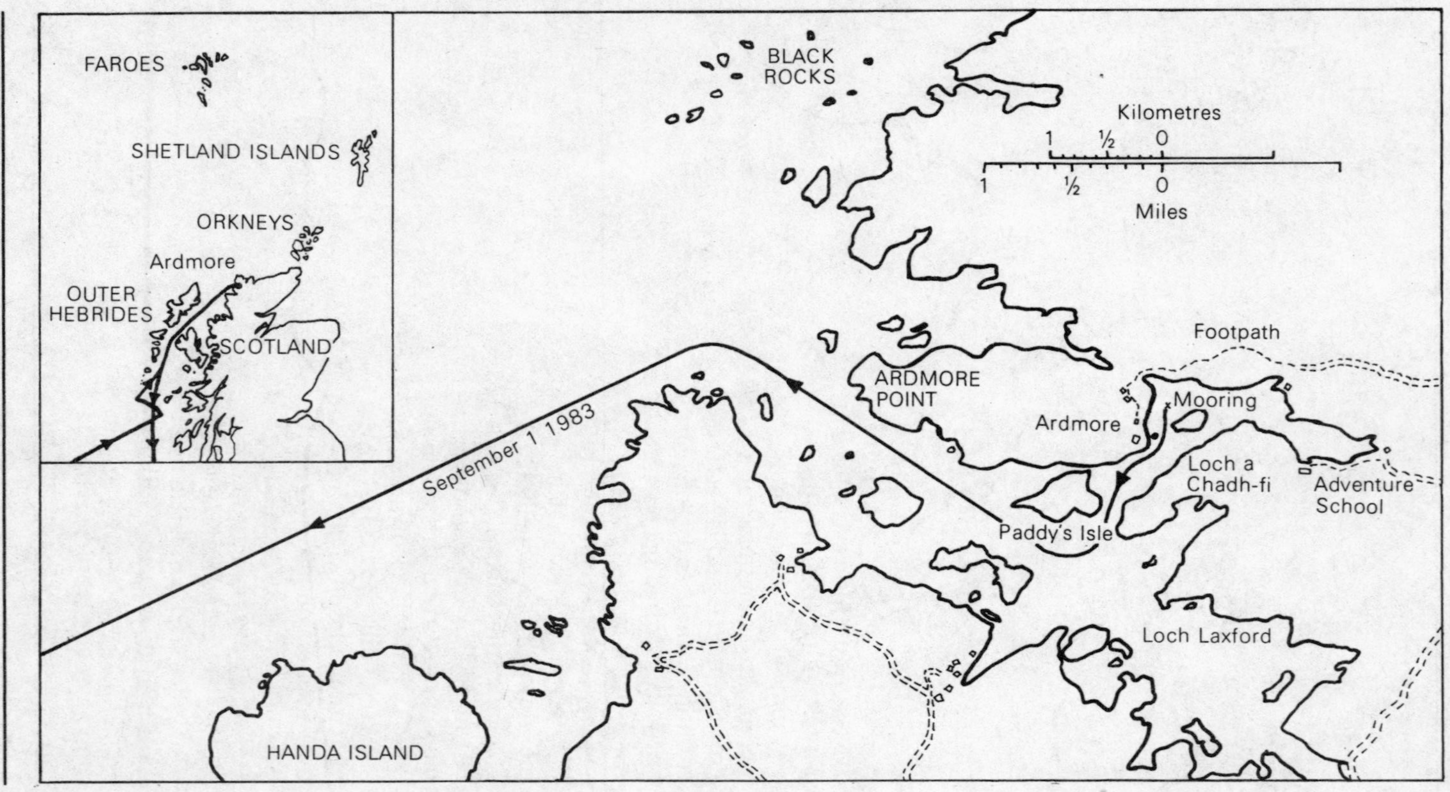
FAROES
SHETLAND ISLANDS
ORKNEYS
Ardmore
OUTER HEBRIDES
SCOTLAND
BLACK ROCKS
Kilometres
1 ½ 0
1 ½ 0
Miles
Footpath
ARDMORE POINT
Mooring
Ardmore
Loch a Chadh-fi
Adventure School
Paddy's Isle
September 1 1983
Loch Laxford
HANDA ISLAND

1

The magic carpet

John Ridgway

It was one of those early June days when anything seems possible. I'd taken the wildlife course down the coast to Handa Island from my home at Ardmore, on the far north-west coast of Scotland. We were aboard our small red trawler, and it was late afternoon. The green-topped island lay astern now, its tall cliffs splashed white by countless thousands of nesting guillemots, razorbills, and kittiwakes. It had been a grand day, and another half hour would see us back at the mooring at the foot of the crofts.

The sea was as calm and blue as the sky above. The horizon, that flat hard line, looked at its most inviting; once more it beckoned me, through the wheelhouse windows.

'Come, my friends, 'tis not too late to seek a newer world' I murmured to myself, over the throb of the diesel. And for a moment I turned the wheel to port, and felt the bow lift gently from the coastline towards the horizon.

'What did you say?' Mig Goulding had half-heard the quotation, close by my left shoulder. 'Oh, I was just thinking its time I set off on a trip again this winter,' I smiled as I brought us back on course for home. A few minutes passed, then I had an idea — I'm always trying to come up with ideas.

'Maybe I could sail the yacht down the Atlantic and join you for Christmas in Luanda, it can't be more than about ten degrees south of the Equator.' 'Eight' he replied, grave and accurate as ever. There was another pause, while we both thought out what such a project would involve.

Mig and his wife Susan, were staying with us for a few days, they'd just returned from a spell with the United Nations in New York. Susan is my wife Marie Christine's sister, and Mig was shortly to take up a new post as British Ambassador to Angola.

'I think we'd better just wait until I've had a chance to weigh-up the situation in Luanda, before we go firm, but it would be lovely if we could arrange something,' he said, and I smiled. Mig clearly thought that in contrast to New York, Angola was about as remote as Mars. Any family visit would be a treat, in the wilderness.

I turned the boat into Loch Laxford and headed for the entrance to Loch a Chadh-fi, an L-shaped sea loch leading off the northern shore of Laxford. No swell ever penetrates as far as our moorings in there. Mig is a keen ornithologist and our conversation turned away to the day he'd so much enjoyed on Handa, but my mind remained on the winter voyage now in prospect.

That sunny day was June 6 1983. At the time, I was hoping to sail for Angola in early October, some four months away. This gave me plenty of time to prepare for a four or five month cruise, and the yacht had undergone a big refit only the previous winter. She is a Bowman 57-foot ketch, built of glassfibre for us in 1975. Her role is sail-training at the John Ridgway School of Adventure at Ardmore, a job she does very well with her powerful rig and 14 bunks. But as well as her trips to Handa and instructional cruises to the Outer Hebrides, St Kilda and the distant Faroes, we'd raced her with a crew of 12, mostly made up of instructors from the adventure school, in the 1977/78 Whitbread Round-the-World Yacht Race.

I let the days drift by, I was intensely involved with the courses at the school. There is practically no darkness in mid-June, in the far north of Scotland, and life is at its most active then. We were running a course for 50 young men and women from the YTS (Youth Training Scheme) at the main school on the far side of the loch, the yacht was on a cruise to St Kilda, while at Ardmore itself we were running a wildlife course. On top of this, our flock of 40 sheep had just finished lambing, and we were in the middle of harvesting the spring crop of salmon from our fish farm. So Mig's letter from Angola came as a bit of a shock. The trip was off. Luanda was almost a Soviet port on the west coast of Africa, and one of strategic importance to the Russians at that. Clearly a yacht with a name like '*English Rose VI*' would hardly be welcomed there.

There would have to be some sort of a re-think. I decided to have a chat with Andy; a cup of coffee at our crofthouse on the hillside one evening would be the best time.

'I'm afraid the trip to Angola is off for this winter . . . how about making a non-stop trip round the world?'

'I'm on' he replied, quick as a flash. Andy Briggs is Head of

Sailing at the School; most of his time is spent on *English Rose VI*, which he skippers on all her cruises away from Ardmore. But he also takes out *English Rose IV*, a 30-foot sloop I sailed alone across the Atlantic, several years ago, and in which we entered one of the school instructors in an *Observer* singlehanded transatlantic race. Then there are the Wayfarer dinghies and the *Rebecca*, a gaff-rigged Shetland model we had built in those northern isles: Andy will sail anything.

A couple of days later we sailed the yacht across the Minch to the tiny crofting village of Mariveg, on the east coast of Lewis. It was fairly breezy coming home next morning, and the crew from the businessmen's course, those hardy souls who thought they would prefer a couple of days on the yacht, to the two-day mountaineering expedition, were not alone in feeling seasick. I wondered if I was crazy, risking everything for another long sailing voyage. But wasn't it always the same? My natural lack of confidence combines easily with seasickness, I'd feel keen enough once we reached the land. But one thing never changed: the panicky feeling of over-commitment.

I find the rhythmic swing of the scythe, during the odd stolen hour of bracken-cutting, on the steep hillside where the green of the croft runs into the edge of the wood, sometimes helps me sort out the tangle of a problem. One of the big problems at this time, was the size of the crew for a non-stop circumnavigation. Clearly food and water were limiting factors, but I felt sure we could carry enough for up to four people for a couple of hundred days. I drew on previous experience, before discussing it with Andy. The most successful team I'd ever been in, on the sea, was when Chay Blyth and I rowed across the North Atlantic from Cape Cod to Ireland during 92 days of the summer of 1966. We knew each other well before the trip, and we were entirely dependent on one another throughout the voyage. I'd been on less happy trips since, notably the nine months of the 1977/78 Whitbread Round-the-World Yacht Race, when we'd had a crew of up to 13 on one leg in the Southern Ocean, including a television crew.

This time, I thought I'd revert to the old plan of just two inter-dependent men; three would be divisive, four would likely be hungry. Andy agreed. We'd have to sail on September 1, get down the Atlantic, turn east and pass below Africa, New Zealand and Cape Horn on South America. Then it would be a race to get back up to Ardmore in time for the instructors' course for the 1984 season, which was scheduled to begin at the end of March. To be successful, we would have to make the fastest non-stop passage round the world ever achieved by a sailing boat.

As we talked, sipping our coffee, and looking out across the loch to the mountains of Foinaven, Arkle and Ben Stack, I realised I hardly knew the companion with whom I might be stuck at sea for 200 days or more.

Andrew Briggs had answered my advertisement in a yachting magazine: 'Wanted: Skipper for 57-foot ketch'. At 24, he was one of the younger applicants, but he had built his own 25-foot sloop in marine ply while still at school in York. Then he'd sailed her, more or less alone, right round Britain, while studying for a civil engineering degree at Southampton University. I arranged to meet him outside the front door of the Ritz Hotel in London, at 2.30 pm on January 12 1983. To be safe, I also fixed up some other interviews at the Boat Show during that week.

The business lunch at Langan's went on a little longer than planned, and with some alarm I realised it was already 2.25 pm. I made my excuses and left, promising to bring the potential skipper back for coffee. I dashed across Piccadilly and there was Andy, somewhat casually attired, standing rather self-consciously beside the giant doorman. It was raining softly.

'Hello, A. Briggs I presume?' The tall thin figure smiled awkwardly, and swallowed. Woolly hair, specs and a beard; more than a bit shy.

'Look, I'm afraid I've been rather delayed. We're going to have to go back to a restaurant for coffee. It's a 'chi-chi' sort of place and some of the clients are pretty sharp dressers, keep close behind me and we'll go in at speed. Look as if you own the place. Charge straight up the aisle and sit down with your back to the rest of the people, this way they won't notice you aren't wearing a tie.' I set off across the street at a trot, wondering if he'd follow. Months later, he told me he'd read somewhere, that most human relationships stand or fall on the first five minutes of contact.

Andy proved to be a good Skipper. The other instructors called him 'Bamber', after Gascoigne of the *University Challenge* programme. He did look a bit like a professor and took life very seriously. For my part, the single outstanding quality which intrigued me about Andy, was that he was the first person I'd had on the yacht who was not obsessed with a need to go as fast as possible; it was this which drew me to him as a companion for a seven month non-stop voyage. I realised he would find it a little more difficult to go on the voyage than the simple 'I'm on', which he'd given me when I first suggested the idea. For a start, there was bound to be some resistance from his girlfriend Marie. There was also the uncertainty of his career. He'd already worked with a firm of civil engineers in London, and found the life not to his liking. His rather introverted personality made for a continuous agonising about his future on three levels: personal, career, and sailing. This sudden opportunity to sail round the world, would allow him to realise something very close to the childhood dreams which had surrounded the building of his own boat, during his schooldays. In early July, Andy took a few days off, between cruises to the Faroes and St Kilda. He headed straight for Glasgow, ostensibly to buy personal stores for the trip, but more realistically to explain to Marie why he wouldn't be spending the coming winter with her. I remembered the broken engagements and other personal dramas which had accompanied the nine months of the Whitbread Race. And there had been similar problems on the trips to the Amazon, Patagonia, Spanish Sahara, everywhere in fact: there are always so many reasons why one shouldn't do something. On his return to Ardmore, Andy was a bit wobbly, and he spent several hours while I was out at sea, explaining to Marie Christine how he'd decided not to go on the trip after all, but luckily she managed to persuade him to change his mind. When I heard of his uncertainty, I felt a sense of relief, if he'd had no doubts at all I'd have been rather uncertain of his grasp of the task we'd set ourselves.

My own mind was not without turmoil either, but at least I'd been through it all many times before, and as usual Marie Christine was a real dynamo. Also as usual, the real struggle took place in my head, mostly at three o'clock in the morning. While Andy had been away in Glasgow I'd had my 45th birthday, and although I'd managed my fastest time ever, on the morning five-mile run the following day, I could sense some danger of the shutters coming down on many years of physical adventure. I'd had a disc out of my spine four years back, and the injury continued to cause trouble. But I tried to keep one thought uppermost in my mind: when Chay and I had set out to row across the Atlantic, there'd been two other men attempting the same crossing. Their boat was found by a Canadian frigate, it was upside-down in the middle of the ocean, but there was no sign of the crew. This memory has served as something of a benchmark in my life, and I've tried to look on every day since then as a bonus. And now, 17 years later, I was feeling rather desperately that I must try to recapture a similar sensitivity to events and feelings.

Seven months on the ocean, with the solitude of being alone on watch, but without the total loneliness of sailing singlehanded, would be a great solace. Living in a remote place like Ardmore, which can best be reached only by boat, and living a life which leans heavily towards independence, I'd found the five cities of the Whitbread Race: Portsmouth, Cape Town, Auckland, Rio de Janeiro and back to Portsmouth, rather obtrusive on my own personal idea of sailing round the world. So many people in a small place, the commitment to sponsors over such a long period, and the urgency of writing a book and making a TV film as we went along, all these things combined to make the project more of an ordeal than an uplift for the spirit. This is not to say it wasn't a valuable experience, it certainly was — there's no steel without fire, and I got plenty of fire on that trip.

Ever since coming to Ardmore in 1964, I've had a mental picture of the point where the road runs down to the water's edge at Skerricha, which is a solitary croft at the head of the sea loch. In my mind's eye I see that narrow strip of water, glinting gold in the evening sunlight, as a sort of magic carpet which stretches right round the planet. Given the right boat, and it took a long time to

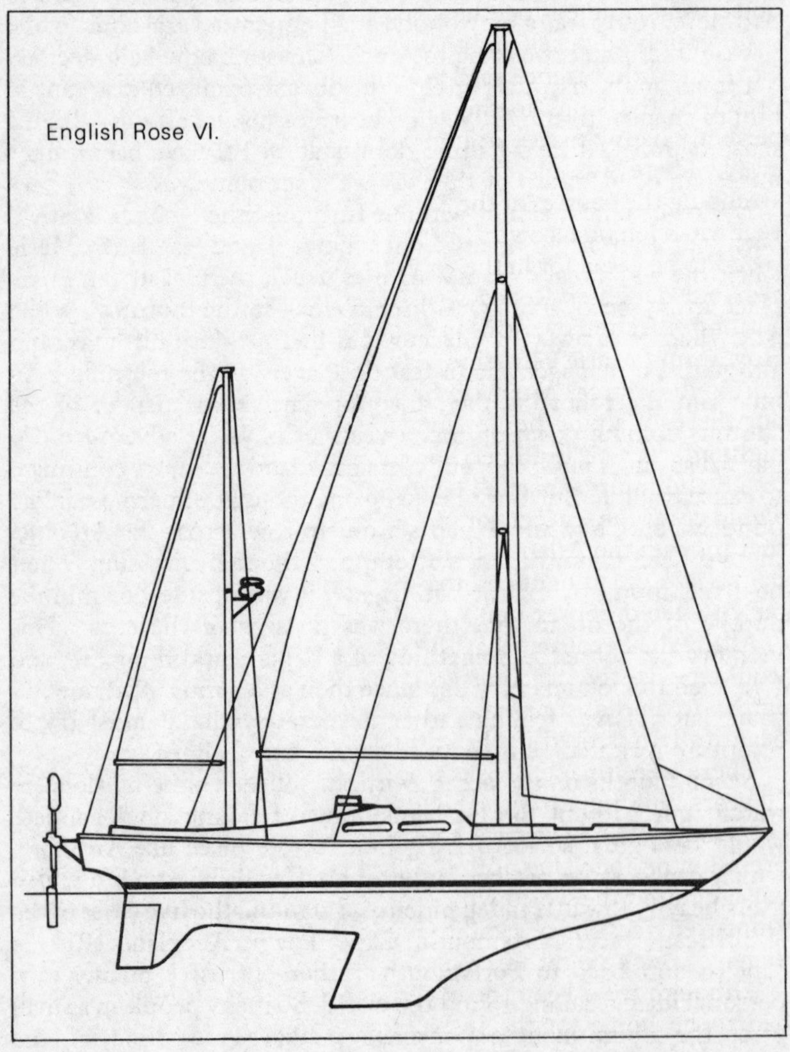
English Rose VI.

get it, I would set off and pick up the unbroken rhythm of the oceans and the seasons, along with the flying fishes, the whales and the albatrosses. I suppose it was originally just a form of escapism, a means of getting away from the pressures I felt as a young Parachute Regiment officer. But 19 years later the pressures didn't seem so different, and now the 57-foot ketch lay gleaming white at her moorings, under the wood at the foot of the croft.

If the Whitbread Race hadn't worked out quite as I'd hoped, well then, this was the time to make the voyage my way — non-stop. There would be no sponsorship, no television crew, and no book to be written. Neither would there be the personality problems which spring from having 13 people, all with differing objectives, jammed together in a small boat for nine months.

Of course such self-indulgence is only gained at a cost. Marie Christine didn't want to sail around the world a second time, she'd preferred the stops to the sailing. This time, she said, she was perfectly happy to stay at home and look after things while I was away. There was plenty to do, the office work concerned with arranging the courses at the School of Adventure for the following year was a job on its own. Then there was the salmon farm, and the sheep to be cared for in the winter months. On top of this, our 16-year-old daughter Rebecca was starting at a new school in the autumn. I fretted over this in the wee small hours of many a night. How would Marie Christine cope with being all alone at Ardmore during the winter? Much of the time she would be the only person out there. Walking home along the rocky snow-covered path at night after a visit to Rebecca at Gordonstoun, she couldn't afford to fall and injure herself. There would be the usual snows, and ice would cover the sea loch for some of the time. Winter storms would roar in from the Atlantic to damage buildings. Worst of all would be the lack of sunlight and the short grey days, she'd need to keep busy to avoid depression.

All in all, I realised that the reality of the next several months would be vastly different from the exciting prospect so easily agreed to on that sunny day in June, when the green hills were so beautifully mirrored in the calm waters of the loch.

There were financial risks too. Marie Christine and I had spent 20 years building up the school, and the yacht was a major part of everything. The insurance company was asking for a 25 per cent premium on the value of the boat to cover her for a seven-month voyage round the world with a crew of only two. I decided to sail uninsured, trusting our ability not to lose the mast or cause similar damage which might force us into a far-distant port.

Although we'd keep the speed down to avoid damage, we still had to be home for the instructors' course in March 1984. To achieve this, we would have to break the record for any vessel to sail non-stop round the world, by about 90 days. According to D.H. 'Nobby' Clarke, the authority on sailing records, the fastest non-stop true circumnavigation, passing south of Africa, Australia, New Zealand, and South America, was a Dutch singlehander by the name of Pleun Van Der Lugt in 1981–82. He sailed his 35-foot ketch from/to Zierikee in Holland in three minutes under 286 days. After we'd successfully completed our circumnavigation, Nobby phoned me at Ardmore, he told me he'd heard the Dutchman had not made his trip without stopping after all, but throughout our voyage, 286 days was the target we set ourselves to beat.

Of course boats have sailed round the world in well under 200 days, but not without stopping. For me, the stopping for rest and repairs at Cape Town, Auckland, and Rio de Janeiro, is like Sebastian Coe running four separate 440 yards races on successive days, and then claiming the world mile record.

As far as we could tell, the furthest any two people had previously sailed non-stop, was the 14,000-mile voyage of Bernard and Francoise Moitessier, from the Pacific islands to Europe by way of Cape Horn in 1966. We would have to double that distance.

While it was to be expected that two men sailing a longer boat should be able to make the passage considerably faster than one man sailing alone, the stresses of the extra speed on the gear would also push the boat closer to failure.

All of this would give us something to get our teeth into during the long empty stretches, but I knew very well from other voyages that comparisons can be odious.

I'd written in my diary for June 13 1983 'better to live one day as a tiger, than a thousand as a sheep', but really I felt much more like a sheep. I searched around for inspiration to help me change from a comfortable sheep into a daring tiger. The World Athletics Championships in Helsinki helped. I watched Daley Thomson on television as he came back from persistent injury to win the decathlon. Then on August 14, Tom Maclean phoned to tell me of his second record-breaking sail across the Atlantic, in the smallest boat ever to make the crossing. He urged me to go ahead with the circumnavigation, life is for living not waiting to die. I thought of the old anti-tank platoon I'd commanded in 3 Para, back in the early 1960s, Chay Blyth had been platoon Sergeant and Tom a young Private soldier. Surely, if Tom could cross the Atlantic in a 7-foot boat, Andy and I could get round the world in a 57-foot ketch?

The days began to run out, and there were the usual delays in delivering vital stores and equipment: it was the time of annual summer holidays. As I worked at sorting out the salmon from the grilse in our small salmon farm, I wondered how MC would manage the sales of the fish, after we'd left on September 1. Andy was away on the final cruise to St Kilda, and when he did return, I still had to make some day-trips down to Handa Island with the final course of the season. The last few days went in a rush: briefing Malcolm Sandals on the long list of maintenance jobs for the winter, while we filled plastic jerry cans with rice, sugar and flour in his workshop down by the water's edge. His wife Jennie helped as well, varnishing pyramids of tins and listening patiently, as I went through the scores of things which could go wrong on the office side of things, where she helped MC.

With only three days left, we laid the yacht against the skeleton pier, and began the loading. I hoped the couple of fresh coats of anti-fouling paint would keep the gooseneck barnacles at bay for seven months. I knew only too well, what a slowing effect these 4-inch long creatures on the hull could have in light airs.

I think few people, seeing all the rush of the last few days, gave us much chance of getting beyond Land's End without having to stop for repairs. Modifications had been going on for so many weeks now, it was difficult to see how everything could stop suddenly, and the boat just sail away for 200 days. But I felt differently. The yacht was now reaching her peak, her work at the school, and all the mileage of her first circumnavigation, had only been sea-trials for this non-stop voyage. We had a very well-proven boat. Other peoples' scepticism was not new to me.

Eventually, the human chain of helpers from the course passed the last box of varnished tins along from the workshop, across the grass and along the short rocky causeway linking the islet with the pier to the mainland. Out over the slippery telephone pole framework of the pier the box was passed, and down into the saloon. Andy jotted down its location in one of the many cupboards and closed his book, he knew where everything was, and he was confident we had everything we needed. And we had beaten the threatening rain.

The yacht left the pier on the evening tide, and returned to her moorings, just a couple of hundred yards away. Next day we heard on the radio that the high pressure system over the British Isles was collapsing, and once more gales were mentioned on the shipping forecast.

On the last evening but one, we gave a small party. Andy's parents arrived, and a number of local friends. We secured the fishing boat alongside the yacht at her moorings, and although everyone did their best to sound cheery, it was a damp and cheerless evening. More than once I caught Andy's eye, it did seem a little bizarre to be sipping champagne, only hours before sailing off for 200 days. Surely there was something still left undone? I'd dived to check the moorings, and I'd got 160 bags of coal, as well as a good stock of logs, up the hill to the houses for the winter fires. We'd booked three new types of course for the following season: for teams of junior, middle and senior managements, and I was looking forward to working up programmes for these during the voyage.

On the last full day, I spent the morning with my daughter Rebecca, washing the paintwork in the Skipper's cabin and storing away the contents of all the heavy bags we'd brought down the hill from the croft during the past weeks. I don't know if she noticed, but I felt terribly sad at the thought of saying goodbye next day.

That evening we gave an end of season party for the instructors in the house. They'd responded splendidly to the extra challenge of getting the boat ready in time, and we'd never have managed without them. Now it was time to see if we'd got it right.

2

From Mirror dinghy to sailing round the world

Andy Briggs

Blinking in its light like a surprised owl, the dazzling searchlight beam of a passing ferry drained all but the last of my enthusiasm for my first circumnavigation. The Isle of Wight is not perhaps the most hazardous land mass to circumnavigate, but as a 20-year-old singlehander I found the trip a major undertaking.

At 24 years of age after several years of adventurous wandering I found myself at sea on board a 57-foot ocean racer bound non-stop around the world. The Skipper was almost twice my age, our interests and characters widely different, I wasn't the obvious choice to go along. But opportunities were in the habit of turning out right for me.

My earliest recollection of being interested in sailing dates back to 1967. I saw on the television the return to Greenwich of Francis Chichester after his epic circumnavigation. Being a mere eight years old I didn't appreciate the achievement so my interest was a fleeting curiosity. Some years passed before the interest was re-awakened.

Sailing is a pastime which neither of my parents pursue, my love for the sport was kindled on holiday in Ireland. For two successive summers, our family of four children, stayed in a cottage close to White Rock Sailing Club on the shores of Strangford Lough. The club held races twice weekly, and I watched through binoculars, fascinated. During the day local youngsters were often out sailing their dinghies in and around the bay. I longed to join in, but instead I reluctantly made do with a tiny inflatable and an old heavy rowing boat.

At the end of each holiday we returned to York, which is 40 miles from the sea, and ideas about sailing were soon forgotten. A large part of my spare time was spent building an assortment of model aircraft, boats and hovercraft. My bedroom served as a workshop, but after several years the smell of resin and paint continually permeating the house, not to mention the chaotic untidiness which frequently cut off my bed from the door, persuaded my parents that a bedroom should be a bedroom. We scanned the local paper and eventually tracked down a reasonably priced second-hand chicken hut, which my father turned into a small workshop furnished with a bench, shelves and electric lighting. It became my workshop, and I guarded it jealously, always preferring to work alone at whatever project was in progress.

At school I became known as a 'sweat', because I seemed to get continuously good grades and never put a foot wrong. I was frightfully shy and usually sat in a back corner with one or two friends, hoping to avoid attention. If my name was mentioned or if I was asked a question, blushing and stammering were the usual results. I dreaded the weekly games lesson: if teams were being picked, it was usually me and two or three others who were left until the end. We were given two choices, either knocking a ball about on a vacant pitch or cross-country running. I chose the latter, and ran until out of sight, then hid. Anything was preferrable to being the goalkeeper in a game, having to stand around until shivering, and then in a rare moment of activity, failing miserably under the glaring eyes of critical team-mates.

Summer sports were tolerable, even enjoyable, since the result of throwing the javelin, discus, or shot, depended on my own efforts rather than teamwork.

Friends were hard to cultivate, and since I was able to do nearly all I wished to do, alone, I became something of a loner. Most of my acquaintances drifted away to seek more agreeable companions.

After the second summer at Strangford Lough, my mother secretly ordered a kit to build a 10-foot Mirror dinghy. To my surprise and delight the parcels arrived one November day, and the little craft was swiftly constructed without a hitch. My father did most of the work while I stood by holding the tools.

We quickly taught ourselves the rudiments of sailing, on a clay pit near home. During the summer holidays we trailed the dinghy to the Lake District. We sailed every day and in the evenings I read *Swallows and Amazons*. What bliss!

With the passing years schoolwork became an increasingly tiresome nuisance, exams were looming but my thoughts were about building a yacht to sail across the Atlantic. At the age of 14

I'd begun trying to raise the capital to buy a kit for a 17-foot Lysander. Two newspaper rounds every day brought in a few pounds each week, and selling eggs laid by two dozen hens added a few more coppers.

The Lysander never materialised. Instead I built a 25-foot wooden sloop similar in appearance to a Folkboat. She was christened *Kinnego*, after my mother's home in Northern Ireland. The project began the day after sitting my final 'O' level exam and occupied nearly all my spare time while studying for 'A' levels; more than once I considered giving up — it was a daunting task.

After completing 'A' levels I decided to take a break from studying. Instead of transferring from school to university straight away, I worked my passage to Hong Kong as a deckhand aboard a container ship, and spent 11 months working at the Outward Bound School there. My parents hoped that dealing with people would help extricate me from the shell of shyness into which I was retreating. Instead of instructing outdoor pursuits, I found myself largely involved with boat maintenance, and this suited me fine.

My university career at Southampton was unexceptional. I gained a degree in civil engineering which might have been better had I sailed less often. Singlehanded sailing had always been my intention, so I didn't look for a crew. Sailing *Kinnego* was a compelling challenge. I loved the freedom of the sheltered Solent and the tranquility of an unruffled anchorage. During the summer vacations I cruised with *Kinnego* to the Channel Islands. I explored Cornwall, and circumnavigated Britain.

They were happy years, despite a solitary existence. I was rarely lonely when sailing. When in harbour I occupied my time walking, reading and listening to the radio. I geared my life to the sun, going to bed early and setting sail at first light. The singlehanding developed resourcefulness and self-reliance, it gave me fulfillment and memories. Nevertheless I longed to find an agreeable first mate, realising that once the elements of seamanship had been mastered, the compelling challenge might degenerate to boredom and loneliness.

A professional career seemed the logical step after university; I joined a firm of consulting engineers, but my time there was short-lived. Three months of cycling into London at 8.30 am, sitting at a desk all day, then returning home at 5.30 pm, left me demoralised and depressed. During the previous four years I had become accustomed to sailing whenever I liked, adjusting my daily routine to suit what I wanted to do each day. I was ill-prepared for an ordered city lifestyle. There had to be more to life. The thought of resigning had been maturing in my mind for some time, I knew it was the only way to regain my freedom. I took the plunge one

Monday morning, and cycled away at lunchtime, carefree and happy.

I had a few hundred pounds and thought vaguely about cruising around Europe with *Kinnego* for most of the next summer, and then see what turned up in the autumn. This idea was abandoned in favour of working as a sailing instructor, a strange choice of occupation for a young man fraught with shyness. The prospect of handling a crew of strangers verged on a nightmare. I needn't have worried, after six months with the Tighnabruaich Sailing School on the west coast of Scotland I no longer lowered my eyes to look at my feet when talking to people. Also I met a girl called Marie from nearby Glasgow.

During the autumn I applied for several jobs, one or two simply out of curiosity. The thought that I could handle a 57-foot ocean racer, when my sailing had largely been confined to *Kinnego*, seemed inconceivable. To my surprise, John Ridgway invited me to an interview, and to my even greater surprise he offered me the position of Skipper of *English Rose VI*.

Arriving at Ardmore for the first time is something of a shock for most people. The barren landscape looks cold and forbidding; Ardmore itself can only be reached by boat, or a half-hour walk along a hilly track. I arrived with Marie in mid-March 1983, and as she turned her car to begin the 300-mile drive south to Glasgow, I felt a twinge of despair. What a place to spend the summer, why on earth had I accepted the job? Several other jobs had been offered, but they didn't sound quite my cup of tea. The thought of beating through gales and exploring the magical lochs on the west coast of Scotland was my idea of enjoyment, rather than cocktail parties and beach barbecues on the windless Mediterranean. While at university I read several of John's books, and he became a personality I admired and wished to emulate; so to be able to work with him was not far short of winning the Pools.

Shortly after my arrival at Ardmore the yacht returned from a winter refit, and I was able to begin the lengthy task of familiarising myself with the miles of rope and numerous sails. The early weeks of sailing were blessed with moderate winds, and there were no disasters apart from two torn sails and a broken stanchion: John was not amused. But by June the summer courses were well in hand and running smoothly.

'Andy, how would you like to sail non-stop round the world?' I was somewhat taken aback by John's suggestion, but found myself saying I thought it rather a good idea. We looked closely at one another, to see if the other was being serious. The basic threads of our plan for the circumnavigation were woven that evening. We discussed the optimum size of the crew: four became three, then finally, a week later, we decided on two. Our starting date needed to be during the first week of September. An earlier departure meant missing the final weeks of the adventure school's season, and leaving later increased the risk of meeting a gear-smashing Equinoctial storm right at the start.

A week after the first discussions, we felt the time had come to announce the planned voyage to the 15 or so instructors. They had all become aware of increased activity aboard the yacht and were sure something was afoot. Their reactions were mixed, several were understandably bitterly disappointed not to be included, and others were full of enthusiasm for the project. Any resentment soon disappeared, and the whole team rallied round to give the moral and practical support without which John and I couldn't have sailed only 11 weeks later.

My parents have never objected to my wandering adventures, but I felt this round-the-world trip might be the final straw. Instead of telling them directly, I wrote to my sister, asking her to break the news to them gently. This she did, and when I next phoned, my father said he'd expected it!

Marie's reaction was less enthusiastic. I have the annoying habit of being tactless or saying the wrong thing, so breaking the news almost resulted in Marie slamming the phone down. But three weeks later I was able to get away from Ardmore to see her and try to smooth things out. We spent two days on Arran, then several days shopping, to buy a year's supply of soap, toothpaste, suncream, clothing suitable for the tropics, and a personal stereo with tapes and a lot of Duracell batteries. A wide angle lens for my Rollei camera, film, two extra pairs of seaboots, a third pair of spectacles, and a growing pile of other gear accumulated as my bank balance plummetted.

John had his appendix removed prior to the 1977/78 Whitbread Race, but now there wasn't time for me to undergo surgery. However I did find an obliging dentist who gave up a lunch hour to fill two suspect teeth.

Six days away from Ardmore was all that could be spared. September 1 was looming alarmingly close. Saying goodbye to Marie, knowing that seven months were to pass before meeting her again was not easy, and we both shed a tear or two.

During my absence from Ardmore, the instructors scrubbed the bottom of the boat and applied two coats of International TBT white anti-fouling, an unpleasant job which I was quietly thankful to have missed. Malcolm Sandals, the school's maintenance engineer, had busied himself fitting the new satellite navigator, and the Pentland Bravo HF/MF radio with which we hoped to keep in contact with our anxious relatives. This radio had been used on the Whitbread Race, then removed from the yacht and stored in a shed. Now it was needed again, the Kelvin Hughes agents in Glasgow tested it and pronounced it still in working order, so our main concern was passing the exam to become proficient radio operators. In the weeks leading up to the start of our voyage, Malcolm worked aboard the boat whenever we were at Ardmore. He serviced the engine, checked the steering and the electrics. The 23-inch three-bladed propellor was changed for a folding one. The alternator was exchanged, and the seals on the fuel tank hatches checked, Malcolm's jobs stretched on and on.

Preparing a yacht for a non-stop circumnavigation is a lengthy task. You have to imagine every problem, emergency, or breakage and then decide if it will actually jeopardise the whole project. For example, if the yacht were dismasted, we would have to make for the nearest port and the voyage could no longer be made non-stop. On the other hand, the loss of electrical power would not be a real disaster, more of an inconvenience. The endless list of tasks has to be set against this standard, and the vital basic tasks completed first. There are of course many grey areas: the loss of the self-steering or the inability to prepare hot food will not prevent the boat from sailing, but will lead to severe hardship and a loss of efficiency in the crew.

Background experience is probably the most essential element in the preparations. John has a string of successful sea-going exploits to his credit: rowing across the Atlantic with Chay Blyth, and sailing it singlehanded; a winter cruise down to the Spanish Sahara and back, and skippering *English Rose VI* round the world in the 1977/78 Whitbread Race, not to mention the countless trips across the Minch with the adventure school. It adds up to a lot of miles.

My own experience was considerably less impressive, but I had built a yacht, and can repair most breakages. John felt I might be an asset. To sail non-stop for 28,000 miles and expect to arrive home intact, is like striking a match on a handkerchief — virtually impossible.

Many yachtsmen feel that when buying a yacht, the second-hand market will provide a well-equipped and proven boat, whereas a new craft will undoubtedly be unfinished and dogged with teething troubles. Francis Chichester was forced to cut short sea trials of his new yacht *Gispy Moth IV*, by shortage of time and funds, with the result that when he left Plymouth bound for Sydney, the craft still had three major undiscovered vices. When she arrived in Sydney after 106 days, she had to undergo a six-week refit before going on to complete her circumnavigation. A non-stop circumnavigation is no project for an unproven yacht.

Built in 1975, *English Rose VI* is a 57-foot ketch of standard Bowman design, but from the start she was fitted out at Ardmore with the Whitbread Race in mind, so her gear is exceptionally strong. At the adventure school she leads a tough life, on instructional cruises from the north-west of Scotland to the Outer Hebrides, St Kilda, and the Faroes. Over the winter before our voyage, John took her to Arun Bose's yard at Tighnabruaich for a refit. Arun knew every inch of her, he'd not only fitted her out from the bare hull, but he'd sailed as a Watch Leader on the Whitbread Race too.

The refit had included one or two modifications for short-handed sailing: an Aries self-steering gear was fitted, and the genoa sheet winches were moved to the aft cockpit by the wheel. A Whitlock steering system for an 80-foot boat was installed. The original rudder had failed six months previously — the stock began to revolve inside the rudder moulding but the makers claimed that their new rudder was built to an improved design, and on many a stormy night to come we were to hope their claim was true. Masts and rigging were removed from the boat and thoroughly checked. The mainmast shrouds and forestay were replaced. On the voyage we carried a reel of rigging wire and numerous bulldog clips, as well as the old rigging stowed in the bilge.

While an efficient self-steering gear is not essential to make an extended shorthanded voyage, the cutting-out of long hours at the wheel undoubtedly pays dividends. The crew is able to rest and remain warm and dry below decks, also they can enjoy some form of hobby to take their mind away from the very small world surrounding them. We occupied many hours, both on and off watch, with cooking and writing. We carried two complete Aries self-steering gears plus enough spares to build a third gear if the need arose. Arun's yard fitted strengthening battens inside the yacht's transom and bolted the Aries on the outside. The positioning looked suitable at anchor, but once under way the stern wave swamped the moving parts, so Malcolm and I raised the mountings by 7 inches. Then we were able to begin experimenting at sea.

The first trials were dismaying — instead of following an accurate course *English Rose* yawed wildly, risking accidental gybes and often putting herself about. My previous experience with self-steering gears was limited to a simple one fitted to *Kinnego*, and the results had been similarly disappointing. I resigned myself to the fact that our mechanical helmsman was a little eccentric. When I told John of the difficulties, he was convinced an improvement was possible, so I persevered, but to little effect. At 57 feet English Rose is perhaps rather large for the Aries, but I didn't think this was the problem — there seemed to be a fundamental fault causing the gear to oversteer continually. I turned my mind to other aspects of the preparations, so as not to become bogged down. I firmly believe that if a problem cannot be solved quickly, then it should be pushed aside for a while and returned to later with a fresh clear mind.

On each cruise I tried the Aries in a wide range of sea and wind conditions, but each time it performed as before. Secretly I wanted to chuck the assortment of tubes and castings overboard, but fortunately I refrained from such dramatic measures. Then, less than two weeks before our departure, the nut was cracked: it seemed unlikely that the instruction leaflet might be wrong, but nevertheless I had the notion of trying the gear with the steering lines and vane connected back to front . . . and it worked! A stiff southwesterly breeze drove the boat swiftly up the Minch, as we returned from a two-week cruise. The Aries now performed

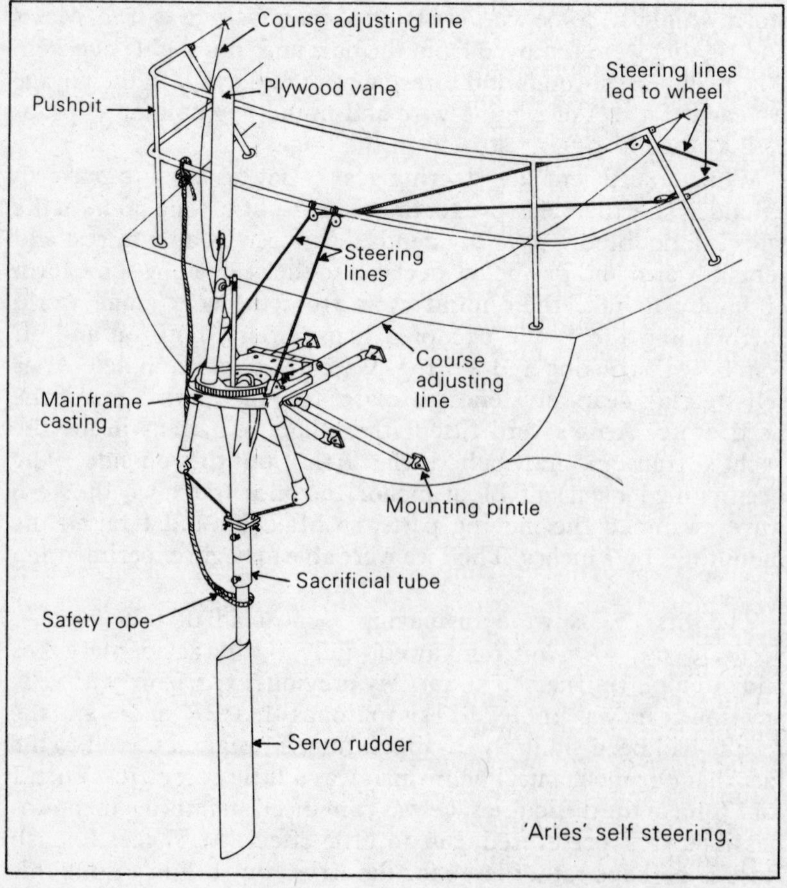

'Aries' self steering.

superbly, holding an accurate course as we began surfing at a couple of knots above hull-speed. I found that sailing on a reach, or to windward, the steering remained inaccurate until the spray dodgers around the cockpit were removed to give a clearer airflow round the vane.

To help ease sail-handling while shorthanded, Arun had moved the two genoa/yankee sheet winches aft, to a position where they were within easy reach of the helmsman, and Barlow kindly donated two self-tailing drums to replace the originals. The remaining 17 winches were left non-self-tailing. David Cripps, a full-time Watch Leader for the season, stripped, cleaned, and greased each winch during the last few weeks before our departure.

Roller-reefing headsails are now widely accepted as an alternative to using a whole wardrobe of different-sized headsails. John considered roller-reefing, but decided against it on the basis that the available gears were insufficiently proven for 28,000 miles non-stop.

Arun had intended fitting a self-tacking boomed staysail so that only the genoa/yankee sheets would need tending when going about, but the boom never materialised in time. This was probably just as well, because we found that each new modification needed time to iron out the snags and we didn't have time to indulge in luxuries. Without the self-tacking staysail, whenever we went about or gybed with only one man on deck, the staysail was left aback while the headsail was sheeted in and the course adjusted. Perhaps this is not a racing technique, but it kept the gear simple. In the confined waters of Loch Laxford we sailed sloop-fashion: headsail and main, with no staysail or mizzen to worry about. Leading the reefing lines and halyards back to the main cockpit was another idea which didn't materialise in time, but we managed perfectly well without it.

We carried 27 Ratsey & Lapthorn sails in all. Only two sails were new for the voyage: a No 2 yankee and a mizzen. These were made in UV resistant cloth of weights 10 oz (USA) and 8 oz (USA) respectively. The No 2 yankee became known as our 'supersail' because it was so heavily constructed, and we often left it up when everything else came down. All the old sails had been thoroughly serviced by a sailmaker during the winter refit, and many of the seams had been restitched with three rows of stitching.

Our sail repair kit included a Reed's sewing machine and several rolls of cloth of different weights. Three weeks before September 1, the older of our two mainsails blew out in a 70-knot squall, requiring a complete new panel. Since we were in the Faroes at the time, far from any sailmaker and the spare mainsail which was back at Ardmore, the repair job fell to David Cripps and myself. After two hours we had fathomed out how to use the sewing machine, and the repair job took two days, thus providing a useful practical exercise in sail mending.

Chafe is the cause of most sail damage on a long voyage, when sail settings remain unchanged for several days, the same small area of cloth or stitching will rub relentlessly against a shroud or spreader. Baggywrinkle, similar in appearance to a mop-head, but made up from strands of old climbing rope in our case, is the traditional preventive. We also wrapped sheepskin rugs round the spreaders, and held them in place with 2-inch-wide linen sticky tape. The newer mainsail had several large sacrificial anti-chafe patches added to it. We planned to use many other methods to combat chafe on the voyage, and these are described fully later on.

There are no formal rules for a non-stop circumnavigation, but we felt that to use the motor when becalmed, would not be fair play. However, to prevent the 80 hp Mercedes diesel from seizing-up through inactivity under the saloon floor, and also to keep the batteries fully charged when we used the big HF radio, we had to endure the throb of the motor for three or four hours once or twice a week. The engine was out of gear and the shaft immobilised by a line running from a nut on the shaft coupling to a strong point on the hull.

For the Whitbread Race the auxilliary had been a small 15 hp Lister diesel, it was converted to run on paraffin with 3 per cent lubricating oil added. The aim was to have only one fuel aboard, and as the cooker, cabin heater, Tilley lamps, and emergency navigation lights all burned paraffin, it made good sense to convert the Lister as well. However time was against us on this occasion, there were too many other tasks more urgent than fuel conversion for the Mercedes, so we compromised and John bought a diesel-fired cabin heater which we hoped to fit along the way. We filled the fuel tank, which lies under the main cockpit, with 180 gallons of red diesel, and carried 50 gallons of paraffin for the cooker in ten 5-gallon jerry-cans.

While I cruised around the Western Isles, John and Marie Christine busied themselves at Ardmore. John bought spare shackles, rope and needles, rivets and cooker parts, every conceivable piece of equipment which might be of use. He compiled a worldwide folio of charts, pilots, radio and weather manuals, as well as a considerable library of nautical books from his own shelves in the croft. Although we hoped to make the voyage without stopping, and so should be able to get round with only about six charts, we had to have a contingency plan for a number of ports of call if we should be damaged; it was here that the charts of the Whitbread Race came in handy, with their coverage of

Cape Town, Auckland, and Rio de Janeiro. We had separate routeing charts of the various oceans for all the months when we should be likely to need them, these American weather charts are very helpful for plotting a broad course in tricky places like the Southern Ocean and the North Atlantic in the winter months.

Marie Christine concentrated on our provisions. A friend suggested we should try the Stevens Lefield range of pre-cooked ready meals, the menus include stews, casseroles, curries, and even haggis. The foil-packed meals are easily prepared by immersion in boiling water for 7 minutes and then eaten with rice or potatoes. This ease of preparation persuaded John to order 300 assorted individual portions.

1,300 tins required the laborious task of stripping labels, marking with a reference number between 1 and 45 and then varnishing to slow the rusting process. Malcolm and his family occupied many hours with this smelly job, assisted by several instructors. All the tins were eventually stowed in plastic bags inside their designated lockers, and registered in the stowage book.

Dry stores like flour, rice and sugar were poured into clear plastic 5-gallon jerry-cans, but fresh fruit and vegetables were left in their original cardboard boxes. We decided not to plan a menu to be repeated weekly, fortnightly, or whatever, instead our meals were to be cooked as the mood took us.

The weeks passed and the yacht was frequently away. I brought the boat back into Ardmore at the end of the final St Kilda cruise early on the morning of Saturday August 27, and went ashore for the rest of the day to begin packing my belongings. Only four days now remained before we were due to begin our 200-day voyage. John took the yacht straight out on a day sail down to Handa Island with some students from the final young peoples' course. On the Sunday he made a repeat trip down the coast, and that evening he brought her in to lie against the wooden pier below the croft at Ardmore, ready to begin loading stores next morning. Marie arrived shortly before dusk.

The mountain of stores stacked in Malcolm's workshop was loaded after breakfast on Monday with the assistance of a chain of helpers from the course. Malcolm was particularly willing, he wanted to use his workshop as a workshop again! By mid-morning their willingness began to wane noticeable, like myself few had realised the quantity of gear that had accumulated. Tea and biscuit refreshment became a necessity!

Loading via the chain greatly exceeded the rate at which John and I were able to properly stow the gear, so the deck soon became a disorganised pile of sailbags, oil drums and blue plastic bread baskets brimming with spares and food. Luckily for us, the

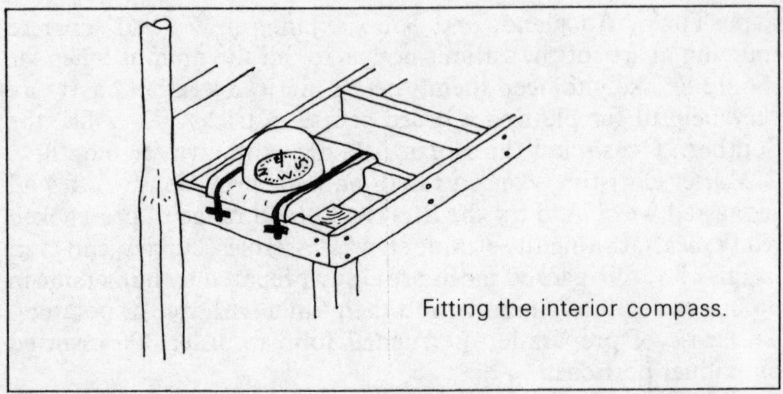
Fitting the interior compass.

forecasted rain didn't materialise. Each item was entered into the stowage book as a suitable home was found for it.

The two freshwater tanks, each with a capacity of 180 gallons, were topped up with peaty water, fresh from the loch on the hill above Ardmore, and an additional 50 gallons was taken aboard in jerry-cans as a precaution against the tanks becoming polluted.

The numerous jerry-cans were hidden wherever possible, in the forepeak and aft locker, lashed under the saloon table and in the bilge. Boxes of paper towels, loo rolls and extra sails were stowed on the vacant berths and tied safely in with lee cloths. By late afternoon the scarlet boot-top stripe, normally about 4 inches above the water, had disappeared beneath the surface.

Marie kept a low profile all day, revising for an important exam scheduled for the following week. At lunchtime and in the evening we were able to talk. Her visit signified an acceptance and belief in the voyage, her presence gave me peace of mind. My parents and youngest brother arrived in the evening.

Tuesday slipped away amid cleaning and gear stowing, a couple of hours in the evening were set aside for a party with a few of John's friends. Twenty-four hours before we hoped to drop the mooring, we concentrated on trying to convince ourselves that despite a lengthy list of unfinished jobs, we were in fact ready to go. Our final job was installing an interior compass, taped onto the boot rack beside the navigation table.

The busy school programme had left no time for John and I to practice sailing the boat together, but John obviously knew the boat well, and I had skippered her for several thousand miles during the season. We both felt that 'where there's a will there's a way', so the lack of trials didn't overly concern us. The majority of the school instructors were unimpressed with our carefree attitude, and visualised us coming to grief within a few miles of leaving Ardmore.

3

Early days

Introduction by John

The first few days of the voyage were to be particularly hard on us. A short-handed crew is never happy close to the shore. We had to sail down the whole length of the western seaboard of Britain in appalling weather, and conditions led us to pass down through the Irish Sea, when we would have preferred to get well out to the west of Ireland.

There was no thought of writing a book. We both felt seasick and my own log book was written simply as a rough diary, in the habit I'd formed in 1958 and have kept up ever since. Andy just recorded events and feelings every couple of days to begin with. Our view of things was quite different in some cases.

John — Day 1, Thursday September 1

Thursday September 1 1983 dawned quiet, grey and rainy. There were a few headaches among the instructors from the night before. I was up as usual at 6.00 am, and after a light breakfast with a couple of Stugeron pills to calm my stomach, I picked up the green enamel kettle from the Rayburn cooker in the kitchen, and said goodbye to the cats, Pussy Ridgway and Fat Oliver. Walking down the hill from the house, I felt pretty miserable. On the shore Andy joined me for a last plod round the boat sheds, checking for any last thing we might have forgotten, then we went out to the boat.

As usual, in spite of all our efforts, there were still last minute things which we could not immediately find a place for, and down below the boat looked a bit of a mess.

There was a steady drizzle from a slate-grey sky. The mainsail and No 2 yankee headsail hung limply in the lightest of breezes. Nobody looked cheerful, the instructors hanging onto the rail from their small boats alongside seemed to have suddenly realised what it was that we were about to attempt. Andy and I were both adamant that a 9.00 am start meant a 9.00 am start. Suddenly the minutes began to run out. A last minute alone with Marie Christine down below, 'I bet you're glad you're not coming' I tried to grin. 'I rather wish I was now' she mumbled miserably.

Everyone clambered over the side and into the little blue boats with their outboards. I slipped below and put the theme music from the film, *Chariots of Fire* at full volume on the stereo system. 'OK, let her go!' I called to Andy up in the bows. There was a dull plop as the mooring line fell through the rails and into the water. We were off.

I turned the wheel hard to port and began a short tack towards the narrow entrance to the loch. The boat felt very sluggish with her heavy load, and the wind was hardly enough to move her. We were both tightly buttoned up in our red Henri-Lloyd suits, and my new extra large Topsider boots felt warm with new socks. Boys and girls on the course were out on the shore to wave us goodbye. Marie Christine and Rebecca stood on a little point further down, both looked downcast in the rain. The light wind dragged the whole ghastly business out, and by the time we had reached the entrance to Loch Laxford my wife and daughter had returned up the hill to the house and were calling on the VHF radio, all three of us were choking on our words. Once in Laxford, we still had a couple of miles to the open sea. The Duchess of Westminster, together with Sinclair and Sandee Mackintosh came out to see us off in a small white speedboat, they took up station astern as we nodded gently to the swell, then after a while they too headed back inshore, leaving a broad 'V' as they sped away.

We felt truly alone for the first time. The cloud hung low on the hills of Ardmore Point, summer looked long gone.

'Best of luck you two... see you next year.' The voice of an unseen instructor boomed down from somewhere up on the misty headland.

'See you next Year? Blimey, this is going to be a hell of a long trip, old top' I called to Andy who was still up in the bows, putting the anchor away until the following spring. I took off my wrist-watch, thinking I wouldn't be needing it for a long time to come. All those programmes of the school courses were a thing of the past, all time now would come from the quartz crystal clock on the saloon bulkhead.

We drifted slowly out past the mouth of Loch Laxford. The forecast was bad, that was why Andy had put up only the No 2 yankee and taken a reef in the mainsail. If the wind got up before we settled into our new life, there shouldn't be any panic with such small sails already set in advance. Looking back one last time at the drab rocky peninsula of Ardmore, I thought how much I loved it, and how little time I'd spent wandering along through its hills and lochs with Marie Christine and Rebecca. Twenty years had slipped by so quickly.

The wind began to freshen as we came into the Minch. Andy suggested that as he was less likely to feel sick then me, because he'd been living aboard for the past five months, he might as well take the first watch as we headed close-hauled for Stornaway, some 45 miles away on the east coast of Lewis. I went below, took off my oilskins, and stretched out on the leeward seat in the saloon and pulled a thick tartan rug over me. I just drifted off to sleep with the influence of the Stugeron pills.

For me, leaving Ardmore was an emotional experience, it completely drained me. For Andy it was a much more practical exercise. He had left home long ago, his girlfriend and his parents had wisely departed well before we sailed. He'd sailed out of countless anchorages during the summer and now he was relieved to be setting sail again.

Andy — Day 1

The mooring chain rattled out of the bow roller at 9.10 am — a mere 10 minutes later than planned on Thursday 1st September 1983, a fine mist of drizzle hung in the air and there wasn't much wind, the lack of wind was the first of many blessings. The morning forecast predicted an early start to the equinoctial gales, force 9 or 10 from the south and this quickly dispelled our optimism for an easy start. We decided to carry the No 2 yankee and 1 reef tied in the main. This is a rig suitable for 25 to 30 knots of wind, not a light breeze, so our departure was far from quick. John skillfully tacked *English Rose* out of Loch a Chadh-Fi, tacking closer inshore than I had ever dared go, but John knew where the rocks were so my apprehension as the shore approached was unnecessary.

As we passed the small gathering of well-wishers grouped together on the foreshore I shouted to them to wave for a photo. Shortly afterwards they began to disperse, only Marie Christine and Rebecca walked along the rocks to keep up with us. I felt a little disappointed that more of the instructors had not stayed with us for longer, obviously they disliked standing out in the rain. I had bade my farewells to parents and Marie the previous day, we all agreed that a tearful departure was not a good idea.

The music from *Chariots of Fire* drifted up through the hatch to add a little cheer. We both enjoyed a hot 'Cup-a-Soup' and hoped the Stugeron pills were taking effect; both of us suffer from sea sickness.

Ardmore slid behind Paddy's Isle, our last sight of home, we didn't know for how long. It was a time of anxiety and excitement, my longest duration at sea had previously been a six-day singlehanded passage, six months or longer was an unimaginable period of solitude.

Before leaving the calm waters of Loch Laxford we stowed the anchor and the boathook below. The anchor usually remains lashed on the bow roller, but with the approaching gales a more secure stowage seemed advisable. Eventually it was hidden under a bunk, but for the first few days while close to land it was kept accessible in the forepeak.

We christened the self-steering 'George' for no better reason than because it was the first name that sprang to John's mind, and then set the wind vane to keep *English Rose* close-hauled on a heading south-west for Stornaway.

The aft locker came under attack next, the Avon inflatable was moved from the top of the pile to the bottom, and the storm sails took the dinghy's place. When all was secure we sat down for a chat, we had dropped the mooring with no firm idea of a suitable watch-keeping rota, but I was quite happy to take the first watch. Over the previous weeks we had occasionally discussed a few ideas about watch-keeping, but it is not until one is actually at sea on a long passage that the true impact of short interrupted periods of sleep is realised. The one point that we both whole heartedly agreed upon is that one or other of us should always be awake, though not necessarily on deck.

John — Day 1

When I came back on deck in mid-afternoon we were going well. The wind had risen to force 6 and veered a little to SSW. Andy had further reduced the sails to a second reef in the main while keeping the No 2 yankee and the No 2 staysail. We were prepared for a bit of a blow, but the boat was moving quite nicely without having to increase sail either. Triumpan Head was abeam now but still half a dozen miles away, so we tacked and headed back across the Minch towards Skye.

Andy said he was feeling very cheery, really looking forward to the voyage. He'd said goodbye to Marie the day before we sailed, and Ardmore meant no more to him than the coast of Skye. He went below for a sleep and I was left looking back towards the blue line of the Foinaven Ridge above Ardmore, already some 30 miles away. The Aries windvane steered the boat from its position perched on the stern, its lines moved to and fro through the blocks leading to the drum on the main steering wheel in the aft cockpit. I watched the spokes move first one way and then the other; the boat kept right on the compass course, as if a ghost was at the helm. I was left with nothing but to feel sorry for myself, there was no work on deck and I didn't trust myself below at the chart table. Seasickness wasn't far away.

I leant back on the starboard rail and wept. What on earth was I doing? I knew all about miserable departures, did I never learn? Would I go on like this for the rest of my days? There'd been the pain of setting off to row across the North Atlantic with Chay in 1966 — that had been a risky venture, and Marie Christine and I had only been married a couple of years at that time. A couple of years later the parting had been even worse, I'd set off from the Aran Isles off the west coast of Ireland to try to sail non-stop alone round the world in a 30-foot sloop; there had been a collision with a television boat right at the outset, and then the wind had fallen calm. Marie Christine had waved forlornly for ages from a trawler, before it finally turned for Galway as I drifted on the tide with a damaged boat. After that she'd always come with me: the Amazon, Patagonia, Spanish Sahara, the Whitbread Race round the world, the Himalayas, and three marathons in America. The seasickness made me feel really glum. As Rudyard Kipling had put it, I'd risked everything we'd struggled for during the past 20 years at Ardmore 'on one turn of pitch and toss', win or lose there'd be nothing to show for it. What a fool I was.

We heated up some lasagne for supper, Marie Christine had made it the previous day knowing full well we wouldn't feel much like cooking on the first night.

John — Day 2, Friday September 2

Andy took over the watch and when he called me at midnight I was most impressed to find he'd taken us through the narrow passage of Trodday, on the north-west coast of Skye. This cheered me immeasurably, the weeks as skipper on the boat had given him that vital feeling of being at one with the ship. We had never sailed alone together and I'd never even seen the self-steering working properly, so this demonstration of prowess in the dark gave me great confidence.

The wind had backed to the south and fallen to a gentle force 3 in the shelter of Skye as I sat in the aft cockpit and watched Vaternish and Dunvegan slip past on our port side. It was a perfect night, my first ever alone on the deck of this boat. The lighthouses blinked yellow, signalling the route south, the 20 tons of boat ghosted gracefully on her way in near silence. There was a great feeling of purpose and achievement in the night air. Then, in the early hours of our second day the glass began to fall rapidly. The forecast gave an increase to force 7–9 with the wind backing to the north. We put the third reef in the mainsail as the wind and sea increased, then we changed the No 2 for the No 3 yankee. Although the wind remained in the SE, I was able to drive hard SSW down past Canna.

A rogue wave on the beam broke the first of the plywood wind vanes on the self-steering at 10.30 pm. For some reason this seemed to worry Andy a little more than it did me. I know we hadn't all that many vanes but I thought we'd have less trouble with the sea once we got clear of the continental shelf and into the more regular ocean swell. I was much more concerned at a near-miss we had with a huge metal 'Special Mark' buoy as we drew near to Tiree. I was down below looking at the chart, trying to set in my mind the exact position of the reefs off the west end of the island. I looked out over the stern from my position at the foot of the companionway steps, and before I knew it we'd shaved close by the enormous yellow buoy, and I realised with a shock that had we hit it the voyage would probably have ended with us limping ignominiously into port for repairs. The self-steering was first rate at keeping us on course, but only the crew could avoid the hazards in our path. How many lives would these cats have? One was already spent, and we'd hardly started the voyage.

Conditions were miserable, Andy was sick but although I felt grim I managed to keep the food down. As we approached the North Channel into the Irish Sea the wind providently eased and finally backed into the north. The night was black and the crests of the waves showed white around the boat.

Andy — Day 2

Our second day at sea passed relatively uneventfully, there was a slight panic when a clumsy wave bumped into the plywood self-steering vane, carrying it away, but it was easily replaced. Not so easily restored was our faith in 'George' if he couldn't look after himself in the 'calm' coastal waters off Scotland how would we fare in the Roaring Forties?

Skerryvore light, on the southernmost island off Tiree, was logged abeam at 14.00 hours. At the time it provided a convenient position fix, 200 days later that isolated granite tower was to take on a different meaning.

The Inner Hebrides to some extent protected *English Rose* from the severe easterly gale that howled out from the mainland. Once out of the lee, my enthusiasm which had earlier persuaded me to lash the storm trisail to the mast, began to be eroded by discomfort and nausea. Foolishly I decided to cook a bacon sandwich, but the bacon never made it to the pan. I was sick. Being sick didn't annoy me, it was the fact that John remained unaffected — his turn would undoubtedly come though!

Towards midnight John woke me from a rare moment of blissful sleep. Outside, the storm had abated to a sail-slatting calm, a damp envelope of fog sealed us in our tiny world.

We raised the mizzen which increased our speed to a slow 3 knots and left the triple-reefed main in readiness for the next rapidly approachig low. John then turned on the radar and explained the use of the anonymous knobs. The set had defied all attempts to get it going during the season, but Malcolm had succeeded in restoring the set to working order a few days before we sailed. The sweeping green arm of light picked out a vessel some way off on our quarter, there was no danger of collision so the set was turned off to conserve power.

A while later, a ship's fog horn had me on deck in a flash. No lights were visible, and I cursed having to wear spectacles, as the drizzle and mist continually obliterated my vision. The horn sounded again followed by the appearance of a white light over a red light fine on the starboard bow. I proceeded to gybe to sail clear then realised that red is a portside light. I had altered course across its bow! The horn sounded yet again. Franticly I turned *English Rose* onto the other tack, and the vessel slid past, throwing out an unpleasant wash. I sat down trembling.

John — Day 3, Saturday September 3

Dawn brought a sharp increase in the wind, a good wash and shave had my spirits soaring, I knew the boat would go well in high winds especially if they came across our quarter as the forecast now suggested. We shouldered down the Irish Sea in NW storm force 10. The ferries were cancelled and we saw no shipping. When we used the VHF radio to call home, the operator asked if we were in difficulties and where were we bound, when I replied we were fine and heading around the world non-stop he cheered up and put us through with some gusto. Secretly I was thanking my lucky stars the wind was from behind us, and another blessing was the performance of the satellite navigator or satnav for short. I hadn't used one of these things before, and I was thrilled with it, I could see that if it continued to work it would be a considerable comfort during bad visibility whenever sights with the sextant proved impossible. We hoped to make very few landfalls during the voyage, and particularly as we approached Cape Horn I knew it would be reassuring to feel confident of our position.

We went about, close off the South Bishop light on the southern end of Cardigan Bay. It was cold, dark, and miserable, and I felt a long way from home. The piston hanks were coming off the luff of the No 3 yankee owing to the slamming back and forth of the sail in awkward seas. With hindsight there is a temptation to think that nothing would go wrong — after all we were setting off to sail right round the world without stopping, but the real situation on the boat was far different. There were two men who hardly knew each other, both extremely tired, not only from a seven-day-a-week season stretching back into March, but also from the last minute preparations. We had left only three days after the boat was released from her commitments with the adventure school and we'd sailed down the length of the British Isles, too close to the land for comfort. It was little wonder we were now beginning to show signs of exhaustion at a time when we could ill-afford to relax our vigilance.

Andy — Day 3

By breakfast the Mull of Kintyre lay in our wake as *English Rose* forged on southwards, the noon forecast promised a freezing north-west storm force 10. I remember asking John if the whole trip were likely to be wet and uncomfortable, if so I would rather get off. He smiled knowingly, assuring me that conditions were unlikely to get worse. Wedged into our bunks or the chart table seat we gained a little comfort from the knowledge that few other ships were at sea; except for old tree trunks and rubbish, a collision seemed unlikely.

Apart from the loss of a mounting nut, 'George' behaved all day. The bolts securing the self-steering mountings to the transom were slowly crushing the iroko-wood strengthening battens, and allowing the nuts to work loose. We should have fitted larger washers or a metal plate.

The saloon and navigation area were drenched from numerous trickles at each window and occasional deluges down the companionway. Our oilskins became a second skin on watch — at a moment's notice one of us could be on deck. The storm wore both of us down physically and hammered *English Rose*. A lifebuoy and attached light were ripped off the rails by a breaking wave.

John — Day 4, Sunday September 4

Next morning, found us bashing to windward in the Bristol Channel. The wind had eased to force 6–8 but it had backed round to the south-west, confused seas washed away a lifebuoy and light from its fixing high on the pushpit, and the radar reflector came adrift at its lower end from aloft on the mizzen mast. We had a close encounter with a container vessel northbound off Tuskar Light. Over-use of our navigation aids caused a serious shortage of battery power, so we ran the engine for charging purposes, hoping against hope that we hadn't got a short somewhere inaccessible.

'Well, I've just about had enough of this' I grunted at Andy, and I thought I caught a look in his eye which wondered if I meant I'd had enough of the whole voyage, or just the weather. Then we found one of the mounting nuts was missing on the self-steering. The one thing we were able to congratulate ourselves on, was the speed we'd mangaged to maintain towards Bishop Rock Light off the Scilly Isles.

Andy — Day 4

Our navigation relied solely on the satnav, plotting the fixes every few hours. Then on Saturday morning the little green numbers disappeared, and we kicked ourselves for not keeping a better check on our whereabouts. The problem was simply a lack of power, a fact which took us several hours to discover. We didn't believe the 500 amp/hr auxilliary bank of batteries could be drained so quickly. After checking fuses, connections, and wiring we tried the engine, a significant click told us something was amiss. Once again the wiring was checked, nothing appeared wrong. Jump leads were connected between the auxilliary batteries and the engine starting batteries and finally the engine started.

The reason for installing two separate banks of batteries is that one is for daily use, the other purely for engine starting. If the bank for daily use becomes discharged, the second bank remains fully charged to start the engine. For some reason the wiring of *English Rose* did not allow this.

John — Day 5, Monday September 5

We chose the famous Bishop Rock as a mark on our circumnavigation, because traditionally it has been used for this by the liners attempting the Blue Riband run across the North Atlantic. The Head Keeper had agreed to log our own start and finish, and I hoped that any future attempt on the record might be timed to and from this point at the western end of the English Channel.

Andy told me he'd reckoned on a week to Bishop Rock from Ardmore, but as it turned out, the Keeper came on the VHF at 09.00 on Monday September 4 1983: just ten minutes under four days out from Ardmore. We were well pleased.

The wind had been falling steadily as we approached the lighthouse from the north, and now it fell away to nothing. So we spent the rest of the day bathed in warm sun, and always in sight of the stern flat-topped tower of Bishop Rock.

The change in the weather added to a feeling, that now we were leaving Britain, we were starting the circumnavigation for real. It had quite an effect on Andy. It was as if some unseen hand had drawn back the sling of a catapult, and now released its missile; he seemed to throw himself into every kind of job, both maintenance and improvement. And, while I just fiddled around with the stowage and worked up a bacon and tomato omelette for supper, still feeling homesick, Andy dashed about the place tackling the possibility of an electrical short and repairing the storm damage to the No 2 and No 3 yankee headsails. He was delighted at our speed to Bishop Rock and now viewed the circumnavigation in a very positive light.

It was already much warmer than home, and the Southern Ocean was still far away on the other side of the Equator.

Andy — Day 5

Our speed has dropped dramatically but we arrived off Bishop Rock at 9.00 pm, four days after leaving Ardmore. During the last 14 hours we have only covered 35 miles. Despite an unpleasant swell we have been able to enjoy a relaxing day: tidying the boat, checking the electrics and making a few adjustments to 'George'. Another mounting-nut worked loose overnight, and while hanging over the stern, tightening the other nuts, I dropped the adjustable spanner. It should have been tied on — John doesn't know yet. Now, using a hammer and cold chisel I have distorted the threads on each mounting-bolt, to prevent the nuts undoing completely if they work loose again.

John cooked a delicious lunch of eggs, bacon and tomatoes, he claims not to have cooked an egg before which I find hard to believe. We began checking through the food lists today, neither of us knows what stores are aboard!

John — Day 6, Tuesday September 6

Most of the night was spent becalmed in the Channel. Occasionally, we nodded south towards Cape Finisterre which lay some 350 miles ahead of us, on the north-west corner of Spain. We put more charge into the batteries with the engine, after some farewell radio calls to friends in the UK. I carried on with sorting the stowage, and made a bacon and tomato omelette for supper. The worry of the minute is the possibility of a short in the electrical system, and I wonder if we will be in radio contact with home again . . .

Andy — Day 6

After three telephone calls to Glasgow I finally spoke to Marie this evening, her exam this morning didn't go too well, otherwise she is happy.

I found my pyjamas this morning and enjoyed a delightfully comfortable couple of hours in my bunk this evening, how civilised it felt, next I will be washing! I've stopped taking the Stugeron, hopefully they won't be needed again.

John — Day 7, Wednesday September 7

(Day's run 101 nm)

Continual headwinds as we claw south. The light genoa is replaced by the No 1 yankee and working staysail. At breakfast I persuaded Andy to put a 10-hour charge in the batteries, I feel they are more likely to be simply run down, than for there to be any fault in the wiring. He spent the day preparing the Aquair 50 log, and it duly went over the stern for its first spell of duty at 20.30 hours. I had to haul it out when we went about by accident, in the dark, after Andy had turned in. I was anxious to stop it from tangling with the self-steering gear or the rudder. When I came to stream the heavy propellor again, I was so intent on avoiding any kinking in the line that I clean forgot to reconnect the cable from the generator to the auxilliary batteries under the chart table seat. And by the time I arrived on the scene, there was considerable 'chattering' from the contact breaker, as well as sparks flying from the terminals as they banged together. However, I managed to sort it out in spite of shocks to salt-wet hands.

It was a long dark night. Feeling barely awake as we bash into endless headwinds, and I feel slightly sick even though it is a lot warmer now. I finished reading *Contact* by A.F.N. Clarke an ex-platoon commander of 9Pl 3Para. He writes from the soldier's point of view in Northern Ireland, and I feel an affinity with him because 9 Platoon was the one I first commanded myself, back in 1959. How cruel and senseless the whole situation is.

Andy — Day 7

I have had a long busy day, coming 'on watch' at 5.00 am, resting between breakfast and lunch, and occupying six hours this afternoon fitting the Aquair towing generator. The generator is now working, providing 30 to 40 amp hours each day. Hopefully an inquisitive shark won't take a fancy to the spinner.

We are both settling into our life aboard. Sharing the workload does not seem to present a problem. This evening I have noticed a slight itch, which I hope is not the dreaded 'gunnel bum', caused by sitting in wet clothing.

* * *

The need to generate electricity while on a long passage brings to mind the question, 'is electrical power really necessary'? For centuries seafarers survived using candles and oil lamps, it is only because yachtsmen are now used to an array of instruments giving boat speed, wind direction etc, that the loss of these aids is looked upon with dread.

The obvious source of power is to run the engine several times a week, it needs to run periodically anyway. Alternators are usually rated to fully charge the batteries after 10 hours running, eg, a 500 amp/hr bank of batteries can be charged with a 50 amp alternator. Fitting a larger alternator may appear a good idea but unfortunately charging a battery too quickly will damage it. Using the engine as the sole source of electrical power has a number of disadvantages. On a long voyage, several hundred gallons of fuel will have to be stored. Running a diesel engine without a load is not generally recommended, and anyway if the engine fails there is no back up. Also having to put up with the engine noise for hours on end is unpleasant.

A number of alternatives are available but, apart from a petrol generator they usually supply only a trickle charge. We carried a small Honda generator but never had need to use it. Carrying petrol presents an obvious hazard.

Windmills, water driven turbines, alternators connected to a free-wheeling propeller shaft, and solar panels are the usual sources of a trickle charge, all have their merits and snags. Windmills are fine in moderate winds, useless in calm weather and vibrate irritatingly in strong winds. Solar panels are expensive and only come to life when the sun shines. A free-wheeling propeller shaft will shorten the life of bearings and possibly the gearbox.

We chose a water-powered turbine, the Aquair 50. The generator within the unit is driven by a spinner which it tows behind the boat on a length of 8 mm rope. The threshold speed required to start generating power is 2 knots and a yacht as large as *English Rose* rarely sails that slowly, so charging is virtually continuous. A small yacht may suffer from loss of performance — at 6 knots the drag is approximately 75lbs, but drag becomes less significant as the size of yacht increases. Fitting the Aquair was relatively easy, it was hung from a large shackle slipped over the pushpit's middle rail and tied down to the toerail to prevent it from swinging wildly. A cable runs down through the deck and forward to the battery unit beneath the chart table seat, where crocodile clips connect it to the auxilliary batteries via a rectifier.

John — Day 8, Thursday September 8

(Day's run 134 nm)

First reef went into the main at 08.30. I feel sick as we bump on in grey clammy weather at 7.5 knots. Andy is in his bunk at 13.00 hours when the 1975 No 1 yankee bursts. The sail is a veteran of the Whitbread Race (it burst off Tasmania) and just too tired to take the slamming in a 30 knot wind. I was exhausted on the foredeck as we hauled down the wreckage and put up the No 3 yankee, plus No 2 staysail and then put the second reef in the main — as well as going onto the port tack to try and get away from the north-west coast of Spain. Egg mayonnaise and tomato sandwiches plus a bit of Christmas cake helped pull me together, but I was only too pleased to get into my bunk at 15.00. Andy spun a few yarns about him meeting Marie at the Tighnabruaich Sailing School last summer and the subsequent sail from Tighnabruaich to Whitby via the Caledonian Canal, in his 25-foot home-built boat. His hero is Tristan Jones. Andy is unusual, he could be another Tristan Jones, and this trip will mark him.

Fine steak and kidney pie and cabbage in the evening. I counted eight ships in sight at once as we near Cape Finisterre.

* * *

The entries would be written in my diary during the night watch. Although I'd wake up around 17.00 from a snooze during the afternoon, I'd not really take over the watch until after supper about 19.30, then I'd be on until 23.00. Andy would do 23.00–02.00 the following morning, and I'd be on 02.00–05.00; he'd do from 05.00–08.00 although this really meant until 09.00 while I had my breakfast, as he'd have had his own earlier. I took over until 13.00 when we both had lunch together, and he was on watch again until 18.00 which was supper time.

At this stage of the voyage we each had time to consider the personality of our companion. I think we were both glad we didn't know much about one another, and I don't think either of us was particularly interested in the other. I was certainly interested in having time alone at the chart table to read, to think, maybe to write my book on Ardmore; but mostly I just wanted to get away from pressure. I wanted to choose what I wanted to do, and I wanted to do small things exactly as I wanted them done; if they didn't work out right I liked to start and do them all over again, without any time limit. I was really tired of asking people to do things, and then seeing them do them badly. This applied to small things like the washing up and the cleaning of the galley. I was very fortunate that my companion was also what I would call a 'particular' person; I think if either of us had been untidy or careless there would have been trouble.

Andy had been the Skipper of the yacht all summer, and he was clearly keen to play an equal role in decision-making on this trip. Here I think it was fortunate that I was twice his age, with a younger man there could have been a struggle for superiority, but with me this didn't matter at all; I was quite happy to let him go about things as he wished I just wanted to see the trip succeed and to enjoy it. I remembered Andy's father's advice to me, 'don't let him push you around'. We met for lunch and supper, and a few times when we called each other for the watch change at nights, otherwise each was free to follow his own ideas on how to pass the time. Apart from continuing homesickness life was spacious, on the grand scale.

Andy — Day 8

A frustrating day of slow progress and damage. At lunchtime, while crashing along closehauled, the old No 1 yankee blew out in a wind of only 30 knots, it was a severe mental blow, how hard can we push the old girl before she falls apart? Instead of changing to the No 2 yankee we clipped on the small No 3 and a tiny staysail, rather like closing the stable door after the horse has bolted. For a while we maintained a reasonable speed until the fresh wind eased to only 15/20 knots. We crawled on all night, reluctant to change sail again because of a gale forecast.

John — Day 9, Friday September 9

(Day's run 112 nm)

We clawed our way up to Cape Finisterre, we are 1,000 miles out from Ardmore with about 27,000 to go. A cold front passed rapidly through with tropical rain and a shift in the wind to a welcome WNW and we slid on our way down the west coast of Spain towards Portugal. On our world scheme for navigation we both felt we should have cut out to the west at the mouth of the English Channel, rather than try to sail diagonally across the Bay of Biscay, it might have saved us a bit of time with the headwinds, but it just didn't seem the right way to treat the weather systems. Near the front of our minds all the time is the coming battle with the 'South Atlantic High'. Weather systems deserve respect if you don't wish them to treat you badly. The headwinds had caused us a lot of pumping to clear the forepeak, water over the bows flooded down through the forehatch because of a damaged rubber seal, Andy held the record with 560 pumps at one time.

Andy — Day 9

The gale passed us by, they always do when one is ready. I came on watch at 5.00 am, two and a half hours later both reefs were shaken out and two larger headsails replaced the storm sails *English Rose* again leapt from wave to wave. I had also tacked, untangled the topping lift from the backstay, taken down the forecast and made breakfast. Who said that sailing is a life of ease?

* * *

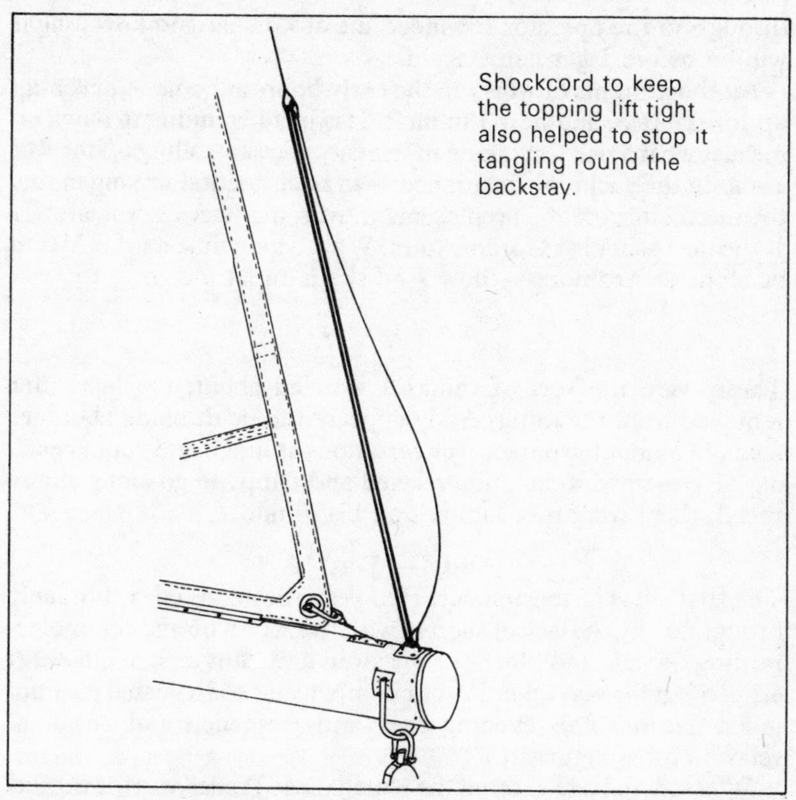

We decided that whenever possible sail changes should be made by whoever was on watch, which allowed the other to remain undisturbed in his bunk. We felt that rest would be a key factor in the success of the voyage, as 200 days is a long time. Continually changing sail to suit conditions increases speed but tires the crew, so leading to less sail changing and subsequent loss in performance. An over-tired crew will make mistakes and cause damage. We aimed to sail *English Rose* at a level that maintained a good average speed without wearing us down. There would be no rest or hot baths at Cape Town to precede three months in the Roaring Forties.

John — Day 10, Saturday September 10

(Day's run 118 nm)

So the seeds of discontent are sowed. A day of slatting sails and very little progress at all. The endless bashing of the sails and chafing of the sheets is a torment all day long. Spent a lot of time trying to get through to Ardmore on the radio — but very disappointed. Over-hearing depressing conversations between other people aboard ships and the shore while I wait to try and get through to the operator reminded me of how far and how long it will be before I get home again.

All those nights of worry in the early hours at home — psyching up for the trip, and now I'm on it. It is just beginning to dawn on me just what a risk I'm taking in so many ways by sailing off for half a year in the yacht. No insurance — so an accidental sinking means the impossible cost of a replacement. Missing Becca's crucial start at the new school at Gordonstoun. What a long time it is for MC to be alone at Ardmore — how kind she is to let me go.

* * *

These were the sort of things I worried about; they were far removed from the things Andy appeared to be thinking about, as far as I could tell from our conversations at lunch and supper each day. He seemed to be quite relaxed and happy to go along at any speed, there were no deadlines on his mind.

Andy — Day 10

The first signs of tension occurred yesterday and today, probably brought on by the lack of success with the HF radio and the endless rattling of sails and blocks in the swell and light airs. We haven't argued but for several hours our company lacked its usual pleasant jovial nature. This evening the wind freshened and an air of relaxation has returned.

We seem to have entered the North-East Trades, during the day it is beautifully warm with a clear sky over a translucent blue sea tempting me to dive in.

John — Day 11, Sunday September 11

(Day's run 117 nm)

A much better day — a real cracker in fact. The wind does seem to have settled into a pale sort of Trade Wind at force 3–4, NW maybe but surely it should be NE? Anyway, after hearing the operator telling Andy twice, that there was something wrong with the 'modulation of the transmitter' on 16 MHZ, we charged the batteries for four hours (off the engine) and tried again on 12 MHZ. Operator said we were nearly hidden under the Russian trawler traffic to Moscow, but all the same he put me through to Ardmore — and delight — MC's voice on the line — HURRAH after four days of frustration.

All well at home and MC going to Brighton (to her Mother between September 18–26, then back to Ardmore so the Sandals can get away for three weeks holiday. 2,000 salmon sold and only 500 more to go. Becca found the first week hard going at Gordonstoun, but now she is 'enjoying it'.

Wonderful to speak to MC and hear her cheery voice, she knows only too well what it is like in the 'radio shack' in the aft cabin, from the 77/78 trip.

Instead of sleeping in the afternoon I got on with the deck jobs, with my new tool box. I moved the danbuoy to the port side, removed the wooden step frame, and removed the twisted lifebuoy frame from the port quarter — the lifebuoy had been carried away in the Irish Sea gales. I tightened the many nuts on the fuel tank top hatch in the Skipper's cabin: we had been losing fuel. I hope that tightening the top will seal the 'Life-Calk' which Malcolm put on at Ardmore. Sorted out the fruit and veg, it is a race to eat it now before it rots. Tomatoes, oranges, lemons, grapefruit, cabbages, onions, all are in danger of rotting. Apples and potatoes do seem to be standing up OK. Bread finished, all mouldy, and butter rancid too. Plenty of work to do on the boat, will I get anything done on 'Ardmore Years'?

* * *

I was homesick, worried about the radio failing and cutting us off from those at home. Everything was at risk. The killing of the salmon was a critical part of the year's programme, and it was easy to get it all wrong. Jennie and Malcolm Sandals had only joined us earlier in the year, when Lance and Ada Bell had retired to their croft through the wood, after 12 years with us; there was no way the Sandals could get through the winter without storm damage, only experience would show them how to guard against the gales. At least I was confident that Rebecca would cope at her new school.

With the onset of warmer weather and smoother seas, we settled down to do the minor jobs and get into a routine for 200 days. Fresh fruit and veg would soon be a memory. One of my main objectives on the trip was to really get down to writing 'Ardmore Years', the story of all the years of struggle since we began in 1968. I felt absence would help the writing, but I did have to get on with it.

Andy — Day 11

The large northerly swell of yesterday has eased off allowing a good day of work. I occupied a few hours rearranging the forepeak, from its clutter of jerry-cans and sails to a more seamanlike sail locker. The rubber seals on the diesel tank hatches are perishing. Now, with the tank full, whenever *English Rose* heels a tiny trickle is polluting the bilge. John has tightened the securing bolts, taking care not to shear any off.

More of a worry are the deck hatch seals. The forepeak, forward cabin and aft cabin hatches were fitted with new rubbers two weeks ago, already the forepeak rubber has come adrift. Three days ago the forward bilge required 1,220 strokes on the bilge pump to empty what flooded below during one afternoon. There must be a solution otherwise all our energy will be expended pumping instead of sailing.

I had my second wash today, my comb remains elusive.

* * *

Will I ever forget the rattling of pulley blocks caused by the sails slatting in light airs? The ceaseless hammering could only be silenced by dropping the sails, but that is a poor solution. A better cure is to support the blocks in some manner. John suggested slipping large diameter plastic tubing over the shackles that secured the blocks to the toerail, but unfortunately we couldn't find any suitable tubing aboard. Another idea was to use shockcord tied to the guardrails, but this idea was thwarted because the shockcord could not be attached to the type of blocks we used. We never did manage to stop the rattling.

John — Day 12, Monday September 12
(Day's run 140 nm)

A bit of an anti-climax after speaking with MC on the radio yesterday. Grey weather. Slipping silently south at only 5 knots — 140 miles is not enough really. We have to average 135 miles/day to do 27,000 in 200 days, and we are some 221 miles down at the

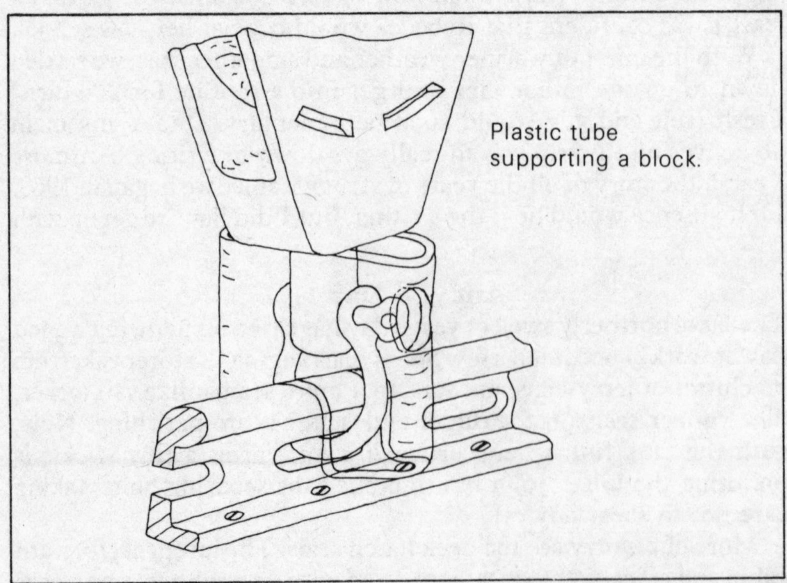
Plastic tube supporting a block.

moment, with all this light following wind. Where are the North-East Trades?

At least I'm able to get to grips with 'Ardmore Years', I'm eager for the book again, and have the typewriter on the chart table, bashing away as good as ever. It's good to have something far away from here to concentrate on.

Andy and I discuss using the after hatch for access to the wheel in the Southern Ocean, I'm frightened of the huge swimming-pool effect of the main and after cockpits. Maybe we'll fill the forward one with the inflated (or partly) Avon dinghy? Approaching the wheel through the after hatch removes that fear of going overboard on the way aft from the main hatch.

John — Day 13, Tuesday September 13

(Day's run 128 nm)

Rolling south under grey skies, its like coming through the tunnel from the dressing room for a boxing match — its leading to the main event!

We have settled into a good pattern of life on board, and both of us seem easy and relaxed with things. I feel it is vital that we continue in this manner, I particularly must work to keep a cheery face on what will be a long, long trip.

I made a reasonable curry in the evening, using Stevens Lefield chicken curry sachets, and boiling the rice in the way John McConnell taught me at Mariveg in 1981. But will this mean we use too much of the precious canned butter? Potential shortages of food, water and fuel are ever at the back of my mind.

I think we'll go through between the Canary Islands of Tenerife and Gran Canaria, it would be good to show Andy Pico de Teide (12,180 feet).

Andy — Day 13

Progress is becoming rather slow. Although we are trying hard, the Trades refuse to blow, rarely exceeding 10 knots. The wind remains between north and north-west. If we used the spinnaker we might do better but until the spinnaker net is finished we are loathe to hoist the beast because it will undoubtedly wrap itself around the forestay.

This afternoon I spent half an hour at the masthead trying to fasten shackles and pieces of line to the forestay, my efforts were in vain. The sickening rolling accentuated 70 feet above sea level, made just holding on a full-time job. I returned to the deck somewhat disgruntled. The spinnaker net will have to wait.

The windows continue to leak, I have smeared a load of Life-calk around each frame which may ease the problem.

Yesterday afternoon saw my first attempts at bread making, using a packet of bread mix given by my sister. Despite the loaf and rolls looking very pale, they tasted delicious. From now on we only have basic raw ingredients so the results may be a little more interesting! John is sorry we haven't brought a supply of prepared mix instead of jerry-cans full of flour.

For supper yesterday we ate steak and kidney pie (from a tin), plus, yet again, cabbage.

We orginally decided to eat all the fresh food, and the tins left from the summer cruises, but the monotony of cabbage every day for over a week has proved too much. At lunchtime we dug around in each locker to produce Ryvita, ham paté, Nutella, fresh orange juice and dry-roasted peanuts, which together with the fresh bread made a tasty lunch.

John — Day 14, Wednesday September 14

(Day's run 122 nm)

Still crawling along, and its beginning to get on the nerves a bit. We are falling behind. We are level with Madeira, so we tacked to avoid running into Islas Desertas, which are only some 80 miles ahead. Began to pick up a bit of speed in the night, and the Aquair generator begins skipping on the end of its 100-foot line.

Andy — Day 14

John is concerned about our lack of progress. When we discovered from her book that Naomi James arrived home in June after leaving the UK in September, I think John felt like turning back. We must return before the school season commences in April, but that is for John to worry about. I am in the fortunate position of having to bear little responsibility.

I miss Marie terribly and occasionally feel seasick, otherwise my shipboard life is carefree, my main concern at present is trying to develop an even suntan.

John tidied all his books off the table today but to my dismay he put them back half an hour later.

John — Day 15, Thursday September 15

(Day's run 180 nm)

Picked up speed in the early hours. I dropped the mizzen staysail at 02.30, and the stern generator sounds rough. We hauled it in, all kinked from skipping, at 08.30. A kink round the shaft of the propellor has done little for the generator. We put it back in again in the late afternon, on 150 feet of rope, but it still skipped, should we add more weight and rope?

At 19.30 we gybed onto a course for the channel between Gran

Canaria and Tenerife. Now only some 130 miles up ahead. It has been a boisterous day with cheery, sunny Trade wind sailing at 8½ knots in NE winds force 5–6, using No 2 yankee-genoa staysail, full mainsail, and mizzen. I feel vaguely ill-at-ease and homesick. Andy is a good fellow, but 20 years younger than me — it does limit the conversation a bit — but he is all, and more, that I could have asked for on this trip: quiet, particular and thoughtful.

Morale did lift a bit with the 180 mile noon-noon run, even though it included a knot of Canary current.

Andy — Day 15

Eight knots in the North-East Trades, we will keep our fingers crossed and hope it lasts. For a week we have made no sail changes except handing and resetting the mizzen staysail at each gybe. Gybing is a long operation taking on average 20 minutes. We drop the mizzen staysail, ease the two boom downhauls, undo the yankee sheet snatchblock, haul the booms in, tighten the running backstay, alter course, reset 'George' and then re-trim the sails with their sheets and downhauls. I wrote two days ago that my life is presently blissfully carefree, I momentarily forgot the nagging worry over the hatch-seals. No amount of cleaning and roughening will make the special silicone glue stick to the rubber.

Our increase in speed has one drawback: the Aquair spinner breaks the surface causing the rope to bunch into twisted balls. The instructions recommend lengthening the rope to 150 feet which we have done.

John — Day 16, Friday September 16

(Day's run 170 nm)

Gran Canaria, maybe the last land we shall see before Cape Horn. It was shrouded in mist and cloud as we skirted half a dozen miles along the north shore and then headed at good speed down between Gran Canaria and Tenerife. I was sorry not to be able to show Andy Pico de Teide (12,180 feet) on Tenerife, but all was in cloud.

The trade wind hit force 6–7 in the afternoon in the channel and we sped south. Many ships coming north from the Canary Passage and so we must keep a good look-out now.

* * *

Andy was working like a Trojan to keep the boat up to scratch and prepare her for the Southern Ocean. I wondered how long it would be before there was a reaction to over-working! We sat down for lunch and supper, and always managed to converse quite happily right through the meal. Although he was 20 years younger than me, and his interests limited to a fairly narrow range of subjects, mostly boats and his future with boats, I found this gave us quite enough material to last almost indefinitely. We were after all engaged on quite a serious venture, and we couldn't think too hard about what lay ahead of us in the Southern Ocean.

John — Day 17, Saturday September 17

(Day's run 140 nm)

Slipping south from the Canaries. Sky bronzed by Sahara dust, but almost no wind during the day, we trickle along at 3.5 knots at best. Andy is well able to deal with this — no idea of racing or any urgency to get anywhere. I am haunted by comparisons with the Whitbread Race in 1977/8 but what am I worrying about . . . Noon saw 2,000 miles logged since Ardmore.

Very hot now, too hot. The heat rash is starting up on my arms, but I'll fight it with Betnovate cream, washing and a clean blue shirt.

Got through to Jennie Sandals at Ardmore at 20.00 on 22 MHZ and all is well there. MC is in Brighton, she went early to give the Sandals an early start to their own holiday as she returns.

Perfect night at 6 knots on a silken smooth moonlit sea. What will the rest of the voyage be like? Southern Ocean . . .

Working away on 'Ardmore Years' its just the thing for the long night watches, while the boat snores along on her own, guided by 'George's sure hand (the self-steering). On a night like this the whole world seems at peace.

Andy — Day 17

The satnav must be right, yesterday Gran Canaria appeared through the haze right on cue.

Today, since our speed has again dropped to a depressing 3 knots, John took the opportunity to try his hand at fishing, unfortunately the bonito or whatever swims around here were too busy to chase the spinner. Instead of a fish supper we dined on canned beef, rice, sweet corn, raisins, peanuts, and potato salad.

The mixture of peat and fibreglass which has previously passed as our fresh water supply is now sweet and clear thanks to a 'Freshness' filter.

My afternoon was again swallowed up with maintenance and preparations for the Roaring Forties. I finished parcelling two bottlescrews, freed two deck-rollers and glued a piece of shockcord onto the forehatch.

⋆ ⋆ ⋆

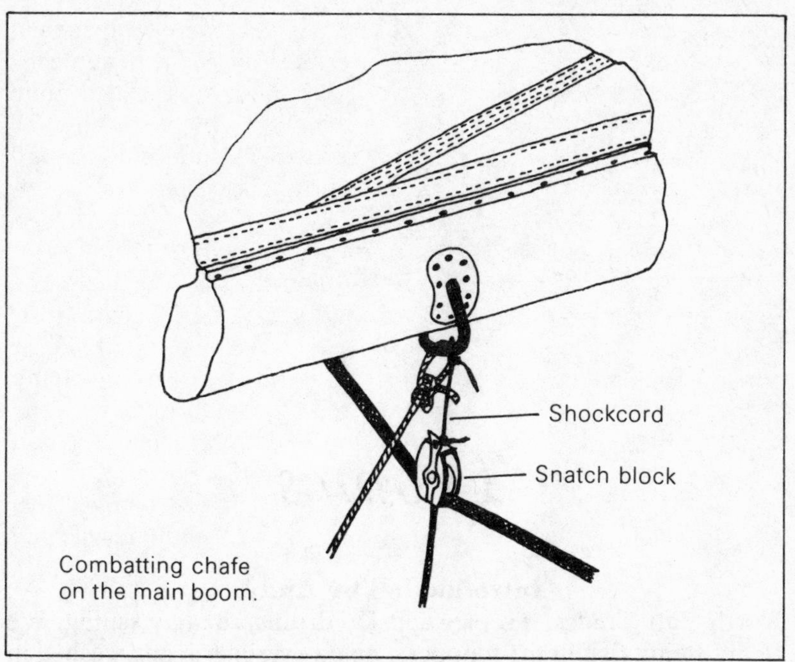

Combatting chafe
on the main boom.

Chafe is the ceaseless enemy to all that moves. Wherever possible we padded rough edges to avoid wrecking our irreplaceable gear. The severity of the problem for someone like me, used only to coastal sailing is hard to appreciate. Finding a sheet one morning almost cut though, simply due to rubbing against the relatively smooth main boom, hammered into me the need for care. We normally pulled the sheet clear of the boom using a snatch block with a rope tail led through a block on the toerail and then cleated down.

On the morning in question neither John nor I had noticed that at some time during the night the block had detached itself from the sheet. Like the No 1 yankee it was a costly lesson. Parcelling the bottlescrews helped to protect the staysail sheets. They were first padded with mutton cloth held in place with plastic tape then tightly whipped with 3 mm line and finally bound with 2-inch-wide linen sticky tape. Slightly excessive perhaps, but it looked neater than plastic tubing and remained intact, as did the sheets.

4

Tropics

Introduction by Andy

North-East Trades, Tropics and Doldrums, dreamy sailing. We found flying fish in the scuppers, dived overboard, and washed in the rain. For John happy memories, for me fascination. Yet we were uneasy, thinking always of the Southern Ocean, the main event.

John — Day 18, Sunday September 18

(Day's run 130 nm)

A number of ships to begin with, probably West African trade. We are 80 miles west of Vila Cisneros on the coast of Spanish Sahara. Memories of our trip down here in the Nicholson 32 in 1974. There were six of us: three instructors from the school, MC, Rebecca and me. It was very hot, and hadn't rained for seven years on one of the Cape Verde Islands we visited; quite a change for seven year-old Rebecca, who'd only known Ardmore.

I'm very pleased with our rig for the trade winds. We have the No 2 yankee, with the genoa staysail forward of the main mast, and the full mainsail and mizzen staysail between the masts, and finally the full mizzen. The great thing about the two-masted ketch rig is the ability to carry as many as five moderate-sized sails, which can easily be dropped in the squalls. With the large single mast of the sloop rig, it would be harder for us. The first sail to go with us, is always the mizzen staysail in 15 knots of apparent wind, that's to say the speed of the wind on the sail, taking into account the speed of the boat either with the wind or against it.

I failed to contact a ship which passed very close to us at 09.45

this morning. I couldn't raise it on either 2182 KHZ or channel 16 VHF. She was south-bound and called *Fionia*. It's a puzzle for us, does it mean we won't be able to speak to other ships at all? We don't like to spend time just calling ships up at random because it uses so much power. At 11.45 we entered the tropics. A large school of dolphins came to us at 14.00, and we also saw our first flying fish.

As it got dark I gybed five sails on my own. I found it hard going. Was this because of the huge amount of 'going-off' bacon in the omlette? Is it better to eat it or throw it away?

Reading Naomi James' *At one with the sea* I'm most impressed with her as a person, particularly her early life.

We are testing our drinking water consumption. One gallon in a plastic 'meths' bottle can last us two days!! Mind you, that is stretching it a bit.

We passed a ship with 'not under command' lights at 02.00 — probably a tanker cleaning her tanks?

* * *

In fact we found we had to fill the gallon bottle every day. Half a gallon was not enough.

Andy — Day 18

Sun, calm seas and sufficient wind to push us steadily southwards at 6 to 7 knots, Marie would love to be aboard now. A score of dolphins joined us after lunch showing off by leaping and splashing around. An amazing creature like a small transparent bird glided over the waves for 100 yards, these flying fish will soon be littering our deck.

The fresh food is lasting surprisingly well; the tomatoes began to mould shortly after leaving Ardmore, but a salt water wash prolonged their life up to two weeks, and there were only a few remaining when the tray was chucked overboard. The boxes of fruit are steadily dwindling; the oranges show slight mould, but the apples are fine as are the grapefuit, onions and potatoes.

I am a little dubious about the bacon especially when the packets are left open for several days and we have no fridge aboard. The sealed packets are probably okay, for a while anyway.

John — Day 19, Monday September 19

(Day's run 145 nm)

Wind still a bit light for the trades I fear. I feel a bit gloomy after finishing Naomi James' book — have I to go through all that again? Will I never learn? Have I the power to still cut the mustard?

My period off watch was spent having a good sleep. Andy is in good form, getting on with his endless job list — might I feel better if I did more myself? But then I'd only feel remorse at not getting on with 'Ardmore Years'.

A brilliant full moon at night.

* * *

Some interesting points here in retrospect. I can see the discomfort ahead, and scold myself for going towards it again, yet at the same time, I'm drawn to it to see if I can still manage. I read somewhere that psychologists divide things into three circles: the child, the adult, and parent. Most creativity derives from the circle of the child, and they urge that this circle be not allowed to wither. I think my feelings above are simple to the point of childishness. I hope I haven't read this thing about 'circles' wrongly!

This was the 18th day without more than three hours sleep at a time; not a shortage of sleep anymore, just an inablity to get the 6–8 hours of unbroken sleep which most adults usually have. Sleep becomes a tricky thing as the voyage goes on.

Regarding the job list, I felt in a bit of a cleft stick. I was well aware of Andy's father's remark to me just before we sailed 'don't let him push you around'. I'd smiled at the time, thinking it to be an unlikely outcome. But I was already realising that Andy had a pretty stubborn streak, he liked doing things his way and if at all possible, on his own. On such a long trip I was especially keen to avoid a clash of personality, and realising that I can be rather stubborn myself, I decided to let him organise things as much as possible for himself. The problem for me was that Andy didn't like discussing the jobs with anyone else, so just occasionally he would do a job which went wrong, and then I'd have to exercise a bit of self-control if I'd seen a way of solving the problem myself.

There really wasn't enough work for two people, certainly not two Andys. He hadn't brought any form of diversion, like my book 'Ardmore Years' to work on. If he had asked me I would have suggested something like a correspondence course, but I'd come to accept that with Andy I would not know how much film he had decided to bring, or if he would have a personal stereo. It was just part of his personality. He liked to keep things to himself, good in some ways, not so good in others. I had 'Ardmore Years' to write, and once into it, I got completely involved, any avoidance of it would feel like slacking.

John — Day 20, Tuesday September 20

(Day's run 157 nm)

Wind got up in the early hours, until the sacrificial tube connecting the servo rudder to the self-steering gear broke for the first time.

Andy replaced it while I steered by hand. Strong winds persist through the morning but fade in the afternoon. Very hot now, and its difficult to do much save keep going. We wonder if it would be a good idea to cut south-east towards Cape Town after the Doldrums. It should save hard wear on the gear by avoiding the Roaring Forties until the latest possible time.

* * *

These sacrificial tubes were limited in number, and were to become the main factor in our calculations for best possible boat speed later in the voyage. To a large extent the duration of the voyage depended on them.

As you will have gathered from the writing so far, the Southern Ocean featured as a central issue of the voyage. All our thoughts were directed towards handling this one big problem. We talked about it almost every lunchtime and then again at supper. If we could put off entering it for as long as possible, then we should do it; the spring squalls before reaching Cape Town on the first leg of the Whitebread Race were etched on my mind. The best thing would be to avoid the temptation of going down the South American coast then have to run before the wind in the Forties all across the South Atlantic. Whatever else, I didn't want to get the boat damaged before we passed Cape Town. If we were forced to call in there I doubted if we would continue the voyage, most likely we would turn back up the Atlantic for home.

Andy — Day 20

Down below an atmosphere of stale humid air is making us lethargic, sleep is difficult with the endless cacophony of rattling blocks. John tells me it gets worse!

Last night 'George' eased his concentration for a moment allowing *English Rose* to broach and snap the servo rudder. It wasn't really 'George's fault. We ought to have shortened sail in a rising wind instead of careering along, occasionally surfing. The servo rudder was quickly repaired, and with the mizzen down and the main reefed, *English Rose* proceeded on her way in a more sedate, ladylike manner.

I suspect there will be a few sail repairs after we change sail, our present rig has remained up for ten days. The headsails in particular are badly chafed along the foot and leech where they rub the shrouds and guardrails. Two piston hanks from the head of the yankee have disappeared.

My daily quota of work began with repairing the sheet locker, the cavernous space is tightly packed with numerous jerry-cans and coils of rope. Overloading had burst the plywood locker side, causing it to bear against the steering gear. I also began to replace the aft hatch seal.

Yesterday evening I hauled out the sewing machine for the first time, the mizzen staysail had chafed against the backstay exposing the luff wire. It was repaired with some difficulty because the infernal machine began to misbehave; breaking and skipping stitches — another repair for tomorrow.

Red Sahara sand and dust forming a low-lying haze blots out the sun until after mid-morning, giving us a few hours of daylight without having to endure the burning rays. The sun is almost behind the sails by lunchtime when I wake, enabling me to work on deck in shade with a cooling breeze.

John occupies his mornings typing at the chart table, taking advantage of the calm weather. I shot the sun twice yesterday to check the satnav position and for practice. I find using a sextant is a satisfying, uncomplicated art, the necessary calculations are easily computed on John's Tamaya calculator. I'm rarely interested in our exact position, and John deals with plotting our noon positions from the satnav and updating the various charts in use.

Night sailing over a moonlit sea is a delight. There are few ships around for we are just off the shipping lane. Twice recently we have passed close to tankers displaying lights for a ship not under command. From the foul smell wafting downwind they are obviously cleaning their tanks. Frequently we sail through large patches of emulsified oil.

* * *

The shockcord hatch seals are a prime example of the unconventional repairs that kept *English Rose* seaworthy. The hatch manufacturers supplied replacement neoprene rubber strips and silicone-based glue which proved totally unsuitable. Though I cleaned the rubber with meths, petrol and acetone the glue simply refused to take hold. I next tried Evo-Stik. That also failed. The Evo-Stik did at least stick to the metal frames giving a glimmer of hope. I lay in my bunk mulling over the problem whenever off watch, something soft and plentiful was needed, similar to rubber: rubber shockcord! Of course, piles of the stuff lay within a few feet of my bunk in the bosun's locker.

An afternoon of work saw the forehatch completed. Shockcord alone didn't quite fill the gap so I used Life-calk on top. The Life-calk was allowed to surface dry, a matter of hours in the tropical heat, then the hatch was closed to squeeze out the excess and form an accurate seal. Life-calk without shockcord would also have worked if I had thought of it earlier.

The aft cabin hatch was similarly repaired, but the two hatches

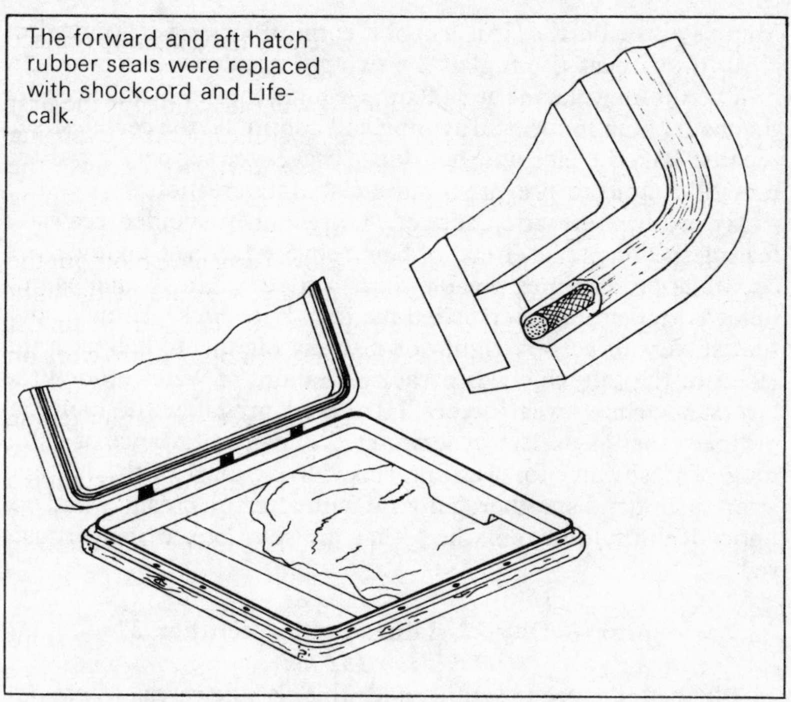

The forward and aft hatch rubber seals were replaced with shockcord and Life-calk.

in my cabin were left alone; provided they were never opened to disturb the seal I reckoned leaks were unlikely.

John — Day 21, Wednesday September 21

(Day's run 105 nm)

A poor day of light winds and great heat near the African coast. Brown water. Did a bit of running repairs on the No 2 yankee while we had the light genoa up, this sail gave a bit of speed in the afternoon as the wind came round to the west. Down to new No 1 yankee for the night and high morale at seven and a half knots. I'm plagued by prickly heat as I expected. The old skin just doesn't like the heat anymore I'm afraid.

Andy — Day 21

Two things worthy of note occurred today: we changed a sail and I enjoyed a thorough wash.

The usually consistent trade wind shifted from north-east to west and accordingly we raised the light genoa, is this the start of the Doldrums? Unfortunately after half an hour the wind died requiring me to sit by the wheel keeping an eye on the course. Luckily I could sit in the shade cast by the mizzen. I wore my straw hat and a baggy white shirt, similar to a nightie, given me by

Marie's sister Bertha. It is a cool if comical looking costume, but ideal in this heat. I am glad the two girls can't see me in it.

When John woke me at 3.00 pm we hung the No 2 yankee under the main boom to form an awning and continued the ceaseless sail repairs. Baked beans and hot dog sausages for supper, it was too hot and humid to prepare a more elaborate creation.

My wash came after supper, I previously avoided seawater fearing the long term effects of being covered with salt. However a combination of interminable heat and a slight aroma which followed me around persuaded me to risk it. Bucket number one sent shivers of ecstasy right down to my big toe, to hell with the effect of the salt, this was paradise. Gallons of water eroded the layers of grimy sweat before I lathered myself with shampoo, ordinary soap is useless in seawater. My daily allowance of half a mug of freshwater for washing rinsed away most of the salt and after an air dry I smothered myself with aftersun cream. I had not noticed, until John remarked, that my skin looked dangerously red.

John — Day 22, Thursday September 22

(Day's run 152 nm)

Much better speed south, and this is the area where we encountered Doldrums in the '77 race. Prickly heat and now sunburn (through two sails) from trying to keep in the breeze. Morale is low with the continuous all-over itch. But we are well south of Cape Verde (Dakar).

Andy is still working like a man possessed. The books of Moitessier (and James before that) make fearful reading for people in our position. Manage to keep plodding on with the typing of 'Ardmore Years' at night.

Sad not to get through to MC on radio, must charge the batteries. Sheet lightning — Doldrums?

Andy — Day 22

Today it was John's turn to burn, I think it is possible to burn merely from reflected light, sitting behind the sails offers little protection. I loaned him my precious cream.

Instead of going on deck I avoided the ultra-violet by working in the stifling galley, turning out a potato salad and caramel pudding for supper and also baking two loaves. The loaves are terrific, they are the first batch using raw ingredients.

In the cool of the evening I re-positioned several blocks on the toerail trying to find positions that avoid the sheets chafing the guardrails. I also eye-spliced the ends of a piece of rope and seized a thimble to the centre. The thimble is shackled to a strong point just aft of the mainmast, the two ends are secured to the forward end of the cockpit on each side, providing a useful jackstay. We can now clip our harnesses to it for unrestricted movement. The original jackstays lead down the side decks together with the sheets, running backstays, downhauls etc. Our harnesses inevitably became entangled in this cat's cradle, thus tempting us to move around unhitched.

The Doldrums are almost upon us judging from the barometer, our latitude, and the appearance of the sky.

John — Day 23, Friday September 23

(Day's run 135 nm)

Are we in the Doldrums? Dark individual clouds and rain showers all round us at breakfast. We get a few brief cooling drops but none to wash in or catch. Wind variable then settles in the west for the day. Fair speed. Charged batteries for four hours, and the Aquair runs all the time. Radio to MC in Brighton on 5 MHZ, but it's still not transmitting properly. Just no signal on transmit at random times. Glad to hear MC — bet she's glad she's not here! All well at home. Will radio again in a week's time, I hope it works OK. Reading *Somme* by Farrar-Hockley.

Andy in great form all over the boat. I'm still near standstill with prickly heat, just got to endure it. Applying Betnovate. Wonderful wash in fresh water at 02.00 at the wheel. I just let the water dry on my skin. Slept well after this.

* * *

The prickly heat was inevitable. It has slowly become a problem as I've got older. Perhaps with access to cold showers it would be no problem. I first encountered it in 1968 when sailing alone from Eire to Brazil, I had nylon sheets on plastic covered mattress, it was not the best thing for absorbing sweat. This time I had cotton clothes and sheets for the Tropics, and the sheets were on woollen rugs. The Betnovate cleared the rash immediately but I always feared the long term effect on my skin. I've found it makes the layers of skin thinner and thinner, until cracks are formed which are difficult to heal. This would not be a good thing on a long voyage.

Andy — Day 23

Late this afternoon the boat virtually stopped, I decided the time had arrived for a swim. With some trepidation I sat on the pulpit then launched myself off in a less than graceful dive, no doubt scaring off every fish for 200 yards. The water felt wonderfully cool and stung my eyes as I opened them to look up at *English Rose*. She looked beautifully sleek and now I know why the dolphins enjoy playing with her. Back at the surface gasping for air I was alarmed to see the boat flying past at 1 knot. I caught the toerail and hauled myself aboard then dived again, even more boldly than before, and swam alongside for a while.

Making baggywrinkle occupied the remainder of the afternoon, the shaggy mop-like bundles of old rope which adorn our shrouds are usually scoffed at and regarded as old fashioned.

Within a few days we will be bashing closehauled into the South-East Trades, so while we are upright I am trying to finish as many jobs as possible.

John — Day 24, Saturday September 24

(Day's run 100 nm)

Much more pleasant day. Humidity has gone, and at 07.30 hours Andy gybed to an easterly wind. Is it possible we are out of the Doldrums? What a stroke of good fortune that would be. Three swallows (just the same as '77) were with us most of the day, on the moving mizzen staysail sheet, and even in the saloon. After they'd gone, a small yellow/green breasted finch-size bird came in the late afternoon; he preferred the radar platform to a seat on the spinning log line.

I cooked up a Stevens Lefield lamb biriani, with potatoes, raisins and planter's peanuts for supper. Then I lowered the mizzen staysail and came up into the wind until we were about 50 degrees off it and sailing just a little east of due south.

Are we in for the long beat to windward now? To get on the African side of the South Atlantic High, we'll have to be hard on the wind for many days.

Andy — Day 24

We seem to be through the Doldrums, can we really be so soon? If we are through it is a terrific bonus, meaning we hardly slowed down. In a way I feel sorry to have missed the experience of calms, thunderstorms and the real chance of fishing. We seem to have missed a number of things, no whales or water spouts, and the North-East Trades never blew consistently.

Keeping my diary usefully occupies an hour or more each night, John advised me to write on alternate lines for clarity, I write so profusely there is a danger of running out of space. Hence I have resumed my old habit of filling every line. Writing daily is vital, early on I frequently missed days, the events and memories are now lost to the sea.

Three visitors arrived today, two swallows and a finch. They are undoubtedly miles off course and will die. The two swallows arrived first, venturing below to my favourite seat, the forward heads. With the hatch open a cool breeze blows down, by far the most agreeable spot in the heat of the day. The birds thought likewise until I appeared with my camera. They objected and left their mark before moving to a precarious perch on the guardrail.

Disaster struck our new water system, the tiny foot pump was not man enough to force water through the filter, now the pump leaks the precious elixir. A bit of lateral thinking suggested the pump need not be at the sink, because we fill a one gallon plastic container daily to monitor consumption. The 'Mk 2' replacement utilises a spare bilge pump neatly hidden in a cupboard under the companionway together with the Freshness filter. It was a sticky sweaty job taking three hours, and involving draining and removing the cooker paraffin tank to reach the plumbing.

By the time I'd finished, the sun had swung well past the forestay enabling me to spend a cool hour reading on the shaded foredeck. John prepared Stevens Lefield lamb biriani for supper. The individual portions allow different meals to be cooked in one pot, however we normally eat the same.

We were treated to a spectacular sunset, it gave the impression of a dividing line between the Doldrums and the Trades. To the north the sky lit up golden yellow tinged with orange, while to the south a clear rich blue faded into the horizon. The clear cut line was probably the edge of the Sahara dust.

Another interesting phenomenon occurred this afternoon: we sailed through several bands of disturbed water each roughly a hundred yards wide, almost like tidal race overfalls.

* * *

The Freshness filter gave sweet clear drinking water, but in the Tropics the water became tepid and lost its appeal.

We had 12 tins of Andrews liver salts and I thought they were a joke from Marie Christine until we added a teaspoonful to a mug of water. The fizzy drink was refreshing despite its warmth.

Another treat from Marie Christine was a slice of fruit cake for every day of the trip. She baked 24 of these rich cakes and wrapped them in aluminium foil. They remained moist and tempting for months.

John — Day 25, Sunday September 25

(Day's run 110 nm)

More or less becalmed all day. The end of the Doldrums? More like the beginning! Towering black clouds of rain which go every way but at us. The wind is light and awfully variable. I recognised a

Chinese trawler, white and antique, on the horizon. It came to us, *No 81 Cheog Yang* (Panama). I couldn't raise it on MF or VHF. It had what looked like tuna drying from the rigging in the bows. Tried trolling Francis Chichester's (1930?) silver and copper Hardy spoon all day, to no effect.

Andy — Day 25

Exhaustion is beginning to take its grip, I haven't slept well recently. My foam mattress is encapsulated within a large plastic bag to keep it dry and covered with a sheet sleeping bag. When heeled slightly I remain comfortably wedged at one side, but rolling downwind my body is continually on the move and sleep is fitful. The ever-present sweat sticks the sheet to my skin — not a lot can be done except perhaps install air-conditioning! I must be grateful to have avoided the prickly heat John is suffering.

A Chinese tuna trawler hove into view passing a few hundred yards astern at lunchtime. It is the first ship sighted in five days. Every eight or ten days I write a letter to Marie with the hope of finding an obliging ship to carry my message of love. The ship's appearance sent me scuttling below to seal the 'mail' into a plastic bag weighted with an old broom head to increase its trajectory. The rust-streaked tramp didn't bother to stop.

I need to start a regular routine of exercises to loosen up my body, my legs especially are weak and leaden.

I poked around inside the radio trying to find the fault which intermittently cuts out our transmissions. The complexity of valves, coils and transistors appeared intact so I reassembled the bits then cleaned the aerial connections.

John — Day 26, Monday September 26

(Day's run 82 nm)

3,000 miles logged since Ardmore, and still in the Doldrums. Pretty poor run of 82 miles at noon. Still heading south. Another swallow and a lone tern.

Satnav had a hiccup at 20.06 and leapt forwards some 60 miles 'IT IS ONLY AN AID TO NAVIGATION' I can hear my navigation instructor at Nautical College, Pangbourne say. 'Get out your sextant!' Maybe. The satnav restarted an hour or two later, on the new distance.

Andy — Day 26

A throbbing headache cancelled all work, so I began to read *The Incredible Voyage* by Tristan Jones. John spent a while stitching the genoa staysail.

Heavy rain and vicious thunderstorms surround us, but *English Rose* prefers to tread gingerly between them.

John — Day 27, Tuesday September 27

(Day's run 150 nm)

My head was just beginning to get heavy at 04.20. I went up the (companionway) steps and poked my head out. We were going straight for an enormous black cloud which stretched to either horizon. I called Andy as the first drops began to hit the hull.

We left the heavy genoa and the mizzen up, careless of a squall. The Australian poncho was rigged from the mizzen backstays to the shrouds, and we had a 5-gallon jerry-can full in a few moments plus five bucketfuls from the booms. All-over wash then washed my clothes plus a sheet and pillowcase in stergene, and rinsed. Delighted with the lessening of the prickly heat.

To bunk at 06.30. Woken at 09.30 'We'd better take down the genoa!' says Andy. Up on deck in tropical rain in the nude. Flailing sails. Andy's a good man to work with. Up went the No 1 yankee and working staysail and two reefs in the mainsail. Comfortable again. Strangely, Andy was easily chilled by the cold rain at 06.00. He huddled in the saloon with a Cup-a-soup while I washed my gear. He's been going flat-out since we left (Ardmore) and may be exhausted or de-hydrated a bit? He was surprised I could keep on going, even in the nude, and this helps our relationship a bit, I think — 'Young Turk' and 'Old Hopeful!'

We had a good noon-to-noon run of 113 miles on the log with an extra one and a half knots from the Guinea Current which gave us 150 on the chart. Greatly encouraged to find we are neck-and-neck with our position in the 1977 Whitbread Race when we had a crew of 13. We are using 'George' (Aries vane gear) to sail much more by the wind than to a set course this time. Dried the clothes a bit at 19.00 hours after I did McConnell rice with nuts and raisins for a Stevens-Lefield lamb biriani. With darkness came a southerly wind at last. We headed ESE, and, helped by the one and a half knot current, we are on our way.

A bumpy night with water gushing down the companionway steps, just like old times. I took Stugeron to keep the seasickness at bay.

* * *

The heat was my opponent, burning hot days with a shortage of water for washing. It was like a furnace down below and necessary to find shade from a sail on deck. Andy did manage to acclimatise fairly well, with the help of quantities of suntan cream and a big straw hat. I was brought to a near standstill with the prickly heat rashes, but I was prepared for this from previous trips in the Tropics, and knew full well that I would just have to endure it. I longed for cool showers. Eventually I found that the best form of dress was no clothes at all, Andy was pretty astonished by this, but then he had no prickly heat. When we finally did have a downpour, it came as a gift from heaven for me, the wash under the torrent of cooling fresh water from the end of the mizzen boom lifted my spirits no end.

By way of a contrast, Andy seemed to find the rain cold and soon retired below looking chilled and exhausted. I wasn't entirely surprised, he had been working so hard that I felt some sort of reaction was inevitable, I doubted if anyone could keep up the tense approach he displayed, for more than a few weeks. I didn't feel it was something we could discuss, Andy had been at full stretch ever since we'd decided to make the trip, back in June. For him every day was a journey further into the unknown, I felt he would do anything rather than discuss fears or anxieties with me, so I never pressed him. I knew from Marie Christine that he had almost decided not to come on the trip after talking it over with his girlfriend but several hours of discussion with Marie Christine had decided him to see the voyage through. After the first month at sea, he was bound to be having second thoughts about another six months, I felt the best thing was to make light of it.

The Chinese trawler put a chill up my spine, we were quite alone on the sea and well off the shipping lanes, the trawler seemed to be steaming aimlessly about the horizon before making for us at full speed. I'd read a bit about piracy, and were more or less defenceless, the emergency flares wouldn't do much good against sub-machine guns. The usual pattern seemed to be to sink the yacht and kill the crew, all for the second-hand value of electrical gear like radar and radio, which could easily be stripped from the vessel. In reality we had a few waves from the crew of the trawler, which hove-to some quarter of a mile off, and I felt disappointed at not being able to contact them on our radio. It was to be many months before we were to even get a wave from another human being. When the southerly wind began to rise I set myself for a long beat into it.

Andy — Day 27

Today the clouds opened, it rained and rained. Whereas before we never could find our way into a decent shower, today we could not find a way out. John woke me at 4.30 am enthusiastically describing an enormous black cloud spanning the horizon ahead. Wary from previous false alarms, I reluctantly got up a half an hour before the watch change. On deck it was already spitting and soon it built into a full bodied tropical downpour lasting three quarters of an hour.

If any ships had passed they would have been treated to a

spectacle; two eccentric Englishmen in the pouring rain clad only in shorts, one collecting water and the other washing clothes. A chill worked its way through my inadequate layer of fat so I retired below shivering, to make a 'Cup-a-soup'.

The sewing machine is operational again thanks to a smear of beeswax on the moving parts and a substitute handle improvised from a piece of plastic tubing. John has just passed on a few helpful hints on how to deal with a giant squid!

John — Day 28, Wednesday September 28
(Day's run 180 nm)

Grim memories of the 1977 race — a fortnight of bumps and living at an angle. Andy was quiet today, it's quite difficult to get him going. Well six months is a short time in a lifetime. Not a lot of fun at the moment. Radio Monrovia is a bit unsettling too — the rhythm is so important on a trip of this length.

Andy — Day 28

A miserable day beating to windward, I feel tired, seasick and homesick. I am missing Marie terribly and spend hours lying in my bunk thinking of her, consequently missing valuable sleep and so becoming more tired, an increasing spiral of gloom. Why did I ever set off with John? I don't feel a great drive to make the trip non-stop anymore, secretly I hope we have to stop at Cape Town and return home.

One of 'George's steering lines snapped at lunchtime, it was badly chafed and ought to have been replaced while we were becalmed in the Doldrums. Hanging over the transom is now like trying to stay on a bucking bronco.

* * *

The steering lines continued to chafe throughout the voyage, we occasionally coated them with lanoline which did help. However prevention is better than a cure. The chafe invariably occurred when the rope rubbed against the shell of a pulley block instead of running smooth on the pulley wheel. The problem was to find the correct position for each block to avoid the rope sliding off the wheel. The positioning was eventually successful, but not before we had chafed to ruin, several yards of rope.

John — Day 29, Thursday September 29
(Day's run 190 nm)

I am doubtful we are hard enough on the wind, nor enough sail — we shall see. Andy's undersail tactics have yet to prove wrong (sail/wind chart should be re-written, 5 mph lower — for all changes). I have a bit of sunburn on the bum.

Could there be a non-stop round-the-world race taking about five months? The wind strength/sail size chart is stuck on the bulkhead by the chart table. It is geared for racing, but with just the two of us, Andy felt we should reduce sail at a lower wind to avoid over-pressing.

Andy — Day 29

Four weeks at sea and to celebrate I cooked a chocolate cake which emerged from the oven somewhat mis-shapen, but tasted delicious.

Sailing hard on the wind the hatches are tightly closed, and below deck it is stiflingly humid. The only respite is a few hours before dawn. John has taken to sleeping on the leeward saloon berth instead of in the pilot berth, which is a nuisance since I used to sit there when on watch. The navigator's seat is hardly designed for comfort.

The oranges are going off, I'll squeeze out the juice for a drink in future, I find eating mouldy food repulsive. The memories of the tomatoes and sliced bread remain vivid.

Andy — Day 30, Friday September 30
(Day's run 147 nm)

Last night I read a few chapters of *An Anthology of Sea Journeys* by Ludovic Kennedy a fascinating collection of stories describing journeys in yachts and open boats, the slave trade and pirates.

My thoughts are back to planning a boat to replace *Kinnego*, I fancy something nearer to 30 feet in which to wander the oceans at a more sedate pace.

I have made a new fitting to secure the two self-steering line turning blocks to the aft toerail. Previously the blocks were attached using tiny lacing eyes with ¾ inch screws. The new arrangement has two large lacing eyes pop-rivetted to an aluminium strip, drilled to take eight screws. The aluminium was cut from an oversize baking tray which now fits the oven.

5

South-East Trades – a test of patience

Introduction by Andy

Then the South-East Trades. Nothing to do except think and hold on as we crashed south, closehauled for ten consecutive days. We both had problems, prickly heat, sunburn and headaches. Our diaries portray the misery.

John – Day 31, Saturday October 1

(Day's run 150 mm)

The first month of the six month holiday is already gone. Only five left. I listened to two hours of Sebastian Coe's taped book *Running Free.* It was inspiring for me, alone in the dark at the chart table — he thought failing his 11+ a great motivator (it was for me too). I still think his winning the 1,500 m in Moscow, after losing the 800 m, the greatest sporting achievement I can remember (maybe the Ali/Foreman fight was its equal). Read more of the Elizabeth Longford 'Wellington' two volume biography, it's very good.

We crossed the Equator at 09.10 BST. First time for Andy. Cooler now, wearing thin white shirt and light blue trousers. 20.00–23.00 at the chart table every night, as Andy sleeps. The light is enough, just. MC's engagement photo taped to the radio bulkhead and Becca's 'Rainbow over the loch at home' is clipped under the engine dial panel above. How often I think of them both. MC was to have taken Becca out from school for the first time today, I wonder how its going, only five months then home — Hurrah!

Andy — Day 31

A new month and we are into the southern hemisphere, the sea looks no different from that of the northern hemisphere!

John sighted a light way off to starboard shortly before calling me on watch and I dashed out to catch a glimpse of the first signs of human life for many days.

Not much work this afternoon, I re-fastened two pipe cots, and began screwing the floor down as a precaution against the inevitable capsize. Also I unscrewed the door to our library in the Skipper's cabin. This door is left open for ventilation but as there is no catch to prevent it banging, John usually wedges his briefcase against it, now we are rid of it and can peruse the 'library' unhampered.

Food is a creative art that I enjoy experimenting with. Our diet could easily become a monotony of eating straight from tins. When chef of the day I decide roughly what we will eat and then study my cook-book to see what variations are possible. Tonight we silenced our rumbling stomachs with chicken in a white sauce with mushrooms, onions, bouquet garni, peas and boiled potatoes.

John — Day 32, Sunday October 2

(Day's run 140 nm)

Boat going along on self-steering like clockwork. Andy and I have nothing to do, save tighten the odd halyard and sheet. Some 350 miles NW of Ascension Island. Thoughts are with the Southern Ocean a lot. 40 degrees south may not be too cold? Or too stormy??

270 pumps on main bilge is a bit of a worry — Loose keel bolts or leaking fresh water?

Andy — Day 32

A solitary flying fish, the first for several days, lay dead in the scuppers this morning. I can never face gutting them first thing so I kicked it overboard, a present for some lazy hungry creature.

I baked a couple more loaves of bread, but unfortunately the oven didn't reach a sufficiently high temperature leaving the dough pale and unappetising. I also baked a few potatoes which are scrumptious.

The radio continues to frustrate us. We tried unsuccessfully several times to call Portishead, then for no apparent reason suddenly got through, only to find that Marie Christine was out!

A chance remark from John has switched my ideas of a new boat to a new vein. He happened to say that I might take to racing! It is perhaps a good idea to take a break from cruising which has recently monopolised my spare time.

Andy — Day 33, Monday October 3

(Day's run 140 nm)

Ten more days of bashing close hauled into these South-East

Trades, a grim prospect. 25 to 30 knots of wind heels *English Rose* right over. She falls off the occasional wave, crashing blindly headlong into the next, throwing pans skittering off the cooker. Shovelling tons of water onto the foredeck to flood aft in a boiling torrent. I feel sick. On deck I get soaked.

I am sure we are over-pressed, John does not agree. I won't argue, I don't really care what happens, if the mast collapses our voyage will end at Cape Town, what a blissful dream.

I got around to re-fastening the two self-steering blocks with the aluminium fitting. To my dismay it began to bend almost immediately.

John — Day 34, Tuesday October 4

(Day's run 150 nm)

Another tedious slamming day in the South-East Trades, the sixth. Bigger seas are heavy on the nerves. Andy fits another set of blocks to 'George', for the steering lines, this time swinging from the pushpit above. I'm amused to see he doesn't consult me at all — he steams on regardless — leaving me to do the washing up and sweep the floor. Still, softly-softly has always caught monkeys for me in the past. I'm just hanging on with the nerves. Trying to apply 'Wellington'!

Most concerned by the play in the steering wheel, Andy says it has always clanked — I wonder — I'm sure it shouldn't.

Andy — Day 34

No headache. Morale is rising, I am not sure whether the headaches are caused by seasickness or anxiety, probably both. We have been sailing closehauled for six bumpy days now. John takes Stugeron to ease the misery.

A fresh drive to get us round the world has come over me. I read *The Longest Race* last night describing the various attempts to sail non-stop around the world in 1968. Numerous men (and a few women) have tried since, few succeeded. The gauntlet is down, it is a challenge I cannot resist.

Revitalised, I continued screwing down the floorboards and had a rethink on the self-steering lines. The solution has the two pulley blocks lashed to the pushpit middle rail. The only snag is the lines chafing where they emerge from the self-steering, I've overcome this by elongating the exit holes. John always said screwing fittings on would fail.

The hint of a chill after dark now forces me to wear tracksuit trousers and a sweat-shirt on watch.

* * *

This burst of enthusiasm was short lived, and the headaches soon returned.

I left Ardmore with rather a vague commitment to the intended voyage, drawn along by my dreams of circling the globe. Outwardly I appeared keen as mustard, raring to go and ready for six months or longer at sea. Inside I felt torn between Marie and the trip.

Marie or the trip? The dilemma came to a head four weeks after agreeing to accompany John. I realised that breaking the promise I'd given Marie to find a job near Glasgow for the winter, might well mean the end for us. Marie was the only girl I had ever felt relaxed with. I dreaded finding myself alone again, and hated the idea of Marie sitting lonely through the coming winter. I regretted my haste in agreeing to accompany John without even talking the idea over with Marie. Would she wait for my return? Our friendship was already bearing scars from my selfish decision. The wound was healing, but it would always remain, even if I decided not to go on the voyage. By going I risked losing the one I treasured more than anyone else.

Marie or the trip? Two voices reverberated inside my head, each debating the choice. A decision had to be made. At one point I decided to forgo the trip, and let down John in favour of Marie. Once made, the decision released me from torment, then another problem arose: how to tell John?

Or should I run away, and forget that the voyage was ever mentioned? No I couldn't do that, I chose to tell Marie Christine and leave her to shatter John's plans. The decision coincided with a day when John was away on the fishing boat for the morning. I climbed the hill to his croft and for two hours poured out my feelings to Marie Christine. She listened, occasionally offered an opinion, and finally advised me to go. She had already sailed round the world and one sentence of hers persuaded me: 'If you are unhappy once the yacht is at sea then stop and get off'.

And so, six weeks later, as we sailed out of Ardmore, a little voice told me 'the six months voyage will probably be cut short at Cape Town'. I waved goodbye feeling happy and at ease.

Shortly, there was another voice. Sometimes shouting, at other times whispering, but mostly shouting 'round the world, round the world'. It was compelling, so during the first weeks at sea I gave in, busying myself with work on the boat. The voice whispering 'Cape Town' was then barely audible. The weeks passed, then suddenly the 'Cape Town' whisper matched the 'round the world' voice: it was then time for another debate. The first round lasted a few days. The outcome was to continue round the world. My first experience of ocean sailing had whetted my appetite and I knew now that I could last a further six months or longer.

But Cape Town still lay ahead, we were barely two thirds of the way there. Another debate was to follow shortly, tearing at my vulnerable mind.

Andy — Day 35, Wednesday October 5

(Day's run 170 nm)

Shortly before daybreak I had to don a polar jacket over my sweat-shirt to keep warm, but, of course, by midday shorts were again sufficient.

The temperatures may be fluctuating but the wind remains as persistent as ever, a steady force 5–6 from the south-east.

Occasionally we meet black clouds, some with rain, then the wind becomes quite squally, keeping us on tenter-hooks.

Living at an angle of 30 degrees we are accustomed to moving around slowly. Leaping from hand hold to hand hold is fatal, as there is always a mischievous wave to knock the boat off balance and fling us against the nearest unyielding bit of wood.

The boat is withstanding unmeasured strain, we are driving her harder than at any time last summer. If I dwell too often on the state of the rigging, sails or keelbolts I will return a white-haired nervous wreck. 'George' is showing the miles, wobbling and creaking at each wave. The steering lines are frayed, occasionally one snaps, promptly putting us about.

We ran the engine today, charging the batteries for our weekly phone call. Two hours of listening to other calls, trying to catch the operator's attention were in vain. I'll try to call Marie tomorrow.

My latest book is *The Hobbit* a gift from Marie, to widen my reading matter from yachting magazines and sailing in general. I find it very entertaining, Bilbo Baggins is currently lost in a cave trying to escape from Gollum. Fortunately he has found a ring which makes the wearer invisible; he will undoubtedly escape, probably with the intrepid Gandalf's help.

John — Day 36, Thursday October 6

(Day's run 170 nm)

Eighth day to windward and 4,000 miles out from Ardmore. Luckily a bluer and a smoother sea, with clouds of flying fish. Another eight days to windward should see us down the South Atlantic High and then the westerlies.

I cooked a curry sauce (white sauce + stuff) Stevens-Lefield lamb biriani and rice (McConnell method). Andy and I spent three hours at the radio, while the crew of HMS *Newcastle* in the Falklands talked endlessly. No reply from MC, spoke with Gran in Brighton — all is well — MC is at Ardmore, but probably out to dinner (with Lance and Ada for supper last week! Maybe Monshalls or Laxford tonight?)

Becca likes Gordonstoun, she and MC are going to Brighton for half-term.

* * *

The bashing to windward during these eight days was a demoralising part of the trip. Heavy on the nerves and on the brink of seasickness all the time. Still sailing straight away from home, with the grim thought of the Southern Ocean springtime storms drawing closer by the day. While we chatted away at lunch and supper, we hadn't really got much in common, and I suppose we both felt a bit 'alone'. Listening to the radio conversations from the ships in the Falklands to the families at home, most of them seemed to be longing for being home at Christmas, and we couldn't help but realise that we wouldn't even be home for Easter, and a lot could go wrong before then. At least the cooler weather helped cure the awful prickly heat for me.

Andy — Day 36

Success with the radio but what a job. Two hours last night, an hour this morning, and three hours this evening, finally led to a call being put through to Marie's number. Her phone is out of order! I can't believe it, instead I spoke to Dad. It was a cheerful interlude talking to someone else but I couldn't help visualising a procession of pound notes as he talked at length about his new Irish Wolfhound 'Tigger'. John had difficulty containing his laughter as Dad described how 'Tigger' rests his chin on the dining room table amongst other antics.

Portishead have deduced that our main 22 MHZ channel is slightly off frequency, hence the difficulty they have hearing us. Also the dials have a tendency to work loose, misaligning the actual and indicated channels. At least the radio is a diversion to ease boredom.

Four ships have passed since 8.00 pm, steaming obediently along the great circle route from Cape Town northwards.

* * *

Ocean Passages for the World, pilot charts and routeing charts all indicate the recommended routes to traverse the oceans. The majority of ships stay close to these routes, thus requiring a vigilant lookout from any yacht in the vicinity. Away from the shipping lanes there is a tendancy for watch-keeping to ease off, a dangerous practice, fishermen roam free, not to mention wandering yachts. I am sure the single-hander's sixth sense, the ability to wake at the approach of a ship is a fallacy. He may wake several times to witness passing juggernauts but he will never know how many pass unseen.

Andy — Day 37, Friday October 7

(Day's run 140 nm)

Venus, the symbol of beauty and love, or more importantly at present, a conveniently bright object to capture with my sextant. Navigation fascinates me.

We eat breakfast separately now, I prefer to eat shortly after coming on watch at 5.00 am. I am experimenting with cooking oats in butter as an alternative to porridge for the colder climes ahead. A small amount of butter, oats and sugar, heated in a pan and stirred until almost burning, produces a delicious quick and unmessy meal served with milk.

John — Day 38, Saturday October 8

(Day's run 160 nm)

A glorious day. Humidity down. Light south-east breezes give us 5–6 knots. Bright sunshine and fluffy white clouds in a giant sky. It fell calm at 11.00, and I took a break from typing 'Ardmore Years'. The typewriter works OK on the port tack, but laid over to starboard the carriage won't work uphill; this makes the letters overprint annoyingly.

Up on deck I saw my first white-tailed tropic bird, it was circling inquisitively on our port side. Its long translucent tail streamed out behind it — truly the 'bosun bird' with a marlin-spike tail. This solitary bird, so white against the blue of the sea, reminded me of the dove of peace, and life seemed not so bad.

Andy rigged the new 8 oz (USA) mizzensail, so stiff and heavy it seems the creases will never come out of the cloth. I cooked liver and onions for supper, with extra fresh onions and tinned peas. Packetted savoury rice too, but I prefer the McConnell-style rice.

Remorselessly we push on towards the Southern Ocean. The duvet comes out onto my bunk, as well as the polar jacket for night watches. A wonderful day of relaxation and peace of mind. Andy planning his North-West Passage voyage. As I write, the moon is a plush grey velvet orb in a silver saucer.

Andy — Day 38

An evil yellow gel, lurking at the bottom of a stowage locker on the starboard side of the saloon, prompted a short discussion over supper about what might have 'gone off'. We guessed correctly, three 10lb cheeses had partially melted in the tropics. These waxed pieces of Scottish Red Cheddar were brought for Southern Ocean snacks, but now they have re-solidified mouldy. I cannot understand how we had not noticed any smell. The clean-up involved removing half of the 300 pint supply of Long-life milk, then lifting the three football-sized lumps of spongy green goo for disposal overboard. An hour of scraping and scouring saw the locker fit for a pantry again.

Today felt like a day off, all I did was to fit the new mizzensail. The 8 oz ultra-violet-resistant cloth defies being rolled into a compact sausage. I suppose it will soften eventually.

My imagination is working overtime, once again I am planning a new boat — one in which to tackle the North-West Passage. Aluminium hull and deck, strengthened bow with an ice-breaker, protected propellor, transom-hung rudder for easy removal, and Aries self-steering. Internal and external steering, two well padded punks, paraffin cooker and cabin heaters, satellite navigation . . . so the list continues. My aim would be to have the hull built professionally next season, then spend the winter and following summer fitting-out, including a shake-down cruise to Greenland. It is a totally impractical notion. Marie would be less than pleased. When I mentioned the idea to John, he suggested I take *Kinnego*. Is he serious, or pulling my leg?

* * *

Cheese and voyaging seem to be an ill-match. John has previously carried the stuff, and experienced a similar fate. He vows never to be sweet-talked into it again.

My thoughts on a new boat were many and varied, ranging from ferro-cement one week to moulded ply the next. A stream of ideas which changed with the wind. John was very patient. Costly and unrealistic though the ideas were, they occupied my mind, as John's book did for him. One must leave the boat occasionally, even if only mentally.

John — Day 39, Sunday October 9

(Day's run 140 nm)

5,000 miles out from Ardmore. St Helena is 672 miles ENE of us at noon, and we are close to the southern limit of the South-East Trades. The wind is patchy, but still always from E to SSE. We are nearly out of the Tropics too, more or less becalmed and waiting for the westerly winds. I lined my bunk on the port side of the saloon with polystyrene tiles to prevent condensation once we reach the cold waters of the Southern Ocean.

Andy — Day 39

Dry and warm in the day, cool at night: a perfect climate, as we slip unhurriedly into the Variables. I spied a white-tailed tropic bird, one of the few species which cannot be mistaken.

Calmer weather induced a day of work. I reeved the new main and mizzen sheets, and tied up the baggywrinkle I made a couple of weeks ago.

John — Day 40, Monday October 10

(Day's run 72 nm)

At last, a fairly steady breeze sprang up at 11.00 from ENE and held all day. Andy and I busied ourselves in the afternoon with changing the 1975 Ratsey mainsail for the heavier 1979 Ratsey sail. We hoisted the 1983 Ratsey mizzensail for the first time as well. I taped the forepeak watertight door handles to prevent rust passing onto the sails, and I oiled the shapshackles for the sailbags therein. Andy went round with the caulking gun to attack the leaks in the saloon from windows and handrails.

Andy — Day 40

We have changed the mainsails. The replacement is not brand new, but has considerably more miles in it than the original, which did the Whitbread Race. A smear of grease on each slide will hopefully ease raising and lowering. We also intend to thoroughly wax the leech stitching to ease the chafe caused by the flapping reefing pennants, when the sail is unreefed. Waxing the reefing pennants themselves may also be a good idea.

Last night I studied *Ocean Passages for the World*, making a few notes about recommended routes through the Southern Ocean. Then using John's Tamaya navigational calculator, I worked out the distance for each option. A composite track taking us down to 50 degrees south will save 430 miles on the straight rhumb line to New Zealand, but carries us to the heart of the Roaring Forties in late spring. We will probably stay on the rhumb line and edge gently south as summer progresses. From New Zealand onwards is too far away to plan a route at this stage.

I have begun reading Shackleton's *Valiant Voyage*, an account of his stranding in the Antarctic pack-ice and subsequent escape in a tiny whaler. By comparison our voyage is a luxury cruise.

John — Day 41, Tuesday October 11

(Day's run 100 nm)

Hurt my back yesterday changing mainsails. Feel sunstroke, back-ache and a cold or chill coming on! Moving very little to the east. NE wind is hot again. Took Lobak (two) in evening and failed to get up for the 02.00–05.00 watch. Back-ache, head cold. Ugh!

* * *

We had an extensive medical kit. In addition to pain killers and the usual bandages and plasters, we had a stitching kit, local anaesthetics and inflatable splints. Dr Sunil, our very helpful local GP, had put a lot of thought into preparing the kit for us, and we found the full range of treatments a real reassurance.

MacArthur Bennie, once again, lent me a dental kit with temporary filling cement, extraction pliers, and a book of instructions! Occasionally I opened the box to look at the instruments, and remembered other trips, but I wasn't keen to let Andy practice with them.

Andy — Day 41

Becalmed with a current pushing us east beneath an awning of blue sky.

Straight after breakfast I re-opened the bakery, determined to improve on the last two batches of bread. With precision I ensured the water, flour, oven, etc, were at the correct temperatures. I even went to the extreme of melting the fat with a Bluet Gaz blowtorch, usually it is simply mixed in. The extra care paid off, rewarding us with two medium-sized white loaves and six rolls, nicely risen and mouth-wateringly light.

After baking, the boat became a laundry. We both hauled out our dirty washing and used the jerry-can of rainwater from the Doldrums. We had left the jerry-can in the cockpit during the intervening fortnight, not realising the sun would 'cook' it, leaving a smelly, faintly brown liquid which is not very appetising.

Once dry, we restowed all our kit in fresh polythene bags, to avoid mould when condensation prevails. Tomorrow I will seal my books in plastic bags too.

* * *

Catching rainwater may well be a necessity on any long or major ocean voyage to supplement the main supply, in which case, topping up the main tanks may be a temptation. Unfortunately, as was shown by our jerry-can, rainwater collected from the sails is likely to be polluted with traces of salt, so shortening its life. So it is better to store rainwater in separate jerry-cans, away from the main tanks. If we had polluted our whole supply, at this stage we might well have had to abandon our voyage; particularly if there had been some other damage as well, to lure us into Cape Town.

John — Day 42, Wednesday October 12

(Day's run 50 nm)

A sort of flash head cold, including green mucus from the nose. I believed one didn't catch colds on such a trip, because of the antiseptic neutral environment at sea. Maybe a chill/sunstroke is different. It all cleared up in the course of the day. My back is v sore. I took two Panadol in the morning, and two Aspirin in the afternoon. I still think it was a chill on perspiration — the old Ardmore digging syndrome. Not easy to 'click' the back into place onboard the yacht.

St Helena is 600 miles NE of us, and we are making use of the calm weather. I cleaned the eight batteries and added nearly two litres of distilled water to the cells.

Andy — Day 42

We appear to be stuck in the South Atlantic High. These calms allow us to continue the vital preparations for the storms over the horizon.

While checking the engine oil, I noticed the battery box forward of the engine looked slightly askew, then I realised it had slid sideways several inches. Our morning was therefore spent removing the saloon table and floor, lifting out the four 100lb batteries and re-securing the box. With the floor up we took the opportunity to check the engine mountings and generally feel around for loose nuts and bolts.

The tool kit was in danger of becoming a box of rust, I hadn't noticed until we needed the hand-drill this morning that several items had already seized. All the tools are now cleaned and oiled.

John's back has started to give trouble, he can scarcely lift a plate of food without wincing painfully. My left eye has developed an itch, probably less serious than John's back injury, but nevertheless an additional worry. I hope it is not infected, at times like this I realise how far we are from help. We are on our own.

A helpful careers advisor once advised me to study marine biology as a hobby, but I ignored the suggestion until now. I am only superifically interested, unlike John, who is also an avid ornithologist. While checking 'George' today, I discovered a tiny striped pilot fish swimming ahead of the servo-rudder. Later on we encountered several Portuguese man-o-war jellyfish, so-named because they have a transparent sail-like membrance above water. They were only tiny specimens, each the size of a 10p piece.

John — Day 43, Thursday October 13

(Day's run 85 nm)

The back is bad, and I have to talk to myself to prevent panic.

Shades of the past, and no Ian Macaulay to 'click' it back into place. I have gone back onto Lobak pills, in the hope they will relax the muscles and let them mend. I only hope it is a case of the lumbago type of injury, resulting from a chill, and not a disc displacement. Must not get sorry for myself.

Andy — Day 43

The engine had a six hour run today, because during the night the lights began to fade, and the satnav went haywire, indicating flat batteries. The auxilliary bank of four under the chart table seat had drained to the stage where the jump-leads were required from the four forward of the engine. We had intended to run the engine anyway, in preparation for our weekly battle of wits with the radio. Reception is often reasonable when we first make contact with Portishead, but it tails off into a background of static as darkness falls. That happened this evening, and I was particularly annoyed because after a four-hour wait, I eventually spoke with Marie, but only just. I went to bed dejected, silently cursing the Falklands' Task Force: one of their warships ahead of us in the queue seemed to have a phone call for each member of the crew.

More bread-baking, and checking the mirror-alignment of my sextant, occupied the afternoon. This evening I took three sights: Jupiter, and two stars.

* * *

The satnav performed faultlessly throughout the voyage, so my interest in celestial navigation was purely a hobby. At no time did we have to rely on my position-fixing ability, except that it provided a convenient means of checking the satnav. I frequently took sights during the day leaving the calculations till the night watch, to while away the otherwise boring hours of darkness.

John — Day 44, Friday October 14
(Day's run 83 nm)

Trickling east. Fixed lee-cloth to port seat in saloon, my new bunk. Tied down seat hatches underneath it, for storm protection. Wind back to SW at dusk increased with black cloud, so we went about and headed south.

Andy — Day 44

We are on the move again slowly, but it is a start.

After breakfast I cooked a small quantity of fudge, flavoured with a packet of instant hot chocolate instead of cocoa. The result is surprisingly good.

John has screwed a lee cloth to the port saloon berth and tied down the locker lids. He decided the new bunk will be more forgiving to his back than the cushionless pilot berth. His back may be on the mend, he 'clicked' the offending joint painfully into place this afternoon.

I made a simple wooden frame to secure the batteries under the navigation seat, if we are unfortunate enough to be capsized, or worse, turned turtle they will hopefully stay put.

Finding myself at a loose end for an hour I laid out the wrecked No 1 yankee to see if it can be repaired. It made a sorry sight a 15-foot seam torn right across the sail; a 6-foot tear along an adjacent seam and 10 feet of the leech missing.

Three days ago I trimmed my beard, today I attacked my hair. Armed with a comb and a small pair of John's scissors pinched from the navigation table I apprehensively clipped away. My over-zealous enthusiasm has transformed my normally conservative appearance into that of a punk rocker.

* * *

My short hairstyle proved a boon. Easily washed in a cup of water, it always dried quickly after a wetting.

6

A test of will

John — Introduction

For the next couple of weeks we slopped around close to the South Atlantic High. The barometer rose to 1,030 and we entered a critical psychological phase of the voyage. My back injury, a re-occurrence of years of trouble, which had included having a disc out of my lower spine and sciatic nerve complications down my left leg, coincided unknown to me with Andy's growing awareness that Cape Town offered a chance to abandon the voyage and return to his girlfriend Marie in Glasgow. On the bright side, we managed to set the boat up well for the coming battle with the Southern Ocean; the long beat into the South-East Trades had not been the best time for this, and the enforced rest now was put to good use. The alternative to this would have been the longer bumpy ride down the west side of the High, with the damaging exposure to the spring storms which causes so many boats to stop in Cape Town; in our case it is easy with hindsight to see that Cape Town would have been the end of the voyage. While the intermission in the South Atlantic High was frustrating, I found it gave me vital time to gather myself for the struggle ahead, and strangely, I'm left with the memory of some of the happiest moments of my life.

John — Day 45, Saturday October 15

(Day's run 128 nm)

Bumping SE along the great circle course for 40 degrees S, 20 degrees E. This our planned rendezvous with the Southern Ocean, for the run from Cape of Good Hope to Cape Horn. I've cut out the Lobak pills for my back and the Stugeron for seasickness. Let's see how we get on.

Making 7.5 knots with No 1 yankee, working staysail, and one reef in the mainsail. I seem to cook supper nowadays, its easy to reach one level, but if I cook it I don't seem to enjoy it. Maybe it is hard to cook well.

I'd like a good following wind now, its three weeks since we beat 150 miles in a day downwind.

Andy — Day 45

What would I give for an oil can? It is the only item of kit that we forgot. Necessity is the mother of invention, so when a loud squeak began to come from the main steering overnight an alternative to the unremembered item had to be found. A plastic tube commandeered from a bottle of distilled water with a small diameter tube from a can of WD 40 taped into the end is our solution. The large tube acts as a reservoir, the fine tube as a jet. Oil is forced out by blowing (hiccupping does not bear thinking about).

I happened to be in the cockpit this afternoon when a sneaky wave broke over the boat, the only splash all day!

John — Day 46, Sunday October 16

(Day's run 102 nm)

The SE wind had us going north of east by 02.30. I decided to put the boat about, with all the back-tearing fumbling about in the dark. Now we are heading nearly due south, into a big splashy swell. I was writing about far-away Nepal in the morning, and managed to sleep in the afternoon. It is getting colder now, I really hope the saloon won't leak too much. The back hurts cruel.

Andy — Day 46

I seem to have spent most of today in bed sleeping from 10.00 am till 2.30 pm and again from 6.30 pm to 11.00 pm. Exhausted and seasick I feel down in the dumps, I long to be with Marie again.

John — Day 47, Monday October 17

(Day's run 152 nm)

Nodding gently south. So slow. Saw my first Schegel's petrel and the first albatross of the trip. Andy is sick with a headache — he's had this sort of thing before he tells me and he looks pretty seedy.

Luckily my back is a bit better. Now we're into the cooler climes I've started to wear paper underpants. Changing them every other day I've enough to last me to the other side of Cape Horn. I've just finished the two volumes on Wellington by Longford and am starting *Walden* by Thoreau. My morale is good but I seem to have lost my appetite for evening meals. Maybe it's too easy going?

Andy — Day 47

Another headache. Since speaking to Marie I have been worrying about her, the anxiety is sapping my strength of mind.

While sitting in the cockpit an albatross appeared, a huge heavy bird mostly white with a thick neck and beak. Every so often it needed a good flap of its wings to keep going, shattering my belief that they glide effortlessly on the wind.

John — Day 48, Tuesday October 18

(Day's run 80 nm)

Slap bang in the South Atlantic High. Desperately slow progress. Washed my hair and put on a white cotton shirt. It is cold enough now for the moleskin trousers and shirt, with a polar jacket.

Andy got the new Ratsey No 2 yankee set up for the first blow, when it comes. It's massively heavy and reinforced as well, in 10 oz (USA) UV resistant Vectis.

Andy — Day 48

A spell of calmer weather has cheered me up. Eager to keep my mind occupied I unfolded the new No 2 yankee to grease the piston hanks. The heavily reinforced sail is a fine example of sail making at its best. Beneath each piston hank a thick piece of terylene webbing is sewn on to protect the luff, while surrounding the hanks triangular reinforcing patches also serve as sacrificial chafe protection. Ratseys had neatly folded the sail to the size of an average suitcase but after the inspection I simply stuffed it back into its bag, now it is so large that the only available home for it is lashed down in the main cockpit.

Next I climbed the mast carrying my camera for an unusual picture, and a screwdriver to check the various fittings. The camera was a waste of time, the wild gyrations made hanging on a full time task, I could not even remove the lens cap. One of eight

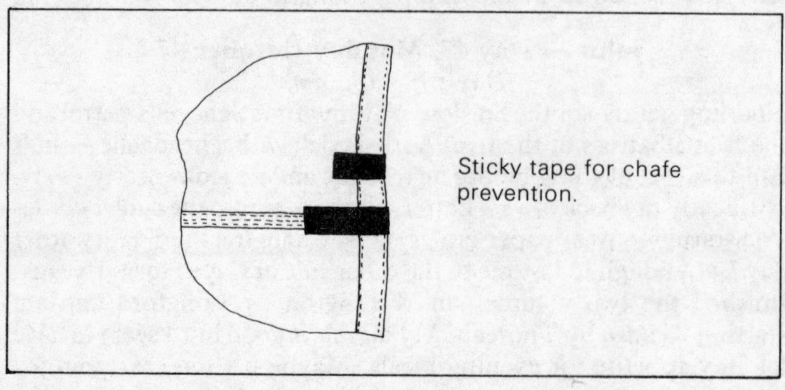
Sticky tape for chafe prevention.

machine screws securing a capshroud fitting had shaken loose, my climb was not wasted.

As *English Rose* rolls drunkenly in light airs alternately filling and collapsing the sails, they continually batter the rigging. The stitching on the No 1 yankee leech tabling was non-existent in places, requiring a few hours of hand stitching to save it from the fate of its predecessor. An added measure of protection is the use of 2-inch-wide linen sticky tape over the stitching. The black tape has found a hundred and one uses. Fortunately half a dozen large rolls are aboard.

A five minute job was to change the main and genoa halyard winch drums to spread wear. The halyards are '7 x 7' stainless steel wire with braided rope tails. The main halyard wire emerges from the wire-to-rope splice at the point where the halyard leaves the winch, thereby protecting the winch. This is a perfectly acceptable arrangement since the wire is buried for three feet within the outer sheath of the braided rope. The wire is therefore still wrapped around the winch drum to take the strain. The genoa halyard has wire on the winch drum which is steadily cutting a groove in the soft bronze casting, the previous drum was crushed last season, we cannot afford another failure.

John's rice is delicious, he has achieved a perfection that an Oriental would be proud of.

John — Day 49, Wednesday October 19

(Day's run 83 nm)

Up in the bows at three in the morning (alone). The boat is bathed in silver moonlight on a smooth sea. A nip of early spring in the air, and Andy's footprints have smudged the dew on the deck during the last watch. Looking back towards the stern, past the slanting slots of the sails, the ropes and wires run hither and thither. Winches, squat powerful and expectant, glinting in the moonlight. A place for everything, and everything in its place — and 'George' in charge. The reluctant whine from the (stern) generator, as its trailing impeller twists it into action. The chart table is dimly lit through the saloon window.

Isn't this the proudest moment of my life? A thing of beauty is truly a joy for ever; 6,000 miles out from home, dead on course, and going better than ever at the quarter-way mark.

Venus a red tear drop on the eastern horizon at 05.00.

Thoreau defines happiness as 'simplicity, independence, magnanimity and trust'. Looking back at the 1977/78 race, I realise I lost all four in the first few days of the nine months. How I felt their loss.

I love the weather, the oceans, the solitude. To have seen Venus that way will be a jewel for the rest of my life.

Gybed after lunch and headed for the heavy weather. The wind blowing NW4 puts a chill down my back. How ready are we? We'll soon find out, I couldn't have a better companion than Andy.

Andy — Day 49

More sail repairs, overhauling and restowing the storm sails, the trisail is now lashed in its bag at the foot of the mast with the slides in the special track.

Albatrosses are increasing in number and variety — we have seen a young wandering, a young sooty and a shy, I hadn't realised there are over a dozen varieties.

An increasing quantity of floating debris, mainly small oil drums, litters our panoramic view.

John — Day 50, Thursday October 20

(Day's run 120 nm)

Another world. Grey and Bumpy. 180 degrees windshift at 09.30. Two hours wrestling to get two reefs in the main; No 2 yankee, and No 2 staysail set, and all the while beating into a SE gale. ROTTEN.

Gloomy — this is the day we got into Cape Town 1,250 miles west of here, in 1977. We're a week behind. Andy tired and gloomy too. He feels tired easily.

No luck with the radio this evening. Galling to think of MC sitting alone at home thinking of the radio shack (on the yacht) — worrying?

Andy — Day 50

Sitting on the loo, looking through the skylight I noticed the sails suddenly go aback so I dashed out expecting a squall. John was

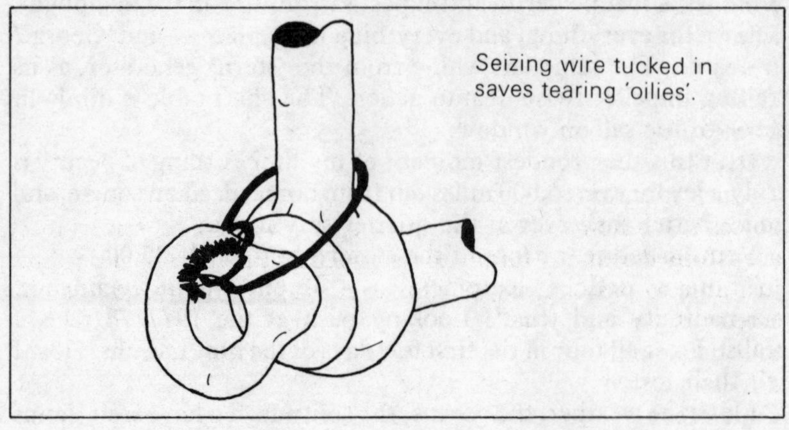

already up from the chart table. We quickly donned oilskins then spent two hours changing headsails, tying in a couple of reefs and tacking twice. The wind peaked at about force 7, the strongest for over a month. I eventually went off to bed at midday, the wind remained strong, it is just our luck to find a headwind where we expect to meet the westerlies.

* * *

John's reminiscing of the Whitbread Race and accounts of yachts in this area convinced me that at some stage a vicious squally front would strike unannounced, I became overly concerned and nervous at the slightest change to the boat's motion. Several days later we were to be caught, in a manner of speaking, with our pants down.

John — Day 51, Friday October 21

(Day's run 160 nm)

1,070 miles west of Cape Town. Northerly gale pushes us 8/9 knots on course for 40 degrees S, 20 degrees E (our preferred point of entry into the Southern Ocean which has 40 degrees S as its Northern limit).

Bumpy and gloomy. Spoke to MC (on radio), delighted to hear her. She sounds pretty cheery — I do hope she's OK. Ten booked on the '84 instructors' course already. Bookings (for 1984 courses) coming in. Fish (salmon farm) OK.

Much more cheery after the call home. Crossed the Greenwich Meridian — only 360 degrees to go! Dismal night, watching the drops of sea water splatter down on the chart table from the window above. No typing now! Bumps but speedy.

Andy — Day 51

John drew my attention to an objectionable patch of rusty iron filings today, precisely where the tools were cleaned with steel wool. Since it was my doing I hunted down a pot of fibreglass cleaner and removed the stain together with an unexpected layer of grime. The clean patch sticks out like a sore thumb, I suppose the whole cockpit will need doing now!

Our transmitter's signal is now so weak that by the time our voices reach home, we are unintelligible. Marie Christine is more accustomed than my family to deciphering the crackle, and John is just able to pass messages. This evening the Portishead operator acted as an intermediary between me and my father, an unsatisfactory arrangement for a personal call, so I signed off with a message that I will call again in three months, after rounding Cape Horn.

John — Day 52, Saturday October 22

(Day's run 157 nm)

A good day for morale. I think Andy and I had thought we had seen the last of the sun for three months. So it was a pleasure to see the wind drop, and blue skies and sun return out of the grey murk of the past couple of days. Andy cheered up.

We think a good suit of sails for the Southern Ocean will be, at top: mizzen, mizzen staysail, full main, genoa staysail, and No 2 yankee — this is for downwind. We'll keep the No 2 staysail hanked and bagged at the inner forestay, the trisail is permanently hanked and bagged onto its own track on the main mast. The mizzen staysail can be taken down fast and stowed in the oilskin locker (aft starboard of saloon). The mizzen can be dropped or reefed to two reefs. The main problem is reefing the mainsail with its big boom.

Andy melted a lead fishing weight and poured it into the pipe of the towed impeller of the Aquair generator. We'll see how it goes! We've been having difficulty with the heavy impeller skipping out of the waves when running before big following seas, the plan is for the extra weight to sink it better.

Fried rice by Andy, with kipper fillets — a success. I'll ask MC to get a Wok and cookbook on the radio.

Still trickling south-east. A 12-inch cuttlefish on deck. First Cape hen and Cape pigeons.

Andy — Day 52

The mizzen mast coat, which forms a waterproof seal where the mast passes through the deck, sprang a leak during the latest spell of wind and it is endangering the radio. I have replaced the old cracked Life-calk with fresh stuff, a good deal did squeeze out, filling the nooks and crannies as the jubilee clip was retightened.

While the Life-calk was at hand I applied more around the window above the chart table, but this evening it is leaking as badly as ever.

Today's most important job involved the cooker, it has been sagging lower and lower until finally today it no longer swung freely in the gimbals, knocking the teak surround instead. Close inspection revealed one of the brass pivots loose, allowing the stainless steel sheet forming the cooker end to literally saw three quarters of the way through the ⅝ inch brass bar. No suitable replacement is aboard. For now the cut has been made good with solder. Re-assembled, the cooker swings freely again though I suspect the problem will arise again.

An occasional glimpse of the sun, and the reappearance of patches of blue overhead, has brought the local bird population

Above *Ardmore—the mooring under the wood.*
Below *John trying to click the back into submission.*

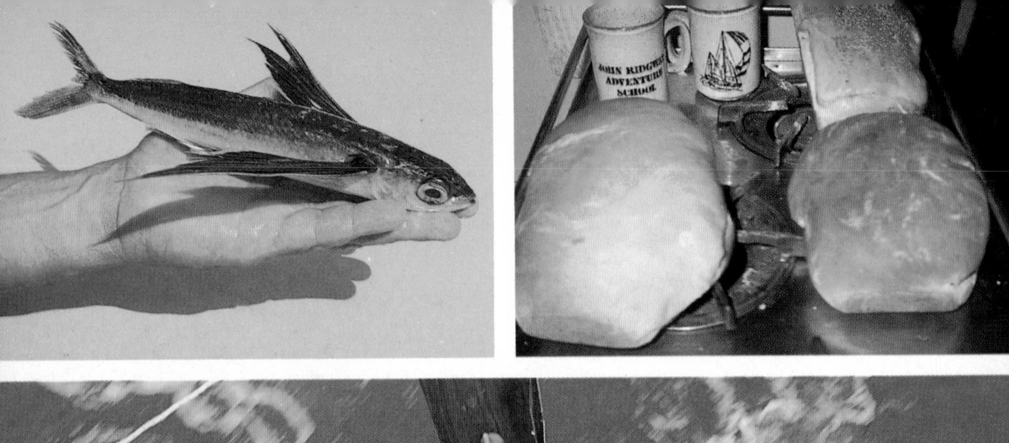

Far left *Flying fish on the deck.*

Left *The staff of life—the tasty results of Andy's trials and errors in the bakery.*

Left *Andy in earnest conversation with 'George'.*

Below left *John steering by hand as a Southern Ocean squall strikes.*

Right *From Shakespeare to Jimmy Durante—John's daily recital in the bows.*

Below *Chez Andy—snug and cozy in the forward bunk.*

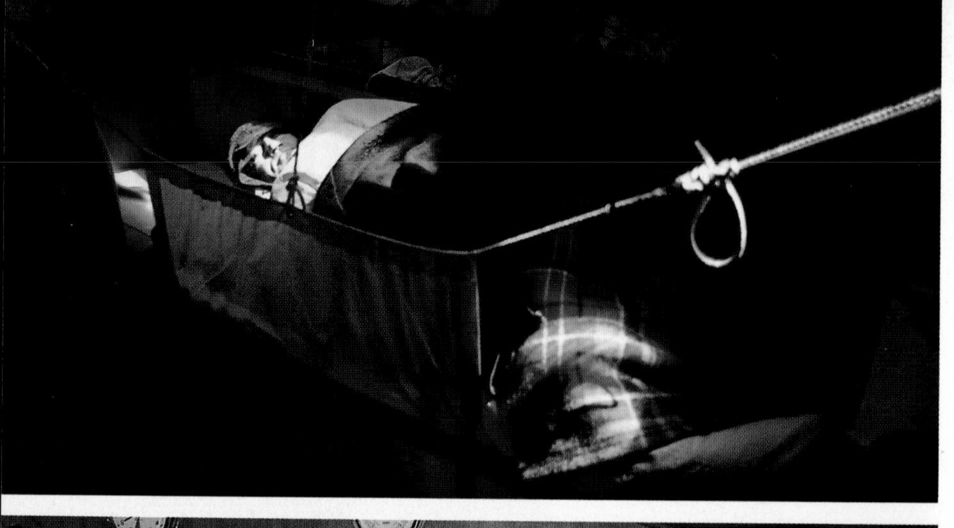

Super Star
HAPPY
XMAS
ANDY

Top left *With no cabin heater, a well-wrapped John in his bunk.*

Centre left *Outside it's foggy—inside it's Christmas, with presents on the saloon table.*

Bottom left *Checking for wear and chafe on the foredeck.*

This page *Virtually becalmed on Boxing Day, sails slatting in light airs.*

Above *Riding the Southern Ocean roller coaster.*

Below *Closing Cape Horn—Andy at the helm to bring us closer inshore.*

Above left *Andy does his washing in the cockpit—viewed through the main hatch.*
Above right *Andy braces the spreaders after the knockdown.*
Below *Once more in warmer seas and three months' washing adorns the rails.*

Above *One of life's small luxuries—John makes use of the toothbrush razor invented and constructed by Andy.*

Below *South Atlantic and homeward bound—John at the chart table.*

Right *The sea seems to stretch on for ever.*

Left *It's John's turn to cook, and it's curry . . . curry . . . curry . . . and curry AGAIN!*

Below left *As the old saying has it 'A stitch in time . . .'!*

Right *Andy checks up on the satnav.*

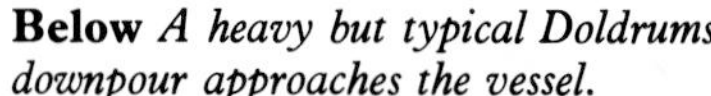

Below *A heavy but typical Doldrums downpour approaches the vessel.*

Above *English Rose VI rests calmly back at her mooring and then we're ashore at last and surrounded by well-wishers.*
Below *Coming home, and those last few miles up Loch Laxford.*

back into existence. During the day their number swells to 10 or 15, obediently following the boat until darkness draws them away.

This morning I found a cuttlefish on deck, an ugly colourless creature with a dark eye. Not unlike a squid, it's about 12 inches long. Cuttlefish are the main diet of albatrosses, if we find ourselves in the liferaft they may become our source of nutrition, an appalling thought. John posed an interesting question this morning, what do the birds drink?

John — Day 53, Sunday October 23

(Day's run 103 nm)

810 miles west of Cape Town at noon, and 913 miles from our intended point of entry into the Southern Ocean at 40 degrees S, 20 degrees E. We are nodding steadily into a wind coming from just where we want to go, and making alarmingly slow progress. Barometer up to 1,029 by dark, near the highpoint for the South Atlantic High. SE wind against us for 24 hours now — frustrating.

Andy — Day 53

It appears that the area of light variable winds is hot on our tail. What wind we have, is a maddening southeasterly; so we find ourselves hard on the wind when we should be running free with the westerlies.

I spent the afternoon cutting out a cover for the radio, using an old piece of sailcloth from the panel of the mainsail which blew out in the Faroes. That was two and a half months ago now, and finding it brings back happy memories.

John — Day 54, Monday October 24

(Day's run 70 nm)

Stationary in a high pressure of 1,030. NOTHING HAPPENED ALL DAY. Andy saw some small dolphins around the boat at dawn. Also he shot the moon and Venus, getting a position only two miles from the satnav. At dusk we saw numerous white forms coming to the surface, and we took these to be the cuttlefish the albatross feeds on. As usual there were albatrosses, white-chinned petrels, prions, pintado petrels and storm petrels about for most of the day.

PATIENCE. I'm really enjoying the voyage. It's wonderful to be able to concentrate entirely on writing 'Ardmore Years', to think without distraction. Touch wood the back is OK.

Andy — Day 54

Incredibly we do seem to be under the influence of the high again. The barometer has stuck at 1,030 mb all day, I'm beginning to find our slow progress very frustrating.

Reading my cookery book, a frequent pastime, has added several ideas to experiment with. Future creations will include: treacle tart, spaghetti bolognese, scones and pizza.

John — Day 55, Tuesday October 25

(Day's run 85 nm)

What satisfaction I'm getting from the voyage — when it is calm. An ocean of time to relax, unwind, reflect, and take stock. My body is functioning perfectly, except for the weak back but even that is OK with the Damart warming pad against the lower spine. The rashes have disappeared for the first time in 15 years. The hearing is coming back in my left ear, after the trans-America drive in 1981. The eyes are as good as ever, and not irritating. Even the clumsiness of age eases with relaxation.

My mind is as fresh as a daisy, full of plans and ideas. This is such a contrast with the 1977/78 race. The craving for food has subsided for the first time in memory, and the fat around my waist has slipped away. Without gorging, the old tiredness and sluggishness has gone.

It has taken all of two months to ease out the knots of tension from all the years, and to give a sense of scale to events.

Dolphins make luminous 'sea-serpent' trails through the water in the black night.

Andy — Day 55

A moderate breeze over the quarter, with sun for most of the day. It is dreamy sailing, although we are no longer warm enough without a jersey.

I measured and whipped the ends of two new yankee sheets after lunch. The previous pair are badly chafed after 12,000 miles. To extend their life they were end-for-ended and the chafed areas served with a light line, a use for them will no doubt be found.

While working in the cockpit, three dolphins appeared playfully riding the bow wave. But by the time I fetched my camera they were out of sight, so I sat waiting patiently for an albatross. One duly appeared, wheeling gracefully across our wake, making an impressive sight. Through the viewfinder of my camera it might have been a common seagull. If we catch an albatross, maybe it will sit on our shoulders with outstretched wings — now that would be a picture!

We often brush our teeth standing out in the cockpit, and last night, as I leant over the side, I was fascinated to see dozens of cuttlefish near the surface. John's book of the sea informs us that they always rise to the surface during darkness.

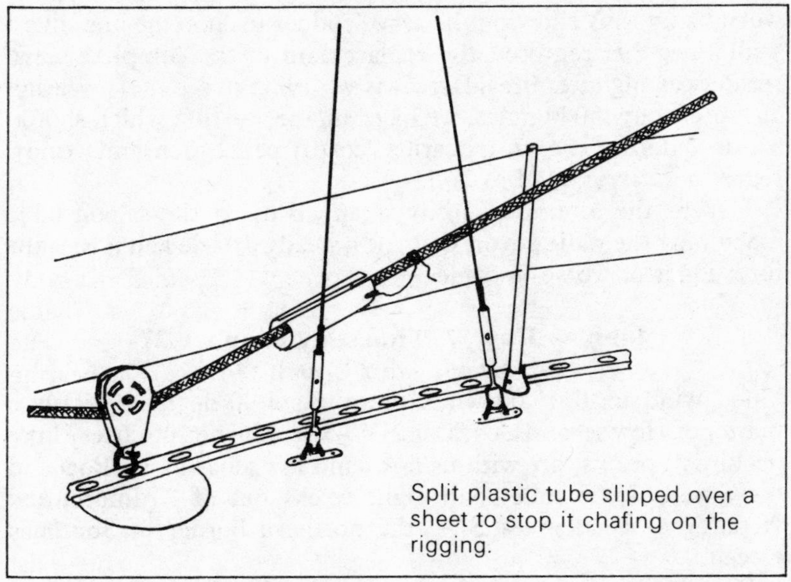

Split plastic tube slipped over a sheet to stop it chafing on the rigging.

We talked at length today about fishing to earn a living. I went off to bed with a romantic idea of becoming a lobster fisherman, working my creels from a large rowing boat.

* * *

The replacement sheets lasted for the remainder of the voyage, and a hard season at Ardmore. Their longer life was simply due to our learning about chafe prevention. The snatch block under the boom has already been mentioned, but another idea commonly used is to slip plastic tube over the shrouds. We also used a short length of split plastic tubing on a vulnerable length of sheet, holding it in place with a lanyard. This was particularly useful if the sheet worked against shrouds or the guardrail under load.

John — Day 56, Wednesday October 26

(Day's run 175 nm)

A grand morning of misty sun. We've had a really good run of 175 miles noon to noon. Straight after lunch, the fog closed in and the wind fell to nothing. Andy replaced a headed bush (Aries steering part no 307) it was badly worn.

Andy — Day 56

05.00 hours found John at the helm and me hanging over the stern to replace a parted self-steering line. Yesterday I cut a worn section off the other line. Looking at the gear I realised two bearings had worn badly thus allowing the servo rudder to chop the lines like a guillotine, this required the replacement of the complete servo rudder casting after breakfast. It is worrying to see parts wearing out after only 8,000 miles; we have another casting which should see us to home. The worn bearings cost 10 pence each, and we now regret not carrying a box full.

I spent the afternoon cosily wrapped up at the saloon table machining the radio cover. Outside a steady drizzle and mist is the forerunner of worse to come.

John — Day 57, Thursday October 27

(Day's run 105 nm)

Good wind until 15.00 when there was a 90 degrees shift in a matter of a few seconds, backing NW–SW. Maybe 100 cheery little 'icebirds' (prions) are with us now, and few albatrosses. Boat and crew well. 7,000 miles and eight weeks out of Ardmore, and virtually at 40 degrees S — the northern border of Southern Ocean.

We altered the planned entry to the Southern Ocean after checking the US Pilot Atlas for Indian and Pacific Oceans. Now plan to follow the November Sail Route to New Zealand, joining the route at 43 degrees S, 20 degrees E, for a rhumb line (almost) to 48 degrees S, (which would be reached just south of New Zealand).

Thrilled to speak to MC and Becca on radio at 21.00 GMT, at Brighton for half-term.

* * *

Looking back now, on nearly three weeks of frustratingly little progress, it is tempting to write it off as all a big mistake, we certainly lost a lot of time here when progress is measured against our first leg time for Portsmouth to Cape Town in the 1977/78 race. But of course we were not going to stop at Cape Town for repairs, and our crew of two was ten fewer than the Whitbread crew. This slow trickle through the South Atlantic High was really part of our plan, and although the reality of the calms made it seem a failure at the time, our route did in fact bring us into the Southern Ocean in fine condition, almost due south of Cape Town. We checked and re-checked everything in readiness for the three months of bad weather ahead, and we came to that bad weather in the knowledge that we were as ready as we ever could be.

I was never aware that Andy was thinking of giving up. He kept his thoughts very much to himself, and although I see from my log that I recorded he seemed gloomy at times, I linked this only with the seasickness we both suffered. And the headaches he sometimes got I associated with the painful glare from the sea on someone who wore glasses. It was a time of apprehension for us both, possibly greater for Andy than for me; I had been through the Southern Ocean before and felt it could only be warmer and easier on the northerly route we planned. I'm grateful to Andy for keeping his unhappiness to himself, I don't suppose it would have taken much urging for me to head for Cape Town if we had broken something, I was feeling homesick too. The occasional snatches of the South African radio programmes I picked up on the lonely night watches, reminded me of the pleasures of home, and the friendly people we had met in Cape Town. The sunshine and massive harbour wall did seem a precious haven from what I knew was bound to come.

All of these thoughts at the time, are what I really felt — not the sober knowledge that we were well on schedule and completely undamaged, without having to cross the South Atlantic before passing into the South Indian Ocean. To anyone following us, I would strongly recommend a determined effort to reach 40 degrees S, 20 degrees E, in an undamaged condition. The Southern Ocean is no place to limp into with a damaged boat.

Andy — Day 57

The pattern of weather has changed to the familiar sequence of fronts and warm sectors that we are used to in the North Atlantic. Except that down here the wind blows clockwise around an area of low pressure instead of anticlockwise. The ever changing strength and direction keeps us busily shifting sails, unlike the lazy Trades.

Since moving the two sheet winches aft, the starboard yankee sheet has a tendency to catch under the deck aerial insulator, one section of the thick brown porcelain has already chipped off. An offcut of plastic tubing taped to the backstay bent over the insulator and wired to the toerail now forms a simple guard. Such ideas are obvious when discovered but often take a long time to evolve.

7

Into the Southern Ocean

John — Day 58, Friday October 28

(Day's run 145 nm)

New rendezvous at 43 degrees S, 20 degrees E, is 450 miles just south of east. Barometer fallen 12 points since yesterday.

A day to remember. Five-hour christening on entry into the Southern Ocean. I steered while Andy replaced the entire self-steering main frame casting unit for a check on wear and tear, and an overhaul. In the course of this operation 09.00–14.00 GMT, the rain poured down and then the wind backed NW–SW, dropped a little from cold 8 to a brief sunny warm 7 and returned a violent SW8/9. We dropped all sail save the Ratsey supersail No 2 yankee, and a No 2 staysail.

Andy, exhausted, slept 14.00–17.30. I cooked a grand curry 17.30–18.15. We ate this quickly and Andy slept 19.00–23.00. I felt not too bad in a rough downwind swell which brought back memories. Rattled downwind (E) all night on the two small headsails 5–8 knots. Like a London tube at speed x 10.

Dozing 17.30–18.00. Vision of self as a spinning metal sphere, varying in both substance, speed and intensity of colour through life. At the end of life the sphere became a gaseous rainbow, through which, in the fashion of *Pentimento,* could be seen a cloud of icebirds against a patch of blue sky in racing cloud. As the gas faded, only the spirit of the birds remained.

There were hundreds of icebirds today.

* * *

I was determined to start the Southern ocean with a brand new self-steering unit, but because we'd disagreed, it was left too late. I chose a very bad day to make the change. This nearly brought about our downfall, the classic 'knock-down' enemy in Southern Ocean, the one thing I'd been trying to avoid all along.

Andy — Day 58

As *English Rose* made her way into the Southern Ocean, the Forties lived up to their name.

Our first real gale leaves me exhausted. John decided yesterday that we should replace 'George' with the second Aries, feeling the original main frame casting will cause the bearings of the second servo rudder casting to wear quickly as before. I vehemently disagreed but finally respected his authority. After breakfast we began, 'George' was disconnected, John took over the helm, then we noticed a tear in the genoa staysail — more work. The sail was lashed on deck. The new Aries parts were thoroughly checked, greased and assembled without a hitch until the final connection — the two castings refused to slide together. I groaned, softly cursing. 'George's brother eventually took control after three hours on deck.

A freshing wind forced us to double reef the main and mizzen and hoist the tiny No 2 staysail. John hauled in the main sheet and tightened the lee running backstay in preparation for a gybe. The backing wind brought a chill, making us shiver. Over our shoulders a low mauve-black cloud stealthily moved in. The mizzen was dropped and no sooner had John finished than an icy blast spun *English Rose* broadside. The Aries was struggling and I straightened the wheel, then John took my place. The next onslaught flicked the anemometer needle off the 60 knot scale, laying *English Rose* over until the cabin windows disappeared beneath a welter of foam. I clung helplessly to a winch hearing John exclaim, 'the main'll rip, we must get it down!' Memories of the Faroes flashed by 'not again?' A moment's lull allowed me to dash forward and cast off the halyard , hauling the wild canvas down with difficulty as it pressed against the rigging while we sped off downwind.

The vigorous cold front passed, easing the wind to force 8 or 9, and we reconnected the Aries keeping our fingers crossed, dreading the prospect of hand steering. This is the real test, we are in mid ocean now, unlike the gales of the Irish sea. We will hand steer if necessary till exhaustion forces us to stream warps.

Below deck as we changed out of oilskins John's grim face told me that his thoughts were the same as mine. What horrors lie further south? Are the next three months going to be like today?

We have been lucky, very lucky, our only loss this morning was a solitary sail tie.

* * *

This was valuable experience. I found out how easy it was to drop the mainsail even when running before a gale.

John — Day 59, Saturday October 29

(Day's run 176 nm)

We kept on all day with just No 2 yankee and No 2 staysail. Our concern is not to damage the gear and to keep boat speed down in high wind. Pleased with 176-mile noon-noon run. Wind died at dusk so we put up the mizzen, not risking the main in slatting calms.

Andy in good form after a good sleep. I didn't achieve much but kept cheerful. There is so much I want to do.

Still rolling a lot. We'll have to get used to it. 11,000 miles to Cape Horn. Bluff in New Zealand is 6,677 miles at noon, but only 6,604 by 23.00 hours. That's on the rhumb line course. On the great circle it is only 5,321 miles, but we'll not try that this time!

* * *

We'd tried to sail close to the great circle on the '77 Whitbread race, and got stuck in the pack ice.

Andy — Day 59

I enjoyed a long sleep this morning to make up for yesterday's exertion.

John — Day 60, Sunday October 30

(Day's run 179 nm)

Awakened by a wave forcing its way through the canvas mainhatch cover and over the top dropboard, and so down into the saloon. Spray hit me on the head, as I lay on my makeshift bunk on the port saloon seats with my feet inside the locker by the bulkhead.

Out with Andy for an hour's steering in force 8/9, while he replaced a steering line on the vane gear. Glorious sailing at 8–12 knots. The old boat loves this sort of downwind gallop. Put the clocks on an hour at noon. Andy has got the sewing machine going like a dream, with a bit of polythene pipe for a handle. Great work on genoa staysail; he also made a fiddle for the galley and set up the Army flask for hot drinks.

Andy — Day 60

A simple fiddle rail for the galley worktop now divides the formica

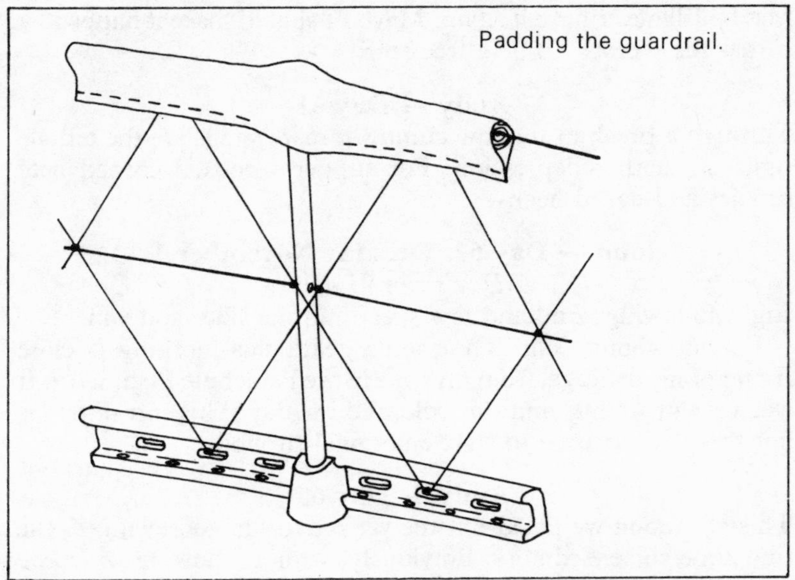
Padding the guardrail.

surface into compartments, rolling and heaving downwind we can at last wedge cups and cutlery in place.

The genoa staysail has undergone a thorough overhaul. Most of the leech is re-stitched, the piston hanks are greased and several sacrificial chafe patches protect the foot. The tear occurred just where the sail frequently presses against a stanchion. The clocks went forward an hour for the first time signifying an appreciable leap east.

* * *

An idea that I read about but never implemented, would be to pad the top guardrail with mutton cloth covered with a strip of sailcloth loosely stitched in place. Such a measure would give useful protection to low-cut genoas.

John — Day 61, Monday October 31

(Day's run 150 nm)

Pretty calm. Rain comes in black squalls, but without the power I remember in 1977. I'm moved by Lillian Hellmen's *Pentimento.* I wish I were a good writer, and able to move about the world at will. I have this feeling that equality and communications in Britain are making us all much the same, are original personalities and free spirits growing scarcer?

I'm loving all this time to myself. Must make the most of it.

Maybe I'll never have it again. Maybe I should make it happen — is that the secret? To be a free spirit?

Andy — Day 61

Through a break in the low cumulus, mare's tails are the telltale signs of another depression. For supper I cooked corned beef rissoles and baked beans.

John — Day 62, Tuesday November 1

(Day's run 75 nm)

Light following wind and low speed in blue skies and sun.

I wrote about Colin Thomson's death this morning [a close friend of my own age, from my time in the Parachute Regiment]. It was very upsetting, and this coloured the day. This sort of trip is not the place or time to start emotional turmoil.

Andy — Day 62

This afternoon we poled-out the yankee to run goosewinged, the first time since Ardmore. Previously, with a following wind, we preferred to tack downwind avoiding the problem of how to handle the large unwieldy spinnaker booms. None of our text books suggest an easy solution so we had to don our thinking caps again. A simple method has evolved. The pole is set up with its usual topping lift and foreguy plus an additional rope leading aft to hold the pole in position. A spinnaker guy is led through the pole end and attached to the sail. This preparation is done with the wind over the quarter to stop the sail flogging, when complete the course is altered to downwind and the sail pulled across. The various ropes are then adjusted to position the pole end at the clew.

Maintenance work today included streaming the mainsheet to untwist it, replacing a few stitches on the No 2 staysail, and dismantling the cockpit wind direction indicator which has decided to have a rest.

A school of dolphins came by this evening. We told them that all is well, and they left to tell their friends.

* * *

Poling out the yankee became a frequent occurrence after our first tentative experiment. Practice reduced the preparation time to 20 minutes if singlehanded — gybing took an hour. If sailing without the pole we often left the spinnaker guy tied to the clew to avoid lowering the sail each time it was goosewinged.

John — Day 63, Wednesday November 2

(Day's run 115 nm)

These days of calm are the worst. So unexpected here. Our average for the six days is only 140 miles per day, which would bring us to Cape Horn in ten weeks. Today we are becalmed.

Passed two large flocks of prions sitting on the water, both flocks each of 100–150 birds are only 200 yards apart. Wandering albatross (mostly juvenile). Shy albatross (maybe they are black-browed albatross, but I doubt it). Always white-chinned petrels (quite large dark birds — 'Cape hens'). Usually stormy petrels. Occasional pintado petrels (mottled bright wings 'Cape pigeon') and rarely, passing terns.

The largest school of porpoises I think I've ever seen passed ahead of us after lunch.

Andy replaced the pintles and gudgeons of the self-steering gear. Very worn, through constant movement. We have spares. This sort of thing is unavoidable I suppose.

Slatting sails. Boomed out No 2 yankee crashing angrily, out and back, out and back. Need to keep calm in this sort of situation.

I wonder about the electrical impulses which operate the brain. The effect of an extremist sort of life like I've led, on depressive two-week cycles, etc. Also the chances of cancer. I think it all depends on morale - and mine is high.

Funny how I seem to dream of everyone I've ever known. I don't dream much at home. Probably it is the routine of life here, and the short two and a half hour periods of sleep. 23.30–02.00 and 05.30–08.00 and 15.00–17.00 at best.

Andy — Day 63

Tonight is possibly the calmest weather of the trip so far, and yet we are in the 'Roaring Forties'. I have just lowered the mainsail to stop it slatting horribly as *English Rose* pitches and rolls, becalmed in the swell. Two nights ago the mizzen staysail poked a hole through itself from continually slatting against the radar. Another lesson learnt, we have always left sails up when becalmed in the hope of being 'pumped' slowly forward. Now we realise this is a foolhardy idea — knocking a sail to pieces for a gain of a couple of miles when 20,000 miles remain.

During the past week I have hardly had a moment to read being so busily involved with maintenance. This afternoon I felt like a rest, so after replacing a mounting pintle on the Aries, and washing my hair, I settled down with a new paperback.

John — Day 64, Thursday November 3

(Day's run 30 nm)

Calm, calm. Slatting sails and bright sun gave me a headache. The run of only 30 miles noon-noon is easily the shortest of the voyage so far. Glum! Picked up a NE breeze after lunch and set the heavy genoa, and by evening we had slipped up to 6 knots. As it grew dark we entered the fog, this persisted all night. I felt anxious with the genoa up in the dark and the glass dropping at a steady rate. However all was still well when I handed over the watch to Andy at 23.00.

All evening I had been trying to contact Marie Christine on the radio. Finally I did get through on 12 MHZ at 23.00, after being sixth in turn. Reception very poor. I don't know how we'll fare with the radio between here and the Falklands. (Three months with no radio in prospect).

Andy — Day 64

Our galley is now sparkling and the cooker gleams after a two hour stint with Jif and a 'J' cloth. John has even polished the kettle bottom with Brasso!

While the main was down I checked the stitching, nothing is drastically wrong. The mizzen staysail is repaired with two patches.

John has spent the evening struggling with the radio, reception is appalling, the operator had to relay messages to Marie Christine.

John — Day 65, Friday November 4

(Day's run 110 nm)

Out on the foredeck at 02.00. Mist swirling around like smoke in the floodlights, as we efficiently lowered the genoa and put up the Ratsey No 2 yankee supersail. The glass fell steadily all day (12 points noon-noon). All is mist until noon, then the wind sprang up from the SW. After a pleasant supper of chilli-con-carne and rice cooked by me, we put a reef in the mainsail and changed down to No 2 staysail, then Andy went off to bed.

At 21.30 the wind rose sharply to 40 knots when we were on top of the swell. I dropped the mainsail, then Andy came up and we strapped it all down. I dropped the mizzen. By 22.00 we were down to No 2 yankee supersail and No 2 staysail alone, and heading ESE at 8 knots — straight for Marion Island, 400 miles away.

I must remember to clip my safety line onto both rings on my harness.

* * *

In an emergency it is all to easy to dash up on deck without first checking the safety harness. I shall never forget struggling with the main boom on a wild night, foot on the guardrail and stretching out over the black sea to tighten the reefing ties. Back down below, feeling exhausted from the effort as we rushed on downwind, I

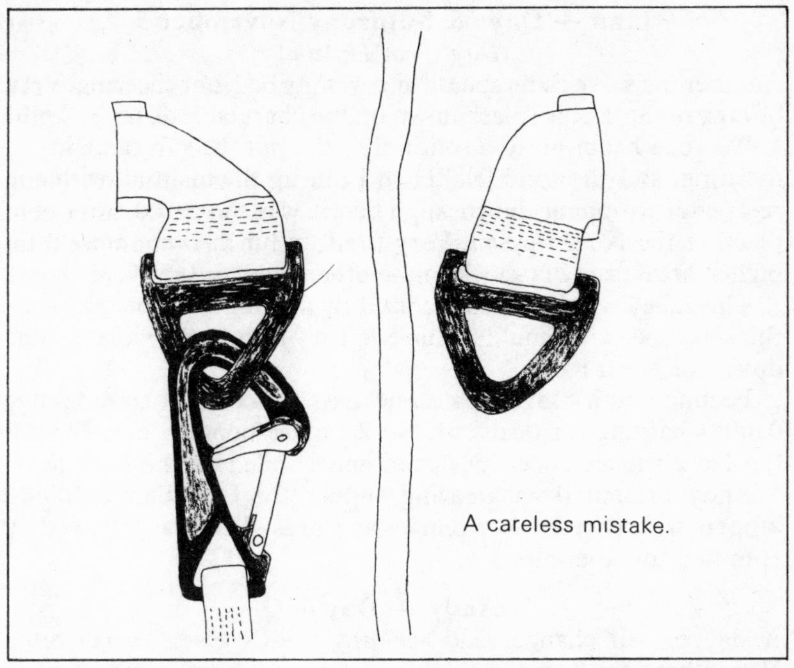
A careless mistake.

reached to unhook my safety line from my harness. Horrified, I realised that in my rush to get on deck, I'd only clipped onto one ring on the front of my red jacket. If I'd slipped or been thrown off that guardrail, my harness could have pulled right through and I'd be a dead man somewhere in the wake. My hands began to sweat as I slumped down on the chart table seat. This kind of carelessness is unforgivable.

Andy — Day 65

Our 'holiday' is once again interrupted with wind howling in the rigging and having to wear oilskins on deck. After supper we reefed the main and changed down a staysail, expecting this reduction to see us through the night. However, at 21.30 John called me as a squall caught hold, he dashed on deck to drop the main, while I dressed hurriedly.

* * *

Reducing sail at night was not our standard practice, although it is a tactic advocated by some. We preferred to crack on at night. Slab reefing is wonderfully quick and efficient, easily done single-handed. Whenever the wind increased suddenly, we simply dropped the main completely.

John — Day 66, Saturday November 5

(Day's run 151 nm)

Another big wave came aboard and wet my bed, not cheering. Very bumpy night. Drips splash down on the chart table all night, Ugh!

We rode beam-on to a southerly gale, but the sun came in the morning, and the wind fell. Then I put up the mainsail with one reef, after dropping the trisail. Then it was the genoa staysail in place of the No 2 staysail. Very tired by lunch-time, must eat a bigger breakfast. Put clocks on another hour to GMT+3.

The galley window is star-crazed by a falling dropboard (inch-thick perspex), I shouldn't have left it on the seat while I came down the main hatch.

Feeling glum. Maybe it's seasickness — took a Stugeron pill at 0200. Charging forward with No 2 yankee boomed-out. First of the No 2 yankee supersail piston hanks failed on the forestay.

Andy presented an amazing supper for Guy Fawkes night: kippers with cheese sauce on rice and peas. This was followed by stunning toffee-apples.

Andy — Day 66

A day of sail changes and seemingly little else. To celebrate November 5th, I made two toffee-apples. John persuaded me to refrain from setting off a flare.

John — Day 67, Sunday November 6

(Day's run 155 nm)

Good progress cheers me. 150 miles a day is good. Andy is now switched very much towards achieving 150 miles per day average for the Southern Ocean.

I finished reading Dostoyevski's *Gambler and Bobok — A nasty story*. I also managed to type a piece on Croft No 78 at Ardmore for 'Ardmore Years'. We had a steady day moving east. Marion Island is 209 miles and the distance to Bluff and the Crozet Islands is dropping encouragingly.

I feel grim on night watch sometimes, but I do cheer up in the mornings — as long as I can see progress.

Andy — Day 67

Blue skies and a crisp fresh following wind are tremendous morale boosters. Still no whales or giant wandering albatrosses, perhaps we are not on deck when they appear.

We encountered our first hail shower last night, and then again this morning. Is it a sign of worse to come? Icebergs?

I cut down a pair of plimsolls this morning, trying to make slippers. The result is a poor imitation of John's genuine pair, which he guards so jealously.

One of the galley windows is badly cracked from a thick perspex dropboard sliding off the cockpit seat. The shards of glass are presently taped over, it really needs a plywood board bolting on.

* * *

On deck and in the cabin I would wear Helly-Hansen polar salopettes and jacket, over cotton Army-surplus trousers, a cotton shirt and a thick woollen jersey. As the temperature neared freezing I added a polar ski suit worn next to my skin, a scarf, a polar balaclava and gloves.

The diesel cabin heater had not been fitted for fear of condensation. It remained in its box while other more important jobs were attended to. So the cabin temperature fell to that on deck but we soon acclimatised and felt little discomfort.

When on watch we wore sufficent clothes to go on deck quickly. A warm cabin might well have reduced the frequency of our round the deck checks.

John — Day 68, Monday November 7
(Day's run 156 nm)

Marion Island is 120 miles south of us at noon, and the Crozet Islands are 669 miles to the east. A good westerly airstream holds. We've done 1,500 miles in the Southern Ocean so far, in only 11 days. Morale is high all round. I cooked supper: liver and onions with rice, then raspberry jam steam pudding. I'm quite pleased with myself, and think I'd enjoy cooking roast Ardmore lamb at home.

Andy is doing great works with the boat. He has all sorts of schemes for maintaining 150 miles a day. Our average creeps up. At 45 degrees S, we worry about icebergs, but from our research, I feel they are south of 50 degrees S.

I'm enjoying writing about fishing on the Dour Loch at home, and I'm also reading *The Riddle of the Sands* by Erskine Childers. I don't think I'll run out of books. I'd like to read Wellington and *Pentimento* again!

Thrilled with the satnav and the Tamaya calculator.

* * *

This was the day when Andy took down the spinnaker halyards. He was awake when I slept, and vice versa. He was certainly not going to wake me before deciding on every job of work, but I feel we might have discussed some of the jobs, and this one in particular, should have been avoided on the basis of my previous experience in the Southern Ocean. Firstly, I should have noticed their absence, and then I should have insisted on something more substantial up the mast. But it isn't possible to go for 200 days and expect to make no errors.

Andy — Day 68

Two piston hanks on the No 2 yankee supersail have burst owing to the violent backing and filling of the sail, as *English Rose* careers downwind. We should have boomed the sail out. I have taken down the spinnaker halyards, they are never used and are chafing badly on the spreaders. To ease their replacement two 3 mm messenger lines are rove in their place.

John has just given me the disturbing news that we are now within the extreme limit of iceberg sightings, as shown on the Polar Ice Chart. It is midnight, and hoplessly difficult to maintain a constant lookout. I am more than a little anxious.

* * *

With hindsight mistakes are always obvious. To remove the spinnaker halyards to prolong their life seemed a good idea but unfortunately the messenger lines proved inadequate, chafing through and blowing away within a matter of days. So we were left with no easy means of replacing the halyards, to act as a temporary forestay or spare headsail halyard if necessary. This was an error of judgement which would soon catch up with us.

John — Day 69, Tuesday November 8

(Day's run 166 nm)

Last evening we saw our first fully adult wandering albatross (f). A good fast night, with No 2 yankee boomed out to starboard and the trisail goosewinged to port. The slatting is hard on the trisail, and a slide broke free on the mast track.

As I was cleaning my teeth over the starboard side this morning, a 50-foot finback whale came up 30 feet out on the port side. I had a wonderful 20 minutes, watching three huge whales cruising alongside the boat. They seemed perfectly content to keep station with us, and I felt they were very friendly. When I decided Andy just wouldn't want to miss seeing them, I went down below to call him, and when I returned on deck they were gone. I think it was my clumsiness with the heavy dropboard which sent them away. Or maybe it was my shouts to Andy?

We are concerned about being south of the mean iceberg limit and so we plan to keep north of the Crozet Islands and Kerguelen too.

Andy — Day 69

Bread making and sail changing kept me from my bunk until 10.30

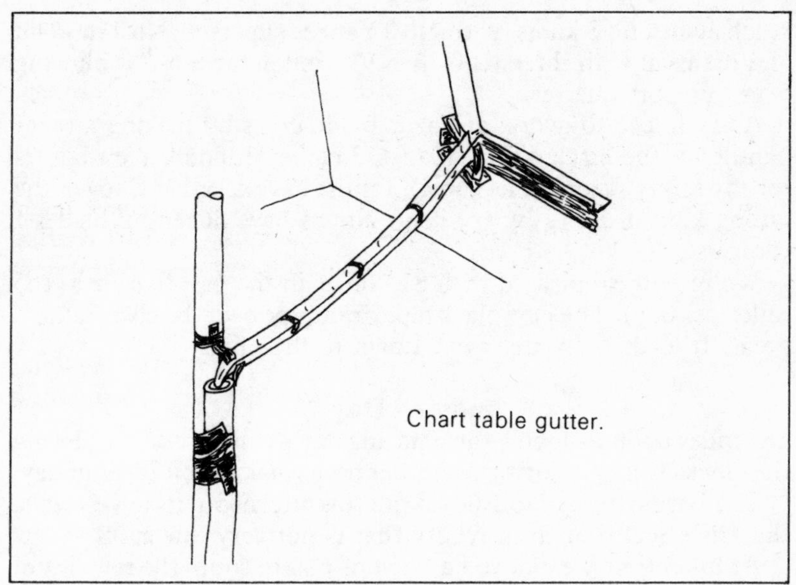
Chart table gutter.

this morning. An hour later, John called me to say three enormous whales the length of *English Rose* were cruising alongside. I leapt on deck dressed in pyjamas, but they were gone, and the cold soon forced me back to my duvet. Again he called and again I missed them.

A primitive gutter and drain for the window over the chart table, has completely cut out the drips which spoiled our charts and books. A strip of the faithful black sticky tape along the window ledge, guides the flow of water to the corner, and from there it flows in a U-shaped gutter in the airspace above the chart table. The gutter is made of the sticky tape too, and this leads into a polythene tube strapped to the stainless steel pipe which supports the chart table itself. The polythene tube leads down to the bilge. The only snag with the arrangement is that it is easy to knock it in the rough weather, but it is easy to rebuild.

John — Day 70, Wednesday November 9
(Day's run 187 nm)

The northern tip of the Crozet Islands is just 178 miles to the east of us, and as we are running more or less straight for them, I hope the satnav is right. The Canary Islands were our last sight of land long, long ago.

We had a surprisngly good run of 187 miles in only 23 hours (the clock went forward an hour yesterday). The barometer reading of 1,002 at noon is the lowest for 62 days. We are bundling along on a reach at around 8 knots, with No 2 Yankee supersail, No 2 staysail, and mainsail with three reefs. A NW wind of force 6–7 is blowing over our port quarter.

Andy hopes to avert my razor blade crisis by making a razor handle for the black double blades. I came with only a few blades for my safety razor (12 left now). I must have asked MC to get the wrong kind in Lairg by accident. Now I have dozens of blades I can't use.

We're both so pleased with 814 miles in the past five days (163 miles per day). The new black tape drainpipe over the chart table is great. It leads the water away down to the bilge.

Andy — Day 70

187 miles noon to noon — an amazing day's run for us, considering the clocks were put forward another hour, making it a 23-hour day.

The barometer fell to 1,001.5 mb this afternoon, its lowest since the Irish Sea, though in reality that is not very low at all.

At lunchtime we enjoyed a bowl of potato soup, the remains of last night's concoction, to use up the potatoes.

John — Day 71, Thursday November 10

(Day's run 151 nm)

Only 70 miles NNE of the Crozet Islands at noon, and heading for Kerguelen 812 miles away.

Light wind until noon veered north and strengthened. Bright sunny day. Warm. Washed hair and changed pillow case. Turned sheet and end-for-ended the duvet. Morale high. 1,000 miles in six days. Andy full of plans as ever, for building new boat or improving his 25-foot *Kinnego*. 9,000 miles out from Ardmore and Andy is a tremendous asset. I enjoy the cooking.

Andy — Day 71

As usual on Thursday, we are trying to make a radio call to Portishead. We find reception is best at twilight. Now that we have a four hour time difference, we are in darkness when Portishead are having a sunny (well maybe) afternoon. The radio waves dislike the change, preferring to linger somewhere over Africa, consequently we are out of contact. None of the crystals in our set is suitable for calling Cape Town, the frequencies have changed since the 1977 Whitbread Race and we didn't think to check.

Sitting by the big HF radio, precariously balanced on a flare container in the gloomy aft cabin, surrounded by jerry-cans, Aries spares, vegetables and sail bags, and with half a gale blowing outside, is mind-bogglingly unpleasant. Then I recall commuting in and out of London: give me the sea any day.

I gave the forward heads a thorough cleaning this morning, but absent mindedly I left the seacock half open. Half an hour later, the floor boards were awash.

John — Day 72, Friday November 11

(Day's run 190 nm)

No luck on the radio last night or at 13.00 today. Maybe no more contact for another ten weeks, until after we round Cape Horn. GLUM.

Wind increased all night and all morning. We are going very fast (9 knots) with No 2 yankee supersail and No 2 staysail only. Heading east with a northerly force 9 wind on our port beam. Too much for the steering gear. At 15.30 the self-steering rudder coupling broke, this is the second of ten in stock. I steered by hand while Andy fitted a new one. No 2 yankee down and trisail up. Wind had backed NW and we run slowly downwind.

190 miles noon-noon is best so far. Too fast.

Andy — Day 72

I let myself become mesmerised by our speed today, with the result that the self-steering broke. Overnight the mainsail was progressively reefed until it had to be lowered completely. We crashed on, a shade south of east willing the northerly gale to ease. It refused to let up and over lunchtime, the gusts touched 50 knots and above. We ought to have changed down from the No 2 yankee supersail since it has a theoretical wind limit of 35 knots. But carrying no main or trisail, *English Rose* was not unduly overpressed, so we left the 'supersail' up.

During the next hour and a half the wind backed to NW, giving us a freer wind to bowl along at 10, 11 and occasionally 12 knots. We hurtled like a bullet through a swathe of spray. I sat by the wheel, totally absorbed and exhilarated by our speed, surfing and broaching; tingling with tension.

Something had to break. I hoped the Aries sacrificial tube would act as a safety valve. Another wave wedged its shoulder under the counter stern, propelling *English Rose* into a spectacular broach. She staggered and didn't recover, a glance astern told me the tube had gone. I rather sheepishly called John, who was asleep down below, to tell him of my misdemeanor. My penance was a jet of cold water up my trouser leg as I hung over the stern replacing the tube.

Yankee down and trisail up, eased our speed to 6 or 7 knots, quite sufficient in the conditions.

* * *

Racing *English Rose* so hard was foolhardy, yet the incident was valuable experience. It proved conclusively that surfing was out. Averaging 8 or 9 knots downwind, occasional surfing was inevitable. A broach may not occur for several hours, but one thing is certain — broaching will lead to damage.

John — Day 73, Saturday November 12

(Day's run 166 nm)

All night, we jogged along at 5 knots on the log, probably 6 over the ground with the surface drift.

I think we both felt slightly bashed by the gale yesterday, and the repairs needed for the self-steering. The lesson once again is to keep the speed DOWN. We'll use the No 3 yankee and No 2 staysail with the trisail more often as the rig, from now on.

A fine sunny morning and warm too, the sea soon moderated. I had the mizzen up with the genoa staysail in the morning, to join the trisail and No 3 yankee.

The glass began to fall after lunch, and we head for another gale by evening. Trisail, No 3 yankee and No 2 staysail this time! We calculate the voyage like this:

Ardmore to Southern Ocean . . . 56 days
Southern Ocean to Cape Horn . 76 days
Cape Horn to Ardmore . . . . 56 days

This gives us Cape Horn on January 11 1984 and Ardmore on March 10.

I'm slightly puzzled by pins and needles in the fingers and thumb of my left hand. This has been creeping on these last weeks, is it the same as my numb left foot, caused by my old back injury? Morale is high, but it is a long way to Cape Horn.

Andy — Day 73

Another stormy day, the barometer foretells a rough night, falling three points in one hour this evening, then a further two points in the next half hour. A drop of one point an hour usually indicates a gale. The wind is at present force 8–9 on the beam, and we are making a steady 6–7 knots with the trisail and staysail.

I did little today, except eat, cook and sleep.

8

Attrition

John — Day 74, Sunday November 13
(Day's run 187 nm)

Glass fell to 985 by 23.00 last night. Andy and I dropped the No 3 yankee and continued under trisail and No 2 staysail. This is the least sail I've ever seen on this boat, and it still gave us 7–8 knots. Very bumpy and very windy, the wind backs round to NW around midnight. I slept in my clothes.

Dawn saw a huge sea building. At 16.00 we broached, throwing me over the saloon table, and my sextant in its box, across from the saloon port bunk, to the oilskin locker on the starboard side. This was a case of very bad stowage by me, a pathetic example. The vane snapped on the self-steering, and Andy replaced it while I sorted out below. A 5-gallon oil drum has punctured against the deckhead in the aft cabin.

Andy got 450 pumps from the aft bilge, and I got 430 from the main bilge. I'm a bit shaken but OK. Find it wearing. 60 more days to Cape Horn, and as usual its a maths problem — have we got the correct sum of resources? I think so.

I did quick spicy beef with rice for supper.

Wind moderates by evening. (I do certainly hope and pray.) Glass back to 1,000.

John — Day 75, Monday November 14
(Day's run 177 nm)

250 miles north of Kerguelen, and delightfully calm after the storm of yesterday. Added to this, I find we are over halfway from our entry point into the Southern Ocean to Cape Leeuwin on the SW

corner of Australia.

The day began abysmally, however. The storm raged on. At 02.00 I was woken for the 75th time at two o'clock in the morning. I staggered to the chart table and a wave hit us on the starboard quarter. A bucketful of icy water sloshed angrily down the mainhatch and right over me. My polar suit was drenched. I was GLUM. No cabin heater or clothes drier on this boat. The next couple of hours were spent mopping up, and I went to bed at 05.00 in my wet shirt and underclothes, to try and dry them.

Morning saw the wind fall, and after lunch I put up the mizzen and genoa staysail. Later on, Andy put up the No 2 yankee supersail, and brightly coloured dolphins played around us as we picked up the pieces after the storm.

Calm and slatting in the evening. Delighted to find that my wet Helly Hansen polar jacket and trousers dried in the rigging in the afternoon. Beat out the salt crystals. Wear damp shirt and long Supa Lifa trousers in bed. Dry and beat socks. The only heat we have is the one ring we use on the paraffin cooker. Our efforts to conserve meths for lighting the cooker has resulted in our using only four gallons of paraffin in 75 days.

I wash and shave every day, and reckon we have used 63 gallons of freshwater in 75 days. We could catch rain, but unless it was a heavy sustained downpour in fairly calm weather, it would probably be brackish off the sails.

Bedding: Sleeping on the port bench seat in the saloon, with my feet poking into the cupboard forward. Beneath me, I have two thick tartan rugs wrapped round two layers of Karrimat closed cell foam, as well as the thick foam cushions which normally cover the bench seat. Between me and these insulating mattresses, I have a cotton sheet folded double lengthways, and I wrap myself up from head to toe in an orange covered duvet. On top of the bunk lies another thick tartan rug folded double, and my head rests on a pillow with a bright flower-pattern case.

I sleep in a long flannel nightshirt, silk scarf, Damart hood, paper underpants, long Supa Lifa undertrousers, and Pied D'Elephant duvet boots. I take my Hardy moleskin shirt and polar socks, into the bunk with me, so they are warm to put on when Andy calls me. Then the polar jacket and trousers are not so bad to put on at two o'clock in the morning. On top of all this I wear a pale blue Henri-Lloyd duvet jacket with High trousers to match. Depending on the temperature at the chart table at night, I might wear duvet mitts with polar bootees inside my carpet slippers.

Andy — Day 75

Three days of continuous gales have been wearing, with little sleep possible. This evening we are back to carrying full sail.

We suffered a partial knockdown yesterday. John was hurled over the saloon table landing in true paratrooper style, his sextant was not quite so lucky. In the aft cabin a 5-gallon drum of engine oil found a bolt in the deckhead, spraying the slippery contents everywhere. On deck the Aries vane succumbed and the aft hatch was forced open allowing several bathfulls of water to flood below. Quickly donning oilskins and my safety harness I scrambled on deck to replace the vane and begin pumping the bilge. John meanwhile returned the cabin to order and pumped the main bilge. We eased the course a little more downwind to keep the breakers astern, thus edging closer to the ice zone.

Prior to the excitement I spent a while on deck trying to capture the scene for my album. My camera is an unprotected SLR, unlike John's semi-waterproof Fujica. Copying an idea from a magazine I sealed the camera within an ordinary plastic bag, with holes cut and taped to the lens and eyepiece.

★ ★ ★

While sorting through the spare wind vanes I came upon two marked 'Southern Ocean'. These were shorter and the plywood was thicker than the others, and therefore less liable to be snapped off. After this discovery we used a thick vane in rough weather and the larger ones in moderate weather.

Waves continually swept *English Rose* during bad weather, so everything on deck was securely lashed down including the mainsail and yankee halyards, but we were careful when tying those ropes with a sail tie to the handrails to ensure the halyard could be quickly released. With the mainsail halyard we developed a habit of leaving about 10 feet of loose rope between the cleat and the coil. This allowed us to shorten sail to the second reef without undoing the coil.

Our sail ties were mostly ½-inch wide terylene tape about 30 inches long. All had a small bowline tied at one end and we used a slip knot to join the free end to the bowline. Tape proved to be more successful than rope in which slip knots have a tendency to untie unexpectedly.

Andy — Day 76, Tuesday November 15

(Day's run 145 nm)

John read out an interesting magazine article at lunchtime describing the use of heavy weather sails. The author suggested stopping a trisail to ease hoisting, no specific details are given. After replacing three slides and splicing a new tack strop to our trisail, I rolled it into a long sausage and seized it with elastic bands as an experiment.

This afternoon, at John's suggestion, I stitched an elastic tie to both sides of the hatch flap, the previous central tie is not very efficient, letting an occasional wave burst into our home. John's bunk is within a few feet of the hatch, so he knows all about the problem.

The barometer has started a downward trend, I hope the weather does not deteriorate too soon as there is still a long list of repairs. A new mounting pintle for the Aries, a small patch on the mainsail, the yankee halyard needs re-splicing and its winch is slipping, together with an endless stream of minor jobs.

* * *

Stopping the trisail with elastic bands in the manner of a spinnaker, worked a treat, allowing us to hoist the sail while sailing downwind without the bother of it catching in the rigging. Strong elastic bands about half an inch wide were required otherwise the sail tended to burst open when only half raised.

Throughout the Southern Ocean and homeward bound in the North Atlantic we kept the trisail bagged at the foot of the mast with the slides slid into its special track. We developed the habit of changing down from double-reefed main to trisail, missing out the third reef, thus saving the mainsail from excessive wear with little loss in speed. Our problem was often how to slow down to a safe speed rather than how to go faster.

Traditionally the trisail is made with cloth reminiscent of hardboard, roped all round and rarely used; it need not be. Because of its small area, the force it has to withstand is correspondingly small, so cloth the same weight as the mainsail is suitable with adequate reinforcement at the corners. Extra slides at the tack and head are advisable.

Sheeting may be a pair of sheets led to quarter blocks thence to a winch or the clew may be lashed to the boom, with an outhaul to provide foot tension. I favour the former idea bearing in mind the conditions encountered in mid-ocean, a far cry from the Solent. Separate sheets allow the boom to be securely lashed down, however if the boom is used with the trisail it is a high risk candidate for damage in broaches or knockdowns.

The canvas hatch flap could have been greatly improved. Aboard *Kinnego* I have a flap which covers the whole space normally occupied by the drop boards. Instead of elastic ties, press studs around the perimeter are a more positive fastening. The centre section is cut out, and replaced with flexible clear plastic of the same material as used for dinghy sail windows. The idea originated in my days as a singlehander, rain is kept out, the window lets light in and allows a view astern. The press studs are easily overcome with a quick push if one needs to dash on deck. In exceptionally rough weather, the drop boards are slid into place as a precaution against swamping.

John — Day 77, Wednesday November 16

(Day's run 213 nm)

Astonishing record-breaking run of 213 nautical miles puts fresh heart into tired bones. A good steady pace, and maybe good drift.

10,000 miles out of Ardmore — seems incredible — only a day since we ghosted out of misty Loch Laxford.

Classic 'front' passed through at 14.00. We were racing along under trisail (hoisted for the first time in rubber bands and burst open like a spinnaker), No 2 staysail, and No 3 yankee. Wind NNE8. Andy alseep. I saw the west horizon fill with black, moving at right angles to the NNE gale. Glass at 1,000 at 13.00 hours. I ate my lunch and glanced at the barometer at 13.45, on my way forward to call Andy — the glass read 998. At 13.50 the black cloud overtook us and torrential rain fell. The wind backed 100 degrees from NNE to WSW (approx). I called Andy and he asked about the barometer: it read 1,001 as I looked at it at 14.05. Up three points in 15 minutes as the front passed through.

Andy — Day 77

213 miles noon to noon, over greatest run by nearly 20 miles: I wonder if the satnav is right, there has not been a chance of a sun sight for several days.

I had a good rest last night staying in bed between 5.00 am and 8.00 am. After breakfast we renewed the Aries mounting, reduced sail, then I went back to bed.

John — Day 78, Thursday November 17

(Day's run 186 nm)

After a peaceful night the wind began to rise from the south. It was cold in the moonlight taking down the mizzen. No radio contact at 04.00 — no power? Charged batteries in morning. Put up trisail to join No 3 yankee and No 2 staysail. Southerly gale all day, it was uncomfortable with a big beam sea by nightfall. Racing along under No 3 yankee, alone half way between South Africa and Australia.

Continued stormy weather makes for difficult conditions to do much except just keep going and reading. Too hard to write the book satisfactorily.

Andy — Day 78

Too windy to work on deck today, instead I busied myself below, adjusting two burners on the cooker, freeing a seacock and cleaning the main bilge pump.

* * *

The paraffin cooker worked well, better than it had during the summer at Ardmore. The delicate needles which automatically clean the burners are easily damaged by inexperienced operators, and so the cooker needed repairing many times before our trip. At the start of the voyage we'd feared it might fail altogether, so we carried two Camping Gaz stoves and 72 Gaz cartridges as a standby. Fortunately the Gaz was only needed for the blow lamp.

Every few weeks the cleaning needles were checked to ensure they still worked. Occasionally they did fail, and then as the burner became blocked so the flame subsided.

John — Day 79, Friday November 18

(Day's run 193 nm)

A bad bumpy night of clenched cheek muscles and anxiety, hurtling beam-on to a southerly gale under No 3 yankee alone. No sleep. At 05.30 the Aries self-steering was overwhelmed, the wind vane clip had slipped out. Seas too big for us. We are forced to bear-off and run NE all day in big seas which break tons of water right over us. The worst yet — though it is becoming one long gale, with just a brief snatch of sun remembered here and there. The wind vane broke at 13.00 and I replaced it. Just waiting for the weather to ease.

The strange thing is the lack of movement of the barometer. Maybe it is easing now (20.00).

We have been under No 3 yankee alone since 15.15 yesterday, and three hanks have been torn off its luff. Praying the Aries holds up.

Andy — Day 79

The storm is over, we can rest again, return to our easterly heading, and raise a bit more sail. Another plywood vane suffered a blow from a breaking crest, the sudden loss of steering started the yankee flapping wildly shaking the whole boat and waking me from a moment's slumber. John was on watch so he nipped out to fit one of the spare vanes which are now kept in a cockpit locker.

Earlier we thought the sacrificial tube had snapped when *English Rose* suddenly came head to wind out of control. The Aries appeared intact. The fault remained a mystery for several minutes until a loose locking pin was discovered.

John annoyed me this evening, moaning about the three dirty saucepans after supper. I had baked two loaves and cooked corned beef hash rissoles and beans for supper with peaches and carnation milk for pudding. The washing-up duty falls on the cook, we agreed on that after a month at sea when John became fed up cleaning the assortment of cooking utensils that remained after my baking experiments. I am quite happy with the arrangement, it is a useful time filler. This evening I simply shut my mind to John's mutterings, his curries leave only one dirty pan. I like curry but not every day.

John — Day 80, Saturday November 19

(Day's run 157 nm)

Half way to Bluff Harbour on the southern tip of New Zealand — from our entry point into the Southern Ocean at 40 degrees S, 10 degrees 40 minutes E: 3,400 nautical miles either way. We are making better progress than we had hoped, averaging 155 miles/day in Southern Ocean as against 140 miles/day forecast. Our overall daily mileage is up to 134 miles/day. HURRAH!

Southerly gale eased and veered to SW6. Seas moderated enough for us to crack on east again with a bit of south to edge us towards 45 degrees S.

The grey skies and huge swell are not very cheering, but we are making progress.

Andy — Day 80

Early this morning I discovered the Aries wheel drum about to detach itself from the steering wheel. One bolt had disappeared, so allowing the drum to move appreciably and sawing into the wheel spokes. Replacing the sticky tape wrapped around each spoke for protection and the bolt took one and a half hours. We remained underway, the wheel twitching to and fro, hampering an otherwise easy repair.

After lunch I found a moment to sew a small patch onto the mainsail using a newly discovered stitch, a flat seaming stitch which allows all the work to be done from one side of the sail. Previously I have always pushed the needle right through then fought my way round to the other side to push it back, a time consuming operation.

The remaining afternoon slipped pleasantly away whipping a few rope ends. I am somewhat pernickety about the state of our sails and rigging, coupled with my passion for ropework. I am happy to employ my time as bosun. The endless maintenance is a blessing in disguise.

While John prepared supper I took an hour off and got

engrossed in a new book, Farley Mowat's *Serpents Coil*, a vivid account of a Liberty Ship disabled by two crippling hurricanes and her eventual salvage. The descriptions of the storms are a little unnerving, especially now the barometer is beginning to tumble.

* * *

After reading the book we carefully checked the Pilot Charts to convince ourselves of the unlikelihood of our running foul of a Pacific typhoon. Typhoons are the colloquial name for hurricanes, they have an uncanny habit of being devastating!

John — Day 81, Sunday November 20

(Day's run 191 nm)

This is the sort of day when nothing is entered in the 'remarks page' of the Ship's Log, save a record of bilge pumping. It's the sort of day, with a falling wind, when we do seem to have a long, long way to go. 81 days in this little cabin, and another 100 or so to go. Just a hint of claustrophobia. My efforts on the radio were a dead loss. We don't have enough power in the batteries, it is now three weeks since we made contact with anyone. A tickle of worry will begin back at HQ (Ardmore). After the radio failure I crept back to the chart table in the dark, and where another man might have a cigarette, I began to eat — the worst thing for morale. Still, you can't be cheery all the time. We'll put a big charge in the batteries and see what we can do.

Andy — Day 81

Bluff Harbour at the southern end of New Zealand is 3,000 miles away, roughly three weeks sailing. We generally regard Bluff as the half way mark, in fact we will already be on our way home. Thinking of sailing for home is unreal at present while we battle through the storms, enjoying only the intervening few hours of calm.

Maintenance took second place today, I had a day of thought: thinking of Marie, home and a new boat. I have an envelope containing 40 photographs which I frequently look through to remember Marie, her smiling face, her defiant look, and so much more. There are pictures of *Kinnego*, my family and home, memories of another world. John also has an album of treasures, we keep our own to ourselves.

John — Day 82, Monday November 21

(Day's run 172 nm)

Slowly falling wind. Andy used the calm spell to re-splice the genoa halyard, and made a tactical error, by running a messenger to the masthead in place of the halyard. It was very cold to do the splicing on deck anyway, but when he tried to run the halyard back up the mast he found the messenger jammed in the sheave at the top of the mast. He spent three quarters of an hour up the mast but didn't solve it... try again tomorrow.

11,000 miles out from Ardmore. The sheave of one of the masthead spinnaker halyard blocks has been blown away, and the red spinnaker pole topping-lift ropes have chafed on the mainmast decklight too.

A ten-hour battery charge from the engine today, but still no contact with anyone on the radio.

* * *

I should have foreseen this from '77. I would make it a cardinal rule for those sailing in the Southern Ocean: Never be without spare halyards at the masthead, you never know when you may want an extra halyard, or a temporary forestay in an emergency. I've been caught out on this one on both occasions in the Southern Ocean.

Andy — Day 82

I often think the maintenance is a blessing in disguise, but the problem we have at present is anything but a blessing.

Early this afternoon I pulled the yankee halyard down onto the deck, sending a messenger line up in its place. It was too cold to re-splice the wire to rope join-up on deck. The messenger promptly did a side step off the masthead sheave, and jammed solid right at the top of the mast. My eyebrows raised, and with a sigh, I slid below, trailing the halyard behind me.

The splice was straightforward though time-consuming, and I finished towards evening. John's delicious-smelling supper was shortly to be served, when I announced I wanted to make a quick trip to the masthead to clear the sheave before it got dark. Three quarters of an hour later, unsteady with fatigue and with fingers numbed to an unfeeling blue, I returned to the deck, defeated. We ate our supper in solemn silence, the chef's speciality had been spoiled.

Now, at midnight, we dodder east with no headsail. The spinnaker halyards are in the aft locker.

John — Day 83, Tuesday November 22

(Day's run 129 nm)

Andy up the mast at first light. He managed to reeve the yankee halyard OK. Terrific performance by Andy.

Grand day of sun in clear blue sky. No 2 yankee supersail boomed-out as we stream downwind, eating up the miles. I typed chapter 19 of 'Ardmore Years', the fishing story on the 'Dour Loch' so far away (but rushing nearer). 160,000 words done in the last two years.

Masses of drifting weed in the sea, we think it must be from Kerguelen Islands — I'd like to visit them! Thinking of a cruise in the Pacific with MC & Bec, also to British Columbia? Dreams come easily here, when you've seen no land for two months.

Huge pizza supper and trifle. Andy in great form.

We have given the batteries a really good boost — running the engine for 18½ hours (out of gear of course) yesterday and today. Andy got through to Perth Radio on 4MHZ at 01.30 in the morning. Telegram to MC 'All well. Horn January 14. Message Wellington'.

Andy — Day 83

John called at 3.30 am, first light, we wanted to relead the halyard before another gale. Mast steps are a great help, though a little tricky in the subsiding swell which did its utmost to flick me off. I can well appreciate the courage of schooner top-men fisting canvas in a blow. Yesterday I expected to spend five minutes at the masthead, this morning that is all I needed. Using a long strand of stiff wire hook shaped at one end, the mischievous messenger was fished out in a jiffy. John pulled the halyard through, then we breathed a sigh of relief.

Shortly after raising the No 3 yankee it was lowered. The halyard winch was stripped to clean the pawls, they were sticking due to an over enthusiastic application of grease. Oil is the recommended lubricant for the delicate ratchet.

After consulting the sky and barometer, the No 2 yankee

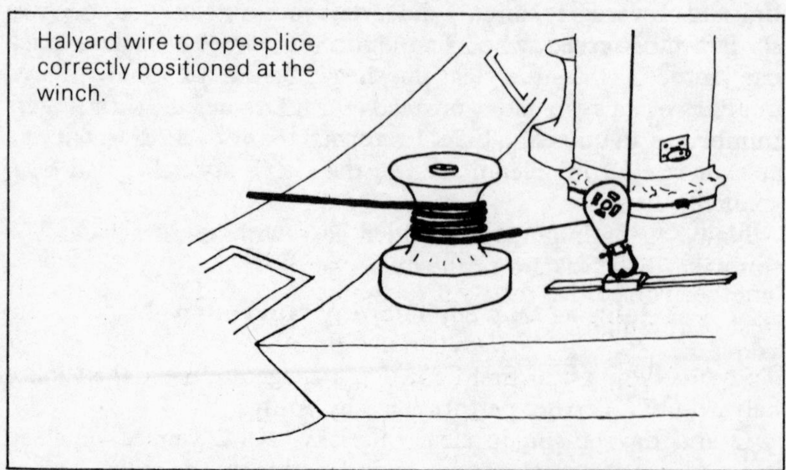

Halyard wire to rope splice correctly positioned at the winch.

boomed to starboard soon had *English Rose* on her way.

I tried to sleep after breakfast but without success. For lunch we had bacon grill and spaghetti — a change from our usual midday meal of bread and jam.

I swapped my Bosun's woolly beany for a chef's hat after lunch, turning out the usual two white loaves plus a trifle, a sponge cake and a pizza for supper with baked potatoes. The pizza tasted remarkably good, topped with ham, chicken, tomatoes, tomato paste, peas and sweet corn, adding a touch of flair to my conservative repetoire of stew ten different ways or corned beef hash. Baked potatoes are a regular treat, they are simply chucked into the oven after bread making and are ready one and a half hours later. Best of all they don't need peeling!

A patchwork of blue overhead is a rare treat, enticing us out of our polar-wear suits. This brief spell of calm has allowed John to clatter away on the typewriter again.

John — Day 84, Wednesday November 23

(Day's run 180 nm)

Much relieved by Andy's success on the radio to Perth. Hope the telegram goes through alright — is the position going to be included? We have Wellington 2,700 miles ahead and should be able to get through there again I hope. This was a calmer, damp day, grey with the barometer rising back to 1,015 in a 'high'. I made a curry in the morning with a tin of stewing steak. Uncertain if two teaspoonfuls of Madras curry powder is enough. Does more make it hotter, or just waste the powder? The curry was a success with lime pickle from a little jar from Inverness.

One third of the way from our entry (40 degrees S 10 degrees 40 minutes E) into the Southern Ocean to Cape Horn — HURRAH!

This has taken 25 days, so the Horn should be reached in 75 days — Jan 11?

Today I saw the smallest stormy petrel I've ever seen: grey and white and flying quick as a bat.

Andy — Day 84

Our three week silence is over, Perth radio sifted our signal from the ether and will pass a telegram to Marie Christine. Hearing another voice filled me with excitement, I could not sleep for the rest of the night.

John — Day 85, Thursday November 24

(Day's run 171 nm)

Grey wet day, with the wind rising from the north. Twelve weeks at sea. A long time since we saw a ship or land. Now we hear Perth and Adelaide on the Brookes and Gatehouse receiver; we must be somewhere near Australia!

Struggling to keep the old heart up a bit. It's a war of attrition, one day is rather like another, and it seems so far to go. Andy is very bright though, and we keep each other going OK.

Andy — Day 85

I made a welcome find in the forward heads this morning, a bottle containing seven pints of meths. The paraffin cooker needs priming with meths each time it is lit, and until now we have tried to limit ourselves to using only one ring at a time fearing we might run short. This find increases our supply by 50 per cent. We can look forward to exotic meals requiring 2 burners now.

John also made a discovery, a fourth layer of apples in the last of two boxes. After three months at sea they remain deliciously crunchy, a daily treat.

Continual use of the pump for the cooker paraffin tank has fractured the soldered joint where the pump enters the tank. A delicate repair, trying to melt the solder in a small area without melting all the seams holding the tank together.

While the cupboard housing the tank was empty I took the opportunity to clean it and all the plastic bottles stowed there. A bottle of washing up liquid had emptied itself leaving everything slimy and horrible.

John — Day 86, Friday November 25

(Day's run 203 nm)

More grey misty weather. Steady barometer and a fair N–NW wind. Almost directly south of the west coast of Australia at noon. 203 miles was a very good run. I think we're eating too much — will cut down and see if it cheers me.

Moving steadily forward, with things in hand at the moment.

Andy — Day 86

No moon, we run goosewinged, leaving a furrow ablaze with phosphorence.

John — Day 87, Saturday November 26

(Day's run 183 nm)

A surprise roll put the mainsail aback, just before midnight last night, when we were going with No 2 yankee poled out to windward. No problem. Andy stowed the pole during his watch 23.00–02.00. At 05.00 I made an alteration to the course. Andy didn't turn out at the start of his watch, but lay on in. At 06.00 he called me and told me the snap shackle on the yankee tack had broken, and the No 2 yankee was half way up the forestay.

We are both jaded — we've averaged 166 miles a day since entering Southern Ocean 28 days ago.

Two days of sunshine are gems in heaven. We left the mainsail with one reef for too long, and paid for it in the mess this morning.

Flogging about in the wet NW8 gale. Anyway, on we go, it's about 12 days to Bluff? It's a long way to go.

Andy — Day 87

Another day of drama. At first light the snap shackle securing the yankee snapped allowing the sail to shoot up the forestay.

Tonight, as John woke me, the sacrificial tube broke, throwing *English Rose* into a confusion of flapping sails. I was particularly annoyed about the tube incident, feeling John should have reduced sail, I scribbled comments in the deck log, and will leave it at that.

* * *

The sail up the forestay incident persuaded us to swap the halyard snap shackle for an ordinary screw shackle, fearing another failure might send the halyard to the masthead. The halyard is a 65 foot length of 9 mm wire which whips violently in any kind of a sea. When fully crewed two men are required at the bow, one to hold the halyard whilst the other attaches it to the sail. We managed singlehanded with the aid of a 3 foot length of rope, attached to the deck and having a large snap hook at the free end. The halyard required two shackles instead of one. In use the halyard is eased until the snap hook can be engaged into the upper of the two shackles, then the halyard is tensioned leaving both hands free to work on the lower shackle.

John — Day 88, Sunday November 27

(Day's run 170 nm)

A setback! At 23.00 last night when I woke Andy, the wind was rising and I thought we should drop the mainsail. He said he could do it. I got started to turn in when the self-steering failed. The third tube was broken. Only seven left. I should have dropped the mainsail. It is no use waiting. We had a rotten time for an hour while I steered, stupidly forgetting my gloves. Andy dropped the mainsail and replaced the tube. Rotten.

At 03.45 the front went through, and the wind backed 90 degrees to SW. I gybed in cold heavy rain, in grey, grey dawn.

Wind dropped calm while I slept, then came up from the SE. Awful cold rainy day. Luckily the wind began to veer to the south in the afternoon.

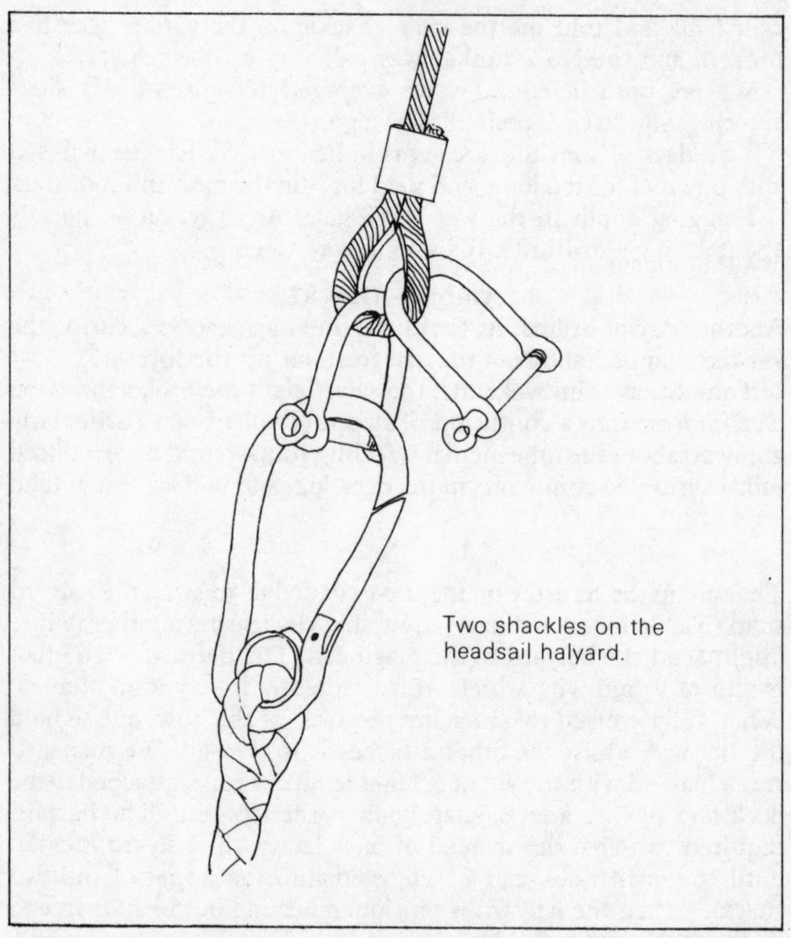
Two shackles on the headsail halyard.

My heads (the aft lavatory) failed while I was cooking supper. Now I'll have to work the outlet pump with pliers. Ugh! Not the best day — homesick.

Andy — Day 88

Continuous rain kept me below deck, except for sail changes and washing a few clothes in rainwater collected in a bucket slung under the boom.

John — Day 89, Monday November 28

(Day's run 111 nm)

Rotten calm day. Bound to happen occasionally. Andy drilled the pump head on my (aft) heads and it works again. Wind got stronger in the evening and I dropped the mainsail. Only seven tubes left! Cape Horn is only 6,234 miles ahead — not as far as Bluff was when we entered the Southern Ocean 30 days ago (6,677 miles on October 29).

Andy — Day 89

John's loo finally gave in yesterday evening, the threads on one part had stripped. Fortunately it and the mating piece are brass, easily drilled through to take a split pin.

A few hours without rain or spray allowed my washing to almost dry this morning. After lunch, rain returned accompanied by a variable wind that boxed the compass settling to south this evening. A full gale howls now.

Bright elongated patches of light the size of a man's shoe surround us at night. We assumed they were cuttlefish bathed in phosphorescence. John's books reveal that to glow like a bulb is their defence mechanism. *English Rose* must appear a mighty predator as she thunders past.

John — Day 90, Tuesday November 29

(Day's run 163 nm)

There seem to be no entries in the other log [Ship's Log] just figures. Sunny in the morning, are we wearing out? No! Quite a lot of sail-changing. Passes the time and tiring.

Hobart is not far. 90 days — doesn't seem long since we left Laxford really, only more and we shall have circled the planet.

Not much to say really. Struggling with doubts about myself as usual.

Andy — Day 90

Exhaustion and fatigue are noticeably settling in, both John and I no longer automatically get up when on watch at night. We tend to lie in our bunks clinging desperately to the warmth. During settled weather our 'lie ins' are a fairly safe practice, but in rough or

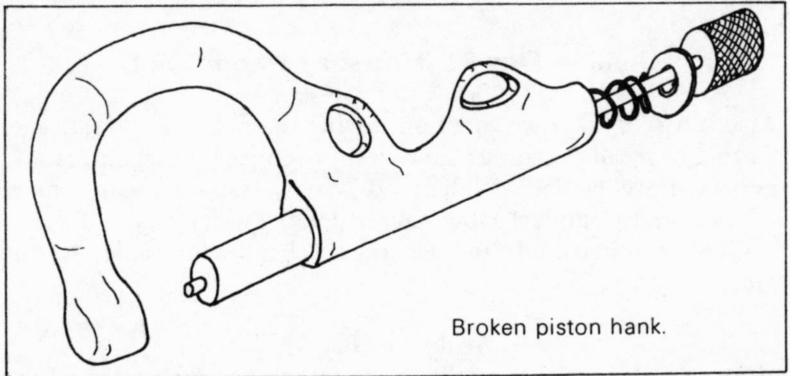

Broken piston hank.

changeable conditions, not having one of us dressed, ready for action could lead to unnecessary damage. We will have to make an effort to keep getting up.

The No 2 yankee 'supersail' is showing signs of wear now, and requring an occasional stitch replacing. More of a worry are the piston hanks of which seven have broken. We used the last spare several weeks ago. At first sight they appear more than adequately substantial, unfortunately when the sail flogs violently the spring-retaining washers are dislodged leaving one or more hanks broken. At present we simply wrap masking tape around the plunger to hold it shut — crude but they stay on the forestay.

John — Day 91, Wednesday November 30

(Day's run 166 nm)

Again a day of sun and fair wind at high barometer saves this old bag of bones. I must never forget the storm will always end and the sun shine again (and vice versa) — life.

Morale high and progress good. Andy sawed off the ends of the No 2 yankee supersail's broken piston hanks and refitted and soldered them. What a pleasure to be with someone able to think creatively.

Andy — Day 91

This afternoon the wind eased, allowing me to finish drying my washing. How wonderful I felt wearing freshly washed pyjamas this evening.

A flash of inspiration while lying in my bunk this morning has I hope solved the problem of the broken piston hanks. By sawing the end off the plunger they can be dismantled, repaired and soldered back together. I clamped the vice onto the companionway steps, apologised to John for the forthcoming noise then occupied three hours sawing, filing and hammering. Hopefully they are stronger than before.

John — Day 92, Thursday December 1

(Day's run 178 nm)

Also it was 92 days we spent on rowing the Atlantic 18 years ago. Trying to recall the things Chay and I promised we would try and be when we landed. 'Older and wiser', 'Less arrogant, more tolerant and humbler! How have I done? Pathetic.

Good weather holds and we are on schedule for 36 days to the Horn.

Andy — Day 92

High clouds again foretell an approaching depression, John

continues to be amused by my irrepressible weather predictions based on old wives' tales. The pilot chart shows a very high gale frequency in this area.

The prospect of a blow is no longer the nail-biting experience of sitting in a dentist's chair that I used to suffer. We are continually improving the boat, learning how to handle her and gaining confidence.

My afternoon was again swallowed up with maintenance, replacing the boom vangs, whipping sheets to cover chafed areas and re-seizing the repaired piston hanks to the yankee.

John — Day 93, Friday December 2

Sunny and warm. Decided to cut my hair — done in the end with random slashes with the little scissors. Washed hair. Changed shirt and socks. Turned sheet and changed duvet for the first time.

Andy made delicious bread and this has poppy seeds on top. He's really professional at it now. Excellent lunch of tuna fish, new white bread and orange juice.

Andy — Day 93

The engine had a six-hour run today. Two weeks ago we hauled in the Aquair spinner, the fast downwind sailing proved too much, running the risk of breaking it. Consequently the Mercedes is fired into life more frequently, usually in the morning when I sleep. Back in September I found the engine disturbing, now I am accustomed to the steady drone, preferring to sleep through it rather than listen to it when awake.

John — Day 94, Saturday December 3
(Day's run 164 nm)

Glass falling as another low marches east. We spin along nearer Cape Horn now than where we entered the Southern Ocean . . . Onto the chart of West Pacific, and we put the chart of the whole world up on the main bulkhead — we are almost half way home.

Andy in great heart, working like a Trojan. I'm doing well with 'Ardmore Years' (I need something to take my mind off these grey seas). Talk is all of trying to phone home, after a month (November 3) since our last contact. Hope Andy's telegram of November 23 got through OK.

Andy says Harry [Harry Simpson, an instructor at Ardmore] thought we'd never make it without stopping — we'll do our best.

At 22.00 I tried the radio. 4125.0, the safety/call/reply channel was filled with a howl and a faint conversation from Darwin. There looked to be little chance. I got a big sluggish tuning signal, and tried 'Hello Wellington Radio. This is yacht *English Rose VI*

2OVE. Do you read me! Over'.

Nothing happened. I felt we were too close to Australia. All their stations use 4125.0 as well. I thought Andy might have better luck with them later in the night.

'Hello *English Rose VI* 2OVE. This is Auckland Radio.' Clear as a bell. The operator got hold of the Awerua operator (at Bluff on the southern tip of South Island). An Australian operator came in from Gosford (I think it was) but he excused himself when he heard I was working Auckland.

'Good progress report from you. All well here. Love MC.' This was sent via Glasgow on November 27 in response to Andy's radio telegram via Perth Radio of November 23. The Auckland operator was full of enthusiasm and got MC on Radphone on 8 MHZ, but we couldn't tune on 8 MHZ and then our power failed on 4 MHZ as well. So it was all left in the air after a brief chat with Awerua to arrange our calling them on December 9.

I went to bed at 23.45 feeling excited. Half way round the world and talking to Auckland again just as we had in 1977.

The gale subsided in the early hours. Glass bottomed at 998 and started to rise.

Andy — Day 94

John's ceaseless endeavour to call New Zealand was rewarded this evening with a reply from Auckland Radio and Awerua Radio. He enjoyed a chat and received a telegram from Marie Christine confirming our telegram via Perth.

We had Coq-au-vin with rice for supper.

9

Half-way

John — Day 95, Sunday December 4

(Day's run 163 nm)

Stimulated by the radio work last night. We really must be half way round the world. 13,000 miles out from Ardmore. It does seem a long way from that ugly flat-topped concrete pillar called Bishop Rock Lighthouse. There was that distant glimpse of Cape Finisterre and then Gran Canaria shrouded in rain. The satnav blinks out its pale green figures 12 inches from my eyes at the chart table. We might make it!

A day of light wind again after the gale. We can manage force 8 OK downwind, but seas pile up and make it hard to prevent surfing, which breaks the sacrificial tube on the self-steering (three broken and seven left). Nursing our way forward.

The stormy petrels in these waters are the prettiest I've seen anywhere, having a slight purple tinge or sheen on them at a certain angle.

To be a free person means that a person must have the CHOICE to do the wrong thing, as well as the right thing.

Sailing unseen past South Africa and then Australia, I tune into their radio. A distant detached listener. In the midst of an ocean which at times is savage and raw, I find at night I wonder where the world is going. There is both frank pop materialism and American-voiced extreme religion.

Malcolm Muggeridge's 15-minute programme on his conversion to Roman Catholicism at the age of 80, makes me think. His attitude to the certainty of Darwin's Theory of Evolution being wrong is interesting: 'Of course there is a pattern in it all — all things are linked, but there is a Creator.' He reinforces the view that suffering is the only ennobling factor in human existence, and believes ALL humans suffer as part of life. Anyway...

Sent radio telegram to MC: 'Position 48 degrees S 149 degrees E. ETA 200 miles south of Bluff December 9. Horn January 6. Ardmore mid-March. Will try and contact you via Wellington and Falklands. Halfway and all well. Merry Christmas. Love John.'

Delighted at prospect of radio link Awerua and Wellington across the South Pacific.

Andy — Day 95

Some days I feel fed up. Today was such a day — using the radio has a negative effect on me. John is always elated after speaking to someone else. I think he finds me a dull companion whose conversation is limited to boats and Marie. I find the radio upsets our rhythm, reminding me of home, voices sound strained and distorted through the loudspeaker, unreal and unhappy. I would happily throw the blue box overboard and live with my photographs.

John — Day 96, Monday December 5

(Day's run 163 nm)

Beautiful warm NW wind off Australia. 7.5 knots. Boat in terrific shape — we must just NOT get casual, it is up to me to keep us on our toes, with all my experience.

Andy in really great heart and well motivated to complete the trip to succeed in our objective. He is the first fellow of his age I've ever met, who likes to have the boat going sweetly rather than flat out: how fortunate for the boat and me.

The cuttlefish pass in the night, like glowing milk bottles on their sides.

One of the features of this trip for me has been the delicious sweet drinking water from the 'Freshness' filter. We fitted the second one of four last week — no more awful fibreglassy water, like so many times in the past.

Andy — Day 96

Twenty-four hours without an alteration of course. Rarely in the Southern Ocean have we experienced such a steady wind, it is warm and blowing straight off the Australian desert. Last night I slept with a blanket instead of the usual blanket and duvet.

Two books occupy my night watches this week: an illustrated account of Darwin's voyage and Francis Chichester's *Along the Clipper Way*. The latter is packed with useful notes on scurvy, ice, gales and Cape Horn, and an account of Smeeton's pitch-poling twice at the infamous Horn is fascinating but chilling. John refuses to read such matter until we are safely into the Atlantic.

John — Day 97, Tuesday December 6

(Day's run 177 nm)

There is a great feeling of New Zealand in the atmosphere. Maybe we should take a look at the Antipodes Islands up ahead, there's nothing between them and Cape Horn.

Reading Darwin on the *Voyage of the Beagle.* Darwin, aged 22, writing to his sister about his surprise at being selected when so young, to sail with Captain Fitzroy (only 23): 'there is indeed a 'Tide in the affairs of men' — I have experienced it!

There is a tide in the affairs of men,
Which, taken at the flood, leads on to fortune;
Omitted, all the voyage of their life
Is bound in shallows and in miseries.
On such a full sea are we now afloat,
And we must take the current when it serves,
Or lose our ventures.

William Shakespeare

Perhaps 'Flood Tide' should be the title for 'Ardmore Years'. It exactly expresses my own philosophy — if not always my action!

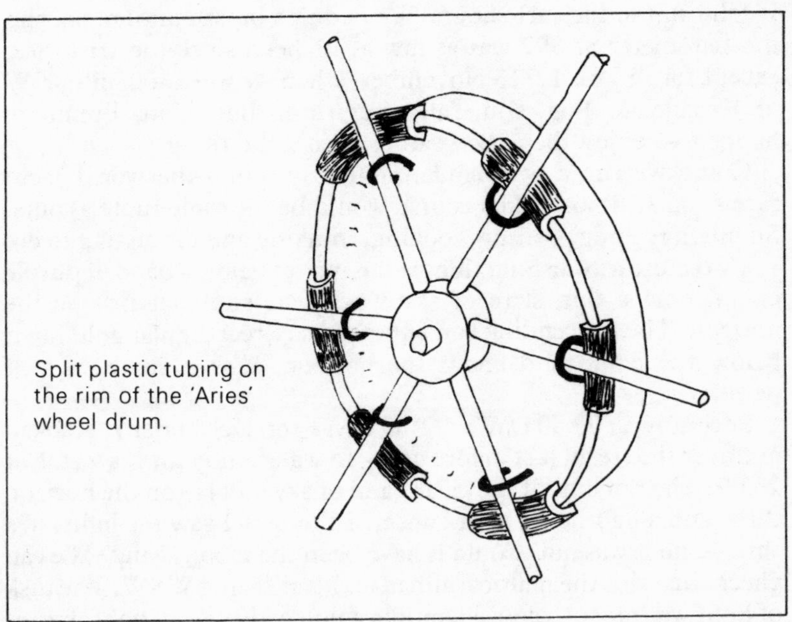

Split plastic tubing on the rim of the 'Aries' wheel drum.

Andy — Day 97

The wind rose sharply after lunch, cancelling my bread baking. Whenever I have tried baking in similar conditions, the mixing bowl has skated around the galley, throwing flour everywhere.

Instead of baking, I wedged myself into the corner of the lee seat in the saloon, and settled down to read a few chapters of *Along the Clipper Way*, by Francis Chichester. The many references to scurvy lead me to wonder if we are at risk. We take a vitamin tablet each day, and regularly eat potatoes and onions. Tinned tomatoes are another valuable source of vitamin C, and we set out with 48 large tins! As we passed south of Cape of Good Hope, my gums developed a slight ache, a primary symptom of scurvy. It wasn't scurvy of course, simply mild toothache, and rubbing Sensodyne toothpaste over my gums eased the pain away.

The Aries has performed so well recently, I hardly dare talk about it, lest it should suddenly fail. This morning I slid short lengths of split plastic pipe onto the rim of its wheel drum to protect the steering wheel spokes. The drum had twice cut through the previously applied plastic tape, and was attacking the spokes like a pastry cutter. The steering lines are occasionally shortened to avoid chafed areas, otherwise the Aries continues to 'stay on watch' in all weathers, 24 hours a day.

John — Day 98, Wednesday December 7

(Day's run 101 nm)

It fell calm in the early hours. We hadn't a breath until noon, and the barometer at 992 was as low as its been since the Irish Sea, except for 985 on 12/13 November, when we were 400 miles NW of Kerguelen. Fog, sun, rain everything but wind. Bound to happen — enjoy the easy weather, that's the thing.

Could we run a two-handed non-stop round-the-world yacht race from Ardmore? The course would be the same route as ours. So much reading, writing, cooking, thinking and discussing to do.

Two more astonishing things: the sun set below a band of purple cloud, only a thin strip of sky was clear, and that just on the horizon. The descending sun appeared as a rectangular gold ingot below the cloud and above the horizon. Was it some trick of parallax?

Secondly, at 22.50 DWT (11.55 GMT) on December 7. I looked out over the stern, just before going to wake Andy for his watch at 23.00. The remains of the clear band of sky still lay on the horizon three and a half hours after sunset. I thought I saw the lights of a ship — no it was not. Could it have been the moon rising? We can check this with the nautical almanac. I was facing WSW. The tusk of light was moon-coloured, or like a domestic yellow light. I went to change into deck shoes, this took 30 seconds, and on my return the light was gone. I was not mistaken in this, I watched it for a minute or more. Rising moon or star?

John — Day 99, Thursday December 8

(Day's run 127 nm)

The glass rose steadily all day and the tail wind returned. The weather has really been much lighter in the past couple of weeks. Our average speed has fallen off a bit, but it is much easier on us. Blue skies and sunshine we'd almost forgotten, it makes the heart rise. The days seem so much longer with the clear skies, we only have about five hours of darkness. Andy keeps saying its like springtime, and I suppose that is just what it is, only we've rather lost track of the seasons. I have a slight twinge in the back — I must out-think it. Back to SW winds, they are much cooler than from the NW.

Andy — Day 99

No gales today, just a fresh wind and lots of sun. We are rapidly approaching land, tomorrow the Auckland Islands will be only some 50 miles out on our starboard beam, that's to say they will be to the south of us. A sun sight confirmed our faith in the satnav, we shall be spared the ignominy of running aground tonight.

John — Day 100, Friday December 9

(Day's run 159 nm)

Established a daily 10.30 GMT schedule with a lady at Awerua ZLB Radio Station at Bluff. Telegram from Gran (All well. Merry Christmas.) What larks!

Glorious day of sailing with boomed-out headsail and full main and mizzen, under blue sky and sun. Auckland Island is 33 miles due south at noon, we couldn't see it for cloud down there.

Andy reveals he had second thoughts about coming on the trip, but MC persuaded him to come. I knew about that anyway. Good old MC.

Andy — Day 100

Great excitement at lunchtime as we passed 35 miles north of the Auckland Isles. We searched the horizon with binoculars, several times imagining low-lying clouds to resemble hills, but clouds were all we saw. Our proximity to land has fired my enthusiasm to see the Antipodes, a mid-ocean pinnacle eroded into several islands which happen to be exactly on the opposite side of the globe from London.

Fine days usually raise our spirits, and today was no exception.

Unencumbered by oilskins I washed my hair and gave it another trim.

John — Day 101, Saturday December 10

(Day's run 146 nm)

14,000 miles out from Ardmore. By afternoon it was spray on the foredeck again, as we bashed along at 50–60 degrees off a fast-freshening SSE wind. Andy went to bed early at 19.00, feeling a bit sick in a rising sea. I went out to put a second reef in the mainsail, we then had the No 2 yankee and No 2 staysail up as well. I saw a big drab fishing-type boat far out on the starboard bow. I'd noticed the continental shelf projects well to the south of New Zealand, and so I asked Awerua if there was a chance of fishing boats down here. They warned me of a permanent fleet of Russian boats. We were at 49 degrees 27 minutes S, and 171 degrees E. Then I saw another big trawler or processing ship, close to the first. We'll have to keep a watch out tonight, over this bank. Its the first sign of human life for 51 days.

Andy — Day 101

A bumpy day which led to me being sick this evening — the shame of it.

We are crossing a shallow bank to the south of New Zealand, four trawlers have passed during the last few hours, our first sight of another ship for seven weeks. John saw the first at twilight, I've only seen a few lights and none approached close enough to cause alarm.

For supper I cooked a steak and kidney pie, baked potatoes and peas. I couldn't finish my helping and what I did eat only stayed down for a few minutes.

* * *

Seasickness plagued us throughout the trip, John never succumbed to the point of being sick, whereas I was physically sick twice. We found a change from calm weather to rough, required a day to acclimatise, after which we were unaffected until the next calm settled our systems.

John — Day 102, Sunday December 11

(Day's run 144 nm)

We saw a total of four trawlers/processing ships. Plagued with ESE winds and so we butt ENE and north of the course for Cape Horn, which lay 4,404 miles slightly to the east of us at noon. Still, we can't have it all our own way, the 'yachtie' will out distance the high and the westerlies will return.

Wish I was home for Christmas with MC and Bec. How many more will we have with Bec? And I'm squandering them. My two dearest.

Andy — Day 102

John sent three telegrams for me this evening, one home, one to my sister, and another for Marie: wishing them all a happy Christmas. The early greeting hopefully will jolt them into sending a reply.

John — Day 103, Monday December 12

(Day's run 145 nm)

A lot more bumpy today. The wind veered 15 degrees at noon and had us crunching over the SE swell. Only 56 miles west of Bounty Island at 18.30 DWT: desolate, barren, rock-infested and low. Discovered by Captain Bligh in the 18th century. I do hope the satnav is working OK.

Andy — Day 103

I spoke to Radio York this evening. After a brief chat, the disc jockey left the phone to prepare a tape; the London telephone operator thought the conversation was over, and pulled the plug. The wretched radio always frustrates me, I don't know why I bother.

John — Day 104, Tuesday December 13

(Day's run 156 nm)

All go last night, skirting round the north of the Bounty Islands. We never saw them in the dark. We've been pushed too far north by contrary winds, but if we headed on the other tack, we'd soon be deep inside the iceberg limit.

Andy — Day 104

Enjoying our food is a major factor in boosting morale, however I'll cut down on quantity — often I go to bed feeling quite bloated. For breakfast I eat toasted oats, that will have to be replaced with cornflakes. A mug of oats, butter and a heaped teaspoonful of sugar is overloading me with unnecessary calories.

Quite a while has passed since any urgent maintenance needed doing, so I can spend an increasing amount of time reading.

John — Day 105, Wednesday December 14

(Day's run 137 nm)

Another day of light and unfavourable wind. Tedious grey day. Have we come too far north (and still going)? I tried fishing with Francis Chichester's 60 year-old spinners, but only caught a bit of moth-eaten seaweed encrusted with gooseneck barnacles.

Will the wind never go west? I asked Wellington to give me a forecast on the radio, but they only asked me to give them our weather! No wonder their forecasts have been wrong these past few days.

John — Day 106, Wednesday December 14

(Day's run 105 nm)

Endless easterly winds (day 6). We head SE to search for a way out. Heavy on the nerves. Hurt my back at lunchtime. Oh Dearie me! Patience, Patience, PATIENCE. Banging into the seas. Crossed the International Dateline, so this is our second December 14.

Andy — Day 106

We crossed the Dateline today, requiring a little book-studying to discover how the new time zone affects us. We are 12 hours behind GMT now, instead of 12 hours ahead.

Today is December 14, yesterday was also December 14. Now yesterday, today was tomorrow, or was yesterday today, or is tomorrow the 15th? It is very confusing. The satnav has more sense, and continues to glare unfeelingly at us with its little green numbers.

John's Tamaya NC-77 navigation calculator is a great asset to route planning, replacing the tedium of transferring courses from Gnomonic to Mercator charts with simple button pushing. Numerous route permutations can be studied in a short time. Although a yacht cannot always maintain the desired course, owing to stress of weather, a generalised route is a fundamental requirement on a long passage. Our planned route between New Zealand and Cape Horn, is to maintain an easterly heading north of latitude 50 degrees S, this should keep us clear of the northerly bulge in the ice-limit. After longitude 115 degrees W we are clear to curve southward to Cape Horn. Headwinds were pushing us 25 degrees north of the desired course, but this seemed better than the 75 degrees divergence south, on the other tack.

John noticed the satnav waypoint distance to Cape Horn has hardly reduced recently, so the Tamaya was hauled out to investigate the missing miles. The answer was obvious: our view of the world is a flat piece of paper, where straight lines appear to give the shortest distance between two points, but in fact the world is a sphere, and the shortest distance between any two points is the great circle distance. Our heading when off course must be compared to the great circle and not the rhumb line course. The present great circle route for Cape Horn approximates to SSE, so ENE is roughly at right angles, and hence the miniscule change in the waypoint distance. We duly tacked, and the waypoint distance is clicking off the miles, yet somehow sailing almost south doesn't feel right, when our course on the chart is east.

A clipper Captain discovered the secret of great circle sailing. To the amazement of his fellow captains, he always seemed to be setting off in a different direction to the rest of them, yet he would beat them all to the destination.

Our latitude at noon was 47 degrees S and our limiting latitude is 50 degrees S, that is only 180 miles away, a day and a bit maybe. If the wind remains in the southeast, we'll have to sail to 50 degrees S, and then short tack in six hour legs along that latitude.

John — Day 107, Thursday December 15

(Day's run 155 nm)

We are about as far south as we mean to go at noon: 49 degrees 27 minutes S, 172 degrees 24 minutes W. Now all we want is a fair wind.

Andy — Day 107

My efforts to improve the efficiency of the cooker nearly led to a disaster this evening. I pumped up the pressure and lit the burner, quite unaware that a leak had formed a pool of paraffin since the afternoon. Everything was engulfed in flame, filling the galley and saloon with smoke. Once I let the pressure off, the flames subsided, and I proceeded with the spaghetti bolognese.

About six weeks ago, John asked me to turn my mind to a small problem, his spare razor blades are the wrong kind for his razor. A mix-up caused by John packing half his kit and Marie Christine the other half. During the intervening weeks I have been turning several ideas over, and with the approach of Christmas I thought it about time I made something. An old toothbrush forms the handle, the bristles are cut off and that end is bent at right angles over a flame. The blade holder is formed from a thin sheet of aluminium, cut from one of our empty butter tins; it is bent to allow the Wilkinson blades to slide on, and its attached to the handle with Araldite and a whipping.

I began reading *Watership Down* by Richard Adams this morning.

John — Day 108, Friday December 16

(Day's run 121 nm)

Perfect day of blue sky, sun and smooth sea, with a force 3/4 wind from the NNE. This gives us a close reach on the port tack, and we glide along, waiting for the westerlies to return. Andy has made me a grand razor — from a plastic toothbrush handle fibreglassed to an aluminium blade holder, which is made from a strip of butter tin! Tomorrow we'll have trials with the Wilkinson blades.

Andy — Day 108

John received a telegram for me this evening: 'So glad all is well. Happy Christmas to both. Will lay on turkey in March. All the best and love from all. The Family.' No mention of Marie, she will probably send her own message.

I presented John with the razor this evening, and for once he was speechless. The gift was meant for Christmas, but like a child unable to keep a secret, I couldn't resist showing off the simple invention.

* * *

The razor was a small peace offering, to settle my conscience. During the previous two months I had developed a progressively more bolshie attitude, believing I knew best, ignoring John's advice. We never argued, and John was right to have opted for a crew of two rather than three. If our hackles were raised, we withdrew into our own thoughts, and conversation ceased for the day. Living in a world of our own, wasn't hard after months of long solitary hours on watch. Our need for the stimulus of conversation, always cleared the air after a period of silence. With three aboard, two would have ganged-up on the third.

What or who caused the disruption? Neither was the sole cause. My solitary nature makes me try to achieve everything alone. To seek help, I regard as an admission of defeat. Changing sail together, usually left me fuming with impatience.

It might appear that our ship was an unhappy one, but on the contrary, we sailed the boat singlehanded whenever possible in our respective watches and *English Rose* maintained a good average speed. Harmony prevailed for 99 per cent of the time, and we chatted endlessly at mealtimes, and never raised our voices in anger.

John — Day 109, Saturday December 17

(Day's run 162 nm)

We are nearer where we came into the Southern Ocean if we continue east now, than if we retraced our course west. 15,000 miles out from Ardmore. Very bumpy day, we are bashing into a NNE wind, and I feel we are too far south really.

The saloon window above my bunk is starting fresh leaks. However, I'm adept at tracing a course for the water with my finger-tip, so I can usually steer them away from dry clothing.

My sprained right wrist is not getting much better, and the back pains are vulnerable to the twisted bumpy position at the chart table. Still, it could be a lot worse.

Andy is in good form in spite of a headache. He's delighted at the amazing blue toothbrush razor he's made for me. A grand shipmate I must say.

I'm racing through the 14 'Bolitho' naval history novels set in the Napoleonic Wars, which Andy has brought with him. On we go: heel for heel, and toe for toe!

Andy — Day 109

Headwinds, and very bumpy. The southerly wind, which lasted a week, has backed to the northeast, pushing us south of Latitude 51 degrees S. Any further south will be too close to the ice for peace of mind.

We experimented with a new rig this morning: two headsails and the mizzen. Our sail changing sequence is somewhat unorthodox here in the Southern Ocean, but our method enables us to sail *English Rose* with only one crewman on deck. The new No 2 yankee is so heavily made it can remain up in winds far in excess of the limit recommended for the old sail. It is also large enough to be of use in lightish winds. We have only used the large genoa once in the Southern Ocean to date, our reason being the rapidly changing weather rarely allows it to remain up for more than a few hours, so why waste our energy unnecessarily. In fair weather our rig consists of No 2 yankee, genoa staysail, full main and mizzen plus mizzen staysail. As the wind increases the mizzen and mizzen staysail are dropped and the No 2 staysail is hoisted in place of the genoa staysail. The working staysail is being kept for the long windward fetch up the North Atlantic, it has been around the world before and is now close to disintegrating.

Further increase in wind strength sees the main reefed, usually straight to the second reef. We found when tying the first reef in, that the second was invariably required shortly after. Downwind there is little difference in speed between one and two reefs. But to windward we still reef progressively, ie, first reef then second. After two reefs the main is dropped and the trisail hoisted, unless sailing downwind when the two headsails alone are sufficient. The No 2 yankee is only replaced by the No 3 yankee in extreme conditions, force 8/9+. All the sail changing bar the No 2 yankee is easily done singlehanded.

The various rigs may not be 100 per cent efficient in terms of sailing performance but they require the minimum of effort. After 110 days of damp, noise, anxiety and little sleep, we are exhausted. Genoas and spinnakers can be kept by racing men, we are not on a race, it is a test of endurance and seamanship.

The new rig utilises the mizzen to balance the boat when sailing to windward in a varying wind, reducing the problem of paying off to leeward in each lull when sailing with headsails alone.

John — Day 110, Sunday December 18

(Day's run 158 nm)

Wind rose to NNE 40+ knots at 23.00 to 03.00. Andy lowered No 2 yankee. When dawn came we were gilling along at only a couple of knots. I put up the No 2 yankee again and then we had a glorious day of misty sun in a blue sky. We sailed nicely with full mainsail, mizzen, No 2 yankee and No 2 staysail.

Mare's tails in the evening — wind coming. I made a good curry from a tin of minced beef, a tin of sweet corn, two onions, a clove of garlic, a teaspoonful of salt and a handful of raisins. To this I added a teaspoon of both vindaloo and chilli powder. Andy fried up the popadoms for the first time — these and some mango pickle made for a grand meal.

Andy — Day 110

Last night's gale looked set to remain for another day at least, surprisingly during the early hours it blew itself out. Ironically the lull came after a trying hour on deck dropping the yankee and raising the trisail. John raised the yankee again after coming on watch at 2.00 am.

I jump at the opportunity to do as much as possible during fine weather. This morning my cabin underwent a spring clean followed by sorting the potatoes and onions. The vegetables are sprouting profusely, one entire sack of onions was heaved overboard. This afternoon I enjoyed the fresh air, overhauling the old No 2 yankee. This decaying sail is unlikely to be needed, it certainly won't take the hammering we are giving its successor, however the work is satisfying and a break from reading.

John — Day 111, Monday December 19

(Day's run 186 nm)

First run over 175 miles for 14 days. The misty grey sea looks like the South Indian Ocean again. Our concern now is the icebergs, they lie between us and Cape Horn. Coming out of the Ross Sea they are blown eastward and also north to meet the westerlies and the surface drift. We have to plan a SENSIBLE course. Regretably this means moving a bit north of 50 degrees S, but still it is better to be sensible.

Andy — Day 111

Ice is an increasing worry, John's file of charts includes several giving ice information: pilots' charts, hydrographic polar ice charts, and the US South Polar Oceanographic Atlas. All give slightly different lines to represent the mean limit and the lack of conformity is confusing. Should we sail north of the extreme or mean limit? To be 100 per cent clear we have to sail north of the extreme limit, but that will add 400 miles to the distance to Cape Horn. Our preference is a course between 45 degrees S and 47 degrees S, this track will cross the ice zone for a period of about two days. Our chief worry is another northerly gale which might force us south.

I would love to see an iceberg, but not on this trip. I'll make a journey to the Arctic or Antarctic sometime in the future.

At present we are lucky to see anything, thick mist has closed around us, sailing full tilt has the feel of running through a sparsely mined field. Radio contact with New Zealand is fading, Marie hasn't sent her telegram yet.

John — Day 112, Tuesday December 20

(Day's run 146 nm)

Another splendid day, though without sun. Five sails up, all easily reduced: full mainsail, mizzen, mizzen staysail, No 2 yankee and No 2 staysail. Steadily eating up the miles towards Cape Horn and the home run up the Atlantic.

'Ardmore Years (Flood Tide)' is coming on well. It gives me so much pleasure to have something big and creative to do, just when I have this remarkable opportunity for thought. Andy is busy with gear, sails, survival kit, and endless thoughts about his future and his own boat, *Kinnego*.

Wonderful long Radphone call home on 4 MHZ to Wellington then by telephone to Ardmore. MC, Rebecca and Gran are at Ardmore for Christmas and in fine form. I suggested MC, Becca and I go on a trip to Nepal. Of couse I couldn't sleep when I handed over to Andy at 23.00!

John — Day 113, Wednesday December 21

(Day's run 170 nm)

So pleased with last night's call — I spent most of the day just thinking about all MC and Bec had to say. Another smooth day in fog, covering the distance under five sails.

Brain going like mad on all sorts of schemes as usual — I have to rush and put them down on paper before I'm onto the next thing.

I sent eight cables away on the radio for Christmas greetings.

John — Day 114, Thursday December 22

(Day's run 174 nm)

On and on, is it day 3 or 4 in this interminable fog? Winds lighter today. Thank goodness for Christmas to break the monotony. Fog, Fog, Fog. Working hard at the writing, but its hard to concentrate. Maybe it's just idleness, maybe staleness — probably the former.

Planning a photographic library of the layout of the boat, a hundred shots or more for reference — it will help with the rig in the future.

Andy — Day 114

The fog remains damp, oppressive and chilly, with no hint of the sun. We relax below listening to the steady hum of the Aquair streamed a week ago after its enforced rest. The demands of maintenance upon my time are lessening now, *English Rose* is close to perfection. As the threat of boredom looms alarmingly in the coming weeks I have started another hobby: designing new fittings for *Kinnego*.

An ominous trickle of fizzing oil from the gearbox gasket, led to the dicovery of several loose bolts and no oil in the gearbox this morning. The gears are never engaged, so hopefully no harm has been done.

I don't know what to make of the silence from Marie, perhaps she doesn't know how to send a telegram, but surely in that case she would ask Marie Christine?

For lunch I cooked scrambled egg, using egg powder, an experiment that won't be repeated — scrubbing the pan afterwards was a real chore.

10

Lonely Christmas

John — Day 115, Friday December 23

(Day's run 128 nm)

16,000 miles out of Ardmore and the fifth day in the fog. Total daily average up to 141 and Southern Ocean average at 151 miles per day. Andy is getting the Christmas spirit just in time, he iced his Mum's cake and fixed the saloon cassette player for the carols. Bags of fog.

Andy — Day 115

One more day to Christmas, I feel excited about the anniversary despite the lack of decorations. We both have a sackful of presents to open. This afternoon I iced a fruit cake sent by Mum, nothing fancy, just icing sugar mixed with water and lemon juice. To stop the white coat sliding off the cake at each roll it now resides in the gimballed oven.

The ship's stereo blares out again after two months muted inactivity, the faulty connections had been left unrepaired because we both have a personal tape player with headphones. With the approach of Christmas we can now listen to carols together.

John — Day 116, Saturday December 24

(Day's run 167 nm)

Christmas Eve. Out of the fog in the morning. Bright sun with a high schism of weather system written N–S in the sky. We sail smoothly along on the NW airstream. In the early afternoon there was a 'Bump' and we'd hit something. It could have been a sleeping whale, but I think it was a patch of something draped in seaweed. No damage. Back in the fog again late afternoon.

New Zealand is just finishing Christmas, we shall be among the last to start it.

My thoughts are of home: I've been with Marie Christine at Christmas for the past 19 years, ever since we were married. Without her now, I see how much she put into Christmas all those years.

Listening to the Festival of Nine Lessons and Carols sung on Christmas Eve in King's College Chapel Cambridge, on the tape Jenny Patteson has given us for Christmas. Alone on watch with Andy asleep. I'm probably the furthest human being (awake!) from land, of the 4,000 million of us on this planet. What a place it is. Am I doing enough to improve it? Aren't there so many reasons to let standards drop — to forget the idealism, and settle for easy comfort. But it is not the way — and I know it.

My thoughts turn to the substance of Christmas, and what it means to me to be an Englishman, how privileged. Have I done enough for Marie Christine? No. Have I done enough for Rebecca? No. The lesson I should learn from this Christmas, out here alone, is that charity begins at home. I must do more for those two dear ones. Only from that base will I be able to achieve something of the ideals of my youth. I haven't seen my parents since 1973, it's time I did.

The only radio programme I can receive is BBC Christmas morning in Hungarian, and a snatch of news from Sacramento, California. Also a summary of Socialist Bloc progress in 1983 from somewhere behind the Iron Curtain. I hear acid rain is killing one third of all trees in West Germany, and they'll have no trees left by 1995.

Slipping through the night fog at five knots, the self-steering leaves a broad luminous trail. The water gurgles along the side of the hull, by my ear at the chart table. The rigging creaks and groans gently, where am I bound? 1984.

Cable came through from the Mackintoshes at home; 'We've got the tube flies. Merry Christmas.' Thoughts of the spring run of salmon in the north.

What I had imagined was the only selection of radio programmes available, gradually increased as short wave reception improved with darkness. As well as Marxism and Acid Rain, I now heard from the BBC that 'Cruise' missiles have been in the UK since a month ago, with American fingers on the firing button, NOT British. Britain is close to Orwell's '1984' vision of 'Big Brother', with the country serving as 'Airstrip One' for 'Oceania'.

Christmas makes you think when you are alone.

Andy — Day 116

I finally got around to preparing an emergency kit this afternoon, the essential tools for survival are stowed in two watertight flare containers. While sorting through fishing hooks and string, I naturally began thinking of ice and all the other floating debris we might hit. *English Rose* staggered, then slowed slightly, jolting me from my day dreaming. I rushed on deck to see a large patch of disturbed frothy water astern, John was out of his bunk in a flash. I dived below for binoculars then climbed the mizzen mast but nothing was obvious, no spouting whale or bulky tree trunk. John thought he saw a large patch of weed while I was below. My impression was that we had glanced off a basking whale, which understandably dived in panic, leaving a tell-tale patch of churned up water.

* * *

There was no excuse for our collision, our watch keeping had become lax, we needed the shock to jolt us into shape.

The emergency kit was discussed at length. We studied the Baileys' epic book *117 days adrift* and the Robertsons' *Survive the Savage Sea.* The contents are listed below, it is by no means a standard or exhaustive list.

Container No 1:
4 x red parachute flares; 8 x red hand-held flares; 3 x buoyant orange-lifesmoke flares; 200 waterproof matches; dinghy repair kit; spare inflation valve; spare spectacles and sunglasses; pliers (greased and sealed in tape); screwdriver; 12 clothes pegs; reel of stainless steel wire; 4 large plastic bin liners; whistle; seizing wire; fishing weights; nylon fishing line; reel of wire trace.

Container No 2:
reel of thick line; reel of thin line; knives, forks, teaspoons, dessertspoons (2 of each); waterproof torch; paperbacks (*Riddle of the Sands,* and *Saga of a Wayward Sailor*); 3 note pads; fishing knife; masking tape; Sensodyne toothpaste (for toothache); needles; pins; tweezers; scissors; chalk; plasters; comb; safety pins; 2 candles (for waxing rope, not for light); torch bulb; spare rubber towing eye for dinghy; 2 spare sets of torch batteries; sail cloth; 2 large sponges; 2 bowls.

In addition to the waterproof containers a non waterproof container held 22 tins of corned beef. All three were stowed on the starboard pilot berth, together with two 5 gallon jerry-cans of fresh water, a groundsheet, a short length of plastic tubing with a plastic funnel, and John's box of fishing tackle.

In an emergency we intended to load the gear into both liferafts taking the inflatable dinghy and whatever else came easily to hand. All very well in theory but thankfully, our ability as rapid removal men was never put to the test.

John — Day 117, Sunday December 25 — Christmas Day 1983

(Day's run 130 nm)

Christmas Day is a difficult day. To achieve the aim, I must maintain control. Relax in routine, see it through . . . 200 days is a long time. Its now 100 days since we last saw land. This is no time for Christmas Day as solitary introspection, there is so much which is appalling.

To awake with depression. To try and shake that old black monkey off my back, with a light breakfast, a hot cup of tea, a scrub of the teeth, and a thorough wash and shave. Then its up on deck for the daily recitation, a few poems and songs I've learnt off by heart on the trip:

'This precious stone . . .' Shakespeare.
'He clasps the crag with crooked hand . . .' Tennyson.
'The splendour falls on castle walls . . .' Tennyson.
'There is a tide in the affairs of men . . .' Shakespeare.

The songs were a little less polished:

'What's that! I've got it! I've found it – the lost chord . . .' Durante.
'Mammy, Mammy, I'd sail a million miles, just for one of your smiles . . .' Jolson.
'Zipedeedooda, Zipedeeay, me oh my, what a wonderful day . . .' Uncertain.

Several turns through this routine, delivered fortissimo, and pianissimo, usually releases some of the tension. Then the spirits begin to lift, even on a grey day with grey seas and grey fog. Today not. Carols on tapes, so many presents — I gave not one gift. Too much food. My afternoon spent reading *Second Meadow* by Archie Hill, a disturbing book for this time.

Andy's great Christmas supper: Roast chicken breasts, roast potatoes, peas, and broad beans as well, plus bread sauce and sage and onion. Then Christmas pudding and Christmas cake.

Well, its bad to think too much. We are very well placed. I climbed the mast without a harness — one slip and it would all be gone. So much to be thankful for. So very much to look forward too. So much to give.

Andy — Day 117 Christmas Day

A memorable day spent becalmed in a shroud of mist, no sickness. Peace.

Marie sent a 'St Christopher' together with a note, 'wear this for me', I thought of Marie, home and Ardmore. I left only one present, for Marie of course.

We listened to carols, I hummed silently to myself. Dinner was a feast. Roast chicken, with roast potatoes, peas, broad beans, sage and onion stuffing and bread sauce; followed by Christmas pudding and cake. A rich meal washed down with several glasses of apple juice.

John — Day 118, Monday December 26 — Boxing Day

(Day's run 72 nm)

I awoke this morning with a thought. After yet another dream, about yet another unsatisfactory period in my life.

I realise I've come on this 200 day voyage almost subconsciously. What am I doing? What will I achieve? 'Conquistadors of the useless'. No sponsorship, no insurance — just financial loss. What am I here for? I didn't know . . .

This morning I found out, on Day 118 — clear as a pikestaff. I've come back to the source of my strength, stumbled on it more like. The 92 days on the Atlantic rowing gave me so much. Later I often talked of going on a 'retreat' to Ampleforth Abbey, but I never went. Maybe I feared pressure from Roman Catholicism. I've come here with that old black monkey of depression on my back, I have to master him. I have mastered him — with my routine each morning.

Why I have come on this voyage is now clear, and must not be forgotten. I must realise that there is nothing to be gained from fretting over the past. My life for the next half-century will all be done in the FUTURE. Regret nothing, forget it. Let it all go, and look up ahead into the dawn.

It has been the calmest day we have had for months. Andy is inspired by the Toblerone and Terry's chocs he has been given for Christmas. He gave the self-steering a four-hour overhaul in readiness for Cape Horn. I took the spinnaker halyard up the mainmast, so we'll have a spare forestay in an emergency. Andy has rigged an ice-damage line round the bows for ease of fitting a patch to the hull, just as we did on the Whitbread Race. He also made use of the calm weather to take some photographs of the boat, from the rubber dinghy, and he was surprised at the growth of gooseneck barnacles around the stern.

The glass has started to fall, but the wind still holds off.

Andy — Day 118 Boxing Day

For several weeks the Aries mountings have been wearing badly sending out awful 'graunching' noises. The continuing fine weather persuaded me to thoroughly overhaul the entire unit. While John steered, I lifted the Aries inboard, a simple task taking five minutes thanks to Nick Franklin's cunning method of attachment using spring-loaded catches. It was soon obvious the boat would steer herself, making a couple of knots in the light breeze. Dismantling, greasing and checking each part, as well as bolting on new mountings, occupied the next four hours. The gear is almost as good as new now, ready for the final run into Cape Horn.

John replaced a spinnaker halyard, combining the job with a masthead inspection and a few photographs from the lofty perch.

With the threat of ice still around I prepared the collision mat, a ten-foot triangle of heavy canvas. In use the mat needs to be positioned over the hole and held in place with 3 ropes. Two ropes are already tied to the triangle. The third rope is lashed at its centre to the bow with each end led outside the guardrails and attached to the toerail alongside the shrouds. A lead weight is tied to the rope at the bow. If the mat is required the bow lashing is cut allowing the rope to hang beneath the hull, one end is then tied to a corner of the mat so it can easily be pulled into place.

When all work for the day was finished, an hour still remained before supper, so I inflated the dinghy, heaved it over the side and rowed off ahead to take a photograph. Even in the light breeze, keeping ahead of our floating home required all my energy. John was taking his afternoon nap, so there was no-one to turn *English Rose* round if I dropped a paddle. Back alongside I was horrified to see a thick carpet of gooseneck barnacles up to 3 inches long under each quarter, hidden from view when on deck. No wonder we are sluggish in light airs.

John — Day 119, Tuesday December 27

(Day's run 65 nm)

Poorest two-day run of the voyage so far (137) miles save for the awful 135 in South Atlantic. Wind picked up and backed SE after noon. Gloom with lack of progress. Ah well.

Andy — Day 119

Upsetting our routine of short sleeps soon wears us down, during the last few days I have missed my morning sleep twice. Partly because I didn't want to miss the good weather, and also because sleep is often not forthcoming. As a result I feel exhausted, last night I slept from 20.00 through to 05.00. John had woken me at 23.00, but I promptly fell asleep again, fortunately coming round three hours later to make John his early morning drink.

The lack of wind had begun to irritate us, we tried everything from opening hatches to raising the lightest genoa, taunting an imaginary gale over the horizon.

By evening our efforts were rewarded, we hauled down the genoa and raised the trusty No 2 yankee supersail, still maintaining good speed.

* * *

I found the short snatches of sleep didn't suit my system, and I went from periods of exhaustion to alertness almost weekly. When tired I easily fell asleep, becoming well rested after several days of sound sleeping. But once recuperated from exhaustion, sleep became fitful, leading to progressive tiredness and eventually exhaustion again, from where the cycle was repeated.

John — Day 120, Wednesday December 28

(Day's run 140 nm)

Thumping into the wind and a slight sea, with one reef in the mainsail. Heading NE. Very trying on the weary patience. Still, unreel these difficulties and reel in again when things get better, just like playing a trout. 120 days is a long time, about 80 to go. Three fifths of the task is completed.

John — Day 121, Thursday December 29

(Day's run 150 nm)

At last the wind begins to veer to the south and so it allows us to head east. We push on in pale winds and grey skies. Nothing very dramatic in the way of progress — maybe this is the cause of our gloom — or maybe it is the over-eating of Christmas goodies. Neither of us is keen on beating to windward.

John — Day 122, Friday December 30

(Day's run 140 nm)

Started the day with a good southerly wind, which dutifully veered SSW then climbed rapidly to a gale and backed SSE. Again we are thwarted. We have had nothing but unfavourable winds all across the South Pacific. Ugh! Still, still...

Andy — Day 122

I will remember the Pacific for its contrary winds, either flat calm or we have to sail to windward. Cape Horn in about a fortnight.

John — Day 123, Saturday December 31

(Day's run 158 nm)

Managed to get away a cable 'To all around Loch a Chadh-fi' with

New Year's greetings, via Wellington last night.' Odd to think I've been here with Andy for one third of a year now. Couldn't have a better companion.

Rough all day, makes for a bit of a seasick feeling. Longing to get round Cape Horn and head off up the Atlantic for home.

Andy — Day 123

The lumpy swell from last night's gale made me feel sick this afternoon, so I sat in the cockpit for an hour stitching a sail until feeling fresh again. By supper-time my stomach had settled sufficiently to withstand an hour in the galley while I made chilli-con-carne and spaghetti.

A craze for crossword puzzles, occupying an hour after supper, started yesterday. I have four books of the mind teasers, another thoughtful gift from my sister.

11

To the Horn

John — Day 124, Sunday January 1 1984
(Day's run 162 nm)

Bluff: 271 degrees True 3,245 miles
Cape Horn: 107 degrees True 1,749 miles
A good gale over the starboard quarter had us rolling along towards the Horn in the forenoon but by evening the wind has eased and backed south again. The days are grey and the ocean monotonous. I'm finding it difficult to concentrate for long, on anything. We will benefit from some sun on the way up the Atlantic. Not much else to say.

Andy — Day 124

New Year's Day and as usual I have forgotten to make any resolutions.

Another gale blew up this morning, fortunately from the west so we made good speed. This evening a cold front passed bringing vicious squalls, and we spent two hours on deck shifting sail.

* * *

Days were slipping by unnoticed at this stage, each new day was so like the one before. We lived without Mondays, Tuesdays or even weekends. Early in the voyage I jokingly told John I intended taking Sunday off each week. My philosophy being that working six days a week produces better results than a seven-day week over a long period. After a month at sea I no longer knew what day it was without looking at the deck log. Even then I sometimes made mistakes. Each midnight, since I was on watch at that time, I had the job of printing the new day and date in the log book. To John's consternation and amusement I occasionally looked at the last entry and simply copied it out again, forgetting to add another day. My holiday 'days off' became erratic, taken when the need was felt.

John — Day 125, Monday January 2

(Day's run 121 nm)

It's six o'clock in the evening, and 1,600 miles WNW of Cape Horn. We've had a rough southerly gale since last midnight. I cooked supper tonight, though it's Andy's turn; he's feeling sick and has a headache with this bumping. Now he's gone to bed, and I'm alone in this tiny pool of light by the chart table.

Good old Andy, dour long Yorkshire face, beard and professory specs, with their square silver rims. He looks pretty vulnerable sometimes, with his ginger woollen flower-pot hat pulled firmly down to the nape of his neck at the back, over the ears and a little roll up across his eyebrows. His stock reply to my attempts at opening conversation, is a flat 'Aye' — he tells me this is used whenever a full reply would be controversial — and Andy doesn't like to make waves. He's been a real star on this trip.

Five hours is a long time in the dark, with only the howl of the wind for a companion. The burden is anxiety: should I go up and take her downwind? Should I reduce sail? Is all this too much for the standing rigging?

Little voices pester me 'remember we changed the forestay in Auckland in 1977. Don't forget all those unexpected breakages that year: the boom vang, the masthead sheaves — yes, what do you think it's like up there tonight, after 17,000 miles?'

I can't work on 'Ardmore Years/Flood Tide'. After 125 days; I'm heartily sick of me and my boring past. I'm not only bored with me, but much worse, I'm profoundly disappointed with myself. I don't have a lot of self-respect left.

I never did like talking, writing or thinking of the past, it's such a waste of the time remaining. This book does nothing to help alter that view. Life is TODAY not yesterday or tomorrow (helps himself to a mint humbug — Hurrah, only five left).

What a lot of twaddle. Everything is going dandy — just grin and be grateful. OK — picked up by the bootstraps. I'll do a crossword, that'll take my mind from that whining wind. Will it never veer south-west? Please, oh please!

Andy — Day 125

Another splitting headache that refused to go away, even trying to sleep it off this morning only made it worse.

★ ★ ★

I was never sure what caused the headaches, was it fatigue, seasickness or anxiety? A combination of the three seems most likely. Whenever exhausted or queasy I tended to sit reading or lie in my bunk thinking. My thoughts invariably turned to Marie and home. What were they doing, no real news had arrived for months. Were they worried? Obviously they must be. My decision to accompany John had been selfish, with little thought for those left at home. Concern for friends and family was becoming an increasing burden.

The lack of news from Marie or even a mention of her from my parents or Marie Christine played on my imagination. John's comments were unsympathetic, usually in the style, 'well there are lots more fish in the ocean!' He didn't believe Marie and I would see each other again. It was an idea I could not and would not accept. I gained solace from her final card which was pinned over my bunk. On the front was a message:

'Happiness is having
Someone to love
Something to do
Something to hope for'

Inside a handwritten message gave a spark of hope. The spark ignited a furnace, melting the tattered dreams till they flowed into one.

The headaches cleared, the prevention was simple: remain busy, and occupy my mind with anything, whether it be cleaning cupboards or scrubbing the deck.

John — Day 126, Tuesday January 3

(Day's run 177 nm)

A good noon-noon run of 177 miles, but like riding a switchback with a SSE 7/8 wind and a course of E by N. Still the rig is only No 3 yankee, No 2 staysail and trisail. Occasional beam seas roll across the deck, but Andy's headache has gone, thank goodness.

Very cold in my bunk last night, and I awoke badly chilled. My head and knees were like meat in a fridge (still 1,500 miles down to Cape Horn). New plan for bedding is an improvement: I put on my Damart headcowl and the bootees, brought my Helly Hansen polar trousers and Long Johns into the bunk, wrapped my shirt round my knees and draped the duvet jacket across the top of the duvet and tartan rug — then it was better.

Andy — Day 126

Unceasingly, the wind blows from the south. Holding our course is now a battle of nerves, as waves break and crash alongside, leaving the boat shuddering, and streaming with water. Several times I have hinted to John that I might ease our course a little more downwind. Each time he has been unperturbed by the noise and violence. Perhaps I am becoming jittery and over-cautious. As we continue to wait for a change the boat continues leaping east. Occasionally an upcoming wave meets the descending bow which buries deep, sending water cascading into the cockpit 40 feet away. A boiling torrent to soak anyone on deck, or sweep him into the scuppers.

Below we try to live normally, an impossibility. Rolling from level to 40 degrees, pitching and being lifted and dropped like a toy on a spring. All these movements occur simultaneously an infinite number of times. I occupied my day wedged into a dry corner trying to read.

Using the forward heads I knock my head, becoming weightless as the bow falls off one wave, then I find myself being pressed into my boots as she staggers up the next.

My planned supper of 'Toad in the Hole' was abandoned, so too was the idea of baking bread. I resorted to a simply-heated Stevens Lefield Chicken Supreme.

* * *

As the weather deteriorated so did our stamina. Periodically we had both fallen asleep when on watch. In the approach to Cape Horn we deliberately stayed in bed though still waking each other at three-hourly intervals. Sailing under storm sails we felt an increase in wind requiring us to drop even those pocket handkerchiefs was unlikely. We stayed in our bunks overnight keeping half an eye open for a change in weather when 'on watch'. Chancing our luck that no ships would pass in the night.

John — Day 127, Wednesday January 4

(Day's run 173 nm)

Fourth day reaching close with storm sails gave us a 173 mile run. Cape Horn is all our thoughts now, 1,300 miles to the south-east, like a great barrier between us and home waters, if you can call the South Atlantic 'home waters'.

Glass is still very high at 1,023.5, soon it'll start to fall; then we'll see what we'll see.

John — Day 128, Thursday January 5

(Day's run 161 nm)

Fifth day with storm sails: trisail, No 3 yankee and No 2 staysail. Wind veered through SW to nearer W. The seas grow bigger . . . I get more anxious. By the early evening the glass was down to 1,003 and going fast. Frightening noise outside — still we have STILL got seven tubes for the self-steering (not ONLY seven tubes left, as was the cry as we neared Australia). I'm worried about being rolled most of all I think.

It'll be light in another three hours (at 03.00), it's easier to judge in the daylight. It'll be tricky at the Horn, now only about eight days away if all goes well. Is it this sense of uncertainty which I find so compelling? I'll soon calm down if we break another tube.

John — Day 129, Friday January 6

(Day's run 174 nm)

Quite a bumpy time. 18,000 miles out of Ardmore. Wind up to SW9 or more in the night. At 22.15 the stern generator line fouled the wind vane, and we came up beam-on to a howling gale. When daylight came the seas had grown and were marbled white. At 10.00 the port self-steering line chafed through and there was some crashing from flogging sails.

It was grand to be at the helm in high seas in this lonely place, singing me little heart out at the wheel. The brilliant flashes of grandeur make up for the immense monotony and claustrophobia. It's all worthwhile — grand to feel that now and then.

John — Day 130, Saturday January 7

(Day's run 151 nm)

Black hail squalls batter in. Great wintry black clouds with ragged hazy and ill-defined tops — like winter at home. The wind rises from 4 to 8 or 9 in seconds.

Alone on deck, singing Jimmy Durante's 'Lost Chord' I felt completely happy. This is the finest sailing in the world. I disconnected the Aries and steered by hand. Patches of blue sky, racing clouds, wild blue seas and lots of foam. All I ever wanted from life. What was it the Aran Islanders said about the white-topped waves in the bay? 'The white horses are running in my garden'?

Alone with this super machine driving for the Horn. Fulfilled. There isn't any more.

Andy — Day 130

We've had two days of squally showers, some with hail, and a spate of problems with the self-steering. The steering lines are chafing badly in the harsh conditions. First one line broke throwing the boat into sail-flapping confusion, so I replaced it and the rope around the wheel drum. Then tonight the other line snapped.

Hanging over the stern is not pleasant especially when blowing about force 8. Heading downwind eases the splashes which threaten to shoot up my trousers. John steered north-east but kept drifting back on course not wishing to lose any distance until I growled that he would be hanging over the back if I got a soaking.

* * *

I occupied the storm-tossed days reading many accounts of rounding the Horn under sail. Undoubtedly the stories which attract a writer's attention are the ones fraught with ice, gales, fog etc. John was forever telling me to shut up if I began to recount the horrors.

Chichester recommended heading to a position 300 miles west of the Cape on the same latitude, in readiness for the final run in. So, using the Tamaya I have sketched a great circle from 50 degrees S to that point. As we head south the temperature is falling, and the hours of daylight lengthen. No snow has fallen but hail showers accompany the 50-knot squalls which batter in, keeping us on deck.

John — Day 131, Sunday January 8

(Day's run 156 nm)

Rolling along on our flightpath for the Horn, 689 miles to the SE at noon. We plan to come down in a curve and be on the same latitude as the Horn while still 300 miles to the west of it. This is what the old clipper Captains recommend in my *Ocean Passage for the World*. I think we are a bit cautious now, content with 150 miles per day, rather than pushing for all speed. I'm sure it's right.

Both of us are pleased with the drama unfolding before us as we near the Horn, then there is the Le Maire Straits and the Falklands after that. Then Home 56 days beyond...

It is a time for caution. Most soldiers are killed through carelessness on the RETURN from a patrol into enemy territory...

Andy — Day 131

John raised the mainsail this morning, the first time it has seen daylight this week.

Our ETA at Cape Horn is Friday 13th, I am not superstitious but I wouldn't mind rounding it on another day.

* * *

For six days we had sailed with storm sails. The weather was reminiscent of the Indian Ocean where gales were tagged together.

Except in the approach to Cape Horn the gales rarely blew from the West preferring to batter us from abeam.

The day of moderate weather allowed another thorough inspection of the Aries. The Aquair spinner needed a bolt through its neck like Frankenstein.

John — Day 132, Monday January 9

(Day's run 166 nm)

Andy and I took down the double-reefed mainsail at 05.30, then at 08.10 we put up the No 2 yankee supersail in place of the No 3 yankee.

I was shaving in the after heads, without a stitch on, when at 11.44, the fourth sacrificial tube broke on the self-steering with all the accompanying pandemonium. Andy was out of his bunk in a flash, into his oilskins and out to the wheel. The officer of the watch (me), took much longer... I got all wrapped up and then took the wheel, while Andy went below to get dressed in warm gear to begin the fitting of the fifth tube (only six left now).

We put the No 3 yankee back in place of the No 2 and then the trisail went up for a while, and down again. The wind stayed at force 8–9 all day. Seas confused. By the chart table at night the tension makes my cheeks ache.

John — Day 133, Tuesday January 10

(Day's run 171 nm)

Much bigger seas. Fear chance of capsize. Self-steering in jeopardy. Grey day. White surf. Confused swells. Anything could happen, we hope it won't. Heavy on the nerves — nothing new. Unreel, then reel in. Stay relaxed.

At 18.40 we turned onto the 300 mile run due east for Cape Horn. Batteries under saloon floor breaking loose, Andy put more screws into the box to secure it.

Hope for daylight and a window in the weather for Cape Horn and up into the Le Maire Straits. And again at the Falklands. Better not let it occupy the thoughts too much. Wind moaning, boat rolling. Every 'n'th swell breaks, and pounds the boat. So far, so good. Quietly hoping.

The annoyance — then the sudden pleasure, to discover I've forgotten my post code, something so unlike me... it really is doing me good!

Andy — Day 133

The battery box under the floor looked as though it had come adrift again. Thankfully it hadn't but nevertheless I put three more screws into it. The extra screws have put an end to an irritating squeak at each roll.

After lunch, John laid out several detailed charts of the area surrounding Cape Horn and they are a marvel to study. Names like 'Beagle Channel' conjure a vision of the tough characters who defied the weather to achieve The British aim of charting every corner of the world. The artistically engraved plans give no hint of foul weather. On the contrary Tierra del Fuego looked an inviting cruising area, dotted with islands and inter-connecting channels. The Admiralty pilot tells a different story. Gales every other day, and that in summer, winter is worse. The wind funnels through Drake's Passage, the only gap between the mountains of South America and Antarctica. The ice limit is a mere 50 miles south of Cape Horn. I begin to realise why John dislikes reading such material. South America presents a vast barrier between us and home. Once round the corner, a straight line leads directly to Scotland, and it really will seem as if we are homeward bound.

We have to get there though. The waves are already becoming shorter and steeper (now we're crossing onto the continental shelf), tending to make *English Rose* surf. Another sacrificial tube on the self-steering has broken. I was in my bunk and John was shaving, neither of us was dressed for a lengthy speli outside. There was the usual chaos when the tube broke. John emerged from the aft heads, face lathered with foam, to meet me dragging on my oilskins over my pyjamas. I took the wheel for five minutes, while John dressed properly in warm gear, then he took over from me while I got dressed to reduce sail and replace the tube.

John — Day 134, Wednesday January 11

(Day's run 162 nm)

Rough and grey — ever anything else? About 90 miles south of the nearest of the Tierra del Fuegan islands at 10.00. By 21.00 they were only 50 miles north of us. Hope the wind stays west and visibility clears. Its a long time since that last sighting of land — a fleeting glimpse of the Canaries 119 days ago.

Icebirds are back, the icebergs won't be further south than the land is to the north. The odd wandering albatross visits us. Both excited. It's been a long trip.

John — Day 135, Thursday January 12

(Day's run 166 nm)

What a magnificent day! We had storms to see the Horn at its best. Went as fast as we could with much hand-steering. All the same we broke a windvane and another tube (fifth). Only five left now . . .

I sighted land first, at 05.30, Ile Defonso Islands. Grand to see green land again after so very long. A brown seal four feet long, or sea-lion I think, bounced along in our wake, far from land. It had a seal's tail.

Vicious black squalls brought snow at intervals, all day. We suddenly glimpsed the mainland of Tierra del Fuego around noon, through the squall clouds. As there were just the two of us, we decided to go in really close, hand-steering at high speed close to the Hermite Island. At last Cape Horn came into sight, just south of east, through the cloud and about ten miles ahead.

We passed along the face of the Horn, keeping about half a mile off and hand-steering in gusts up to 70 knots. The Horn was abeam at 15.20 — unforgettable. The beehive light is down near the shore. I can only think of the dramas which have been played out here in the past.

How wonderful it all is. We raced on, to the east, past Deceit Rocks, and then turned for home — NE for Ardmore. Past Barnevelt Island on up towards the Le Maire Straits.

It has been a long tiring day for Andy and me. 136 days and 19,000 miles out of Ardmore. The land could have been the west coast of Scotland in the spring, at 56 degrees south it is almost exactly the same latitude as Cape Wrath is north. All Andy's reading leads him to hope for 63 days from Cape Horn to Ardmore.

Very tired. Wild, wild, wild day. Oh how grand...

Andy — Day 135

A totally unforgettable day of squalls, arguments and excitement at seeing land again.

John's sighting of the Ile Defonso Isles annoyed me slightly, I had wanted to catch the first glimpse of terra firma. The islands soon disappeared behind another squall.

Eight hours later Cape Horn was abeam. Roughly hewn granite with not a trace of life, stark solid and lonely. John visualised a crouching lion, I saw only the rock, we were too close but 'so what' the photographs would be even better. Great Uncle Charles had seen this lonely outpost. He took the first published photo. I felt proud to be taking my own picture home. We toasted ourselves with a few sips of mead then turned north, for home. We slept soundly, in the lee of Tierra del Fuego. 8,000 miles stretch on ahead — it seems insignificant.

12

Turning for home

John — Day 136, Friday January 13

(Day's run 159 nm)

Well, we made it through Friday 13th. It was the reason for our dash to the Horn! A grand sail up the Le Maire Straits in gentle waters with some sunshine. Tierra del Fuego and Staten Island looking as savage as I remember them.

After lunch in the cockpit, with high speed hand-steering, the wind settled down to the strong SW gale, and we rushed on towards the Falklands.

At 21.30 I tried 2182 KHZ on medium frequency, and eventually R/V Hero answered from Palmer in Antarctica. Memories of *Punta Arenas* in 1972, and the view of Captain Lenie, her stocky Flemish-American skipper, on our plan to navigate the Magellan Straits in our ten-foot rubber dinghies. 'We sure hate to lose good men.' Very kindly the operator said they'd send a cable via British Antarctic Survey to Ardmore saying we had rounded the Horn OK.

Andy — Day 136

At our present speed we will be out of the Roaring Forties in a week. For three months we have endured cold and storms, now we are acclimatised. The thought of once again sailing in shorts is beyond my comprehension.

* * *

Our yearning for warmth and calmer waters triggered another push! We had hand-steered in the final few hours to Cape Horn, the prospect of rest within a few days prompted us to hand-steer again. North of the Le Maire Straits under the lee of Tierra Del Fuego the waves were slight. We sailed without oilskins, enjoying a spell of hand-steering under a warming sun. Over lunch the wind suddenly picked up forcing us to don our scarlet suits. We decided it was probably a weak squall lingering well behind the main body of squalls that had passed overnight. Over lunch, eaten on deck, we realised the squall was in fact the forerunner of the next gale. I was enjoying my spell at the wheel and assured John I could cope with reducing sail when the need arose.

Our speed climbed to a steady nine knots, surfing continually on the increasing swell. Half an hour later powering on at full speed the cold southwesterly was chilling my enthusiasm. I didn't believe the Aries could keep control for the few minutes needed to drop the main. A couple of rude blasts on the brass platelayer's horn intruded into John's rest. The horn was our helmsman's alarm, a crude arrangement which I doubted could wake me from a deep sleep in the fore cabin. Fortunately it alerted John, and with both of us on deck the main was soon dropped, allowing the Aries to take control.

Hand steering through squalls became our practice over the remaining short period in the Forties. Previously we had kept the sail area small enough to handle squalls, contenting ourselves with a slower speed in between, and saving ourselves from exhaustion. Now we pushed on faster, disconnecting the Aries and hand steering when squalls hit us. At night when on watch, if the weather turned squally I sat at the chart table wearing boots and oilskin trousers ready to leap into action. Pushing harder was tiring, our long nights in bed became a thing of the past.

John — Day 137, Saturday January 14

(Day's run 181 nm)

A great run of 181 miles in a 23-hour day, had us only 58 miles from the SW corner of the Falklands by noon, but we are well clear to the west. A fine start for the last leg home — we've come north like a bubble from a diver's helmet. Rushing towards a bit of sun to warm and dry us after 72 days in the Southern Ocean. I've a bit of a head cold, chill and sore throat at nights. On we go. Crashing north under the No 3 yankee and No 2 staysail which have seen so much action.

Andy — Day 137

After my early breakfast, I discovered the Aries about to detach itself, two nuts had worked loose on a mounting pintle. Bad weather tends to reduce our number of trips on deck, so we have no idea for how long it had been working loose.

The Aries was easily repaired without having to call John on deck to steer. A pair of molegrips, wedged to stop them turning, gripped the nuts inside the aft locker while I hung over the transom with a spanner to tighten the bolt.

During the afternoon I poled-out the No 2 yankee and began work overhauling its smaller cousin, the No 3 yankee. The piston hanks are in a sorry state, seven have needed re-seizing to the luff during the last few days.

Sitting outside, quietly absorbed in sail repairs, I thought of the Falklands lying a few miles to the east. We debated sailing up Falkland Sound to see Goose Green and San Carlos Water, a macabre sight-seeing tour. But the bad weather has put paid to the idea, just as happened to our planned look at the Antipodes.

My mind drifted on to planning my next boat, I imagined cruising round the islands and visiting the romantic area of Patagonia.

* * *

I nearly had to give my suppertime Leckerli to John that evening. We had discussed the barometer and I was sure it had fallen below 972 mb since the Irish Sea. I checked the log but was wrong. Fortunately for me John had refused to accept my wager.

A tin of the sweet Swiss Leckerli biscuits were put aboard by Walter and Ida Hafner for a Christmas present. We had one each after lunch and supper, a twice-daily treat since New Year.

Andy — Day 138, Sunday January 15

(Day's run 124 nm)

Now that we stand our night watches again I am getting progressively more tired. My lack of sleep has not been helped by changing the clocks an hour a day for three days running.

We only made six miles in six hours this afternoon. However the sea was flat so I was able to potter about without the usual rolling and slatting in a calm. I finished leathering and seizing the piston hanks to the No 3 yankee.

* * *

We hadn't changed the clocks for some time, preferring daylight an hour after midnight.

The human body is at its lowest at 2.00 am. Statistically more people die at that time of day than at any other, and despite our unnatural hours of sleep the early morning still found us at a low ebb. We decided daylight during those few early hours was a sensible safety precaution at the Horn. Fumbling around only half awake in daylight was infinitely preferrable to clumsiness in the dark.

John — Day 139, Monday January 16

(Day's run 100 nm)

Twenty-four hours of light N-NNE winds dropped flat at 07.30 and a fresh WSW wind sprang up in its place. Soon it was a gale, and I spent the forenoon taking down the sails Andy had put up before breakfast. By afternoon we were flying along with only No 2 yankee poled-out to starboard and the No 2 staysail goosewinged to port. By 20.00 we had covered 58 miles on the desired Great Circle course for 40 degrees S 35 degrees W on our track to meet with the old SE Trades as soon as possible, for a ride up to the Equator (after we've crossed the variables and the dreaded South Atlantic High of the first leg).

Much warmer already. 500 miles north of the Horn. Sunshine and following gale is like the trade wind sailing we look forward to. Soon we'll be able to cut ourselves out of our winter woollies and put on fresh clean warm-weather gear... grand.

My carpet slippers have been a real comfort for the old feet down below, even leather sailing shoes are uncomfortable if worn damp all the time, they are so encrusted with salt they never dry. The slippers are held together with black masking-tape wound round them. The polar jacket, trousers and Helly-Hansen blue Long Johns have been worn for two and a half months now. Luckily the paper knickers have been a great success, fresh ones every day or two. My long silk scarf round the neck has kept me warm, and I haven't worn a vest under my moleskin shirt at all — just the polar jacket on top and a Damart cowl hood rolled up into a hat mostly, or down over my head if cold.

In cold times on watch at the navigation table at night, I've worn the Henri-Lloyd quilted pale blue jacket; and in extra cold conditions the long quilted trousers with bootees on top of my socks. The large black Topsider boots have easily taken my socks and bootees on deck, and their otherwise cumbersome oversize has been worth it for these times. The Henri-Lloyd red sailing suit has done all that can be asked of it. With one of his scarves round my neck, to keep the drips out, I've been quite dry downwind all across the Southern Ocean. Andy and I have seldom got at all wet on the whole trip. Running off to change sail has been a grand idea.

No cabin heater and a lot of draught in through the main hatch hasn't bothered me much. The duvet on my bunk and a doubled heavy wool tartan rug has sufficied. Usually, I've taken my clothes into bed so they are warm to put on. I've avoided sleeping in my clothes, and a daily all-over wash with a pint of fresh hot water has kept the skin in good shape. None of the 'Gunnel-Bum' so rife in the 77/78 race. Flannel nightshirts are the thing, heavy and long, and the Damart hood is necessary in cold weather.

Andy — Day 139

John isn't his usual cheerful self at present, perhaps the trip, me, or not being able to contact Ardmore is getting him down.

This morning found us becalmed at the centre of a depression, which like the eye of a hurricane, is an area of light variable winds with blue sky overhead. Pleasant though it was, I found it an unnerving experience knowing there was wind all around and seeing the barometer needle hovering close to the sector marked 'Stormy'. I spent a few hours in the cockpit overhauling the No 2 staysail. All but two of the piston hanks required re-seizing to the luff, and several have a new leather patch underneath to avoid chafe.

John — Day 140, Tuesday January 17

(Day's run 153 nm)

Twenty weeks at sea. It's all much easier now. We no longer count the weeks, rather we try to enjoy the limited number remaining on this great adventure. To feel as we do, needs the 20 weeks behind us.

A grand sunny day. Milky pale blue deep ocean water again, we are just coming off the continental shelf. The price is a lack of real progress, but we are in a mood for the sun on our backs — and looking round the horizon. They certainly won't be having warm sun at home just now!

Andy — Day 140

As the temperature rises life is improving, this afternoon I took my shirt off for the first time in three months.

* * *

Note, it was the first time for three months that I wandered around on deck shirtless — my shirts had been changed several times below! The warmth dried my deck shoes, which, laden with salt had swelled with moisture prior to the Horn. I had had to resort to wearing sea boots above and below deck, cumbersome and not very good for my feet. I envied the slippers John wore.

John — Day 141, Wednesday January 18

(Day's run 151 nm)

When I came on watch at 02.00, Andy said there was something wrong with the self-steering. He thought he'd fixed it, but it wouldn't work for me, so I decided to take the wheel until 05.00, when he came on again in daylight. It was a peerless night, full moon of gold on the port beam, the first duck-egg shade of dawn coming on the starboard beam.

I went through the plot of the novel I'd been working on in my head, and decided there and then to write it before we got home... The first spell on the typewriter yielded 500 words.

A glorious day, so very much warmer, first time I've worn moleskin trousers since October. Up there on deck tonight, five sails, a full moon and the Southern Cross: the world is mine.

Malaysia 1968 was the last time I was away on MC's birthday!

Andy — Day 141

Shortly before 02.00 the Aries stopped working for no apparent reason. I called John up, and checked over the gear with a torch, but could find nothing wrong except for another loose mounting bolt that had nothing to do with its inability to steer. After a brief fiddle with the course-setting lines I thought it was working again, so I went off to bed.

At 5.00 am John called, then scurried back on deck muttering something about getting back to the wheel. 'Rather odd' I thought, 'he can't be hand-steering.' Quickly dressing, I saw John at the helm, from his expression and the musical tones drifting below he was obviously enjoying himself. It transpired the Aries was taking another rest, and John had decided to hand-steer rather than wake me because he wanted to see the sunrise.

I began to suspect this Aries was becoming lonely. Nick Franklin had advised talking to it daily. Whether I swore at it or praised it lavishly the reply was always the same: a series of groans and squeaks with an occasional wave, not very conducive to recounting my life story.

The fault, when I eventually found it, was not obvious. A pin connecting the servo-rudder to the gear had disappeared, allowing the servo-rudder to swivel ineffectively. It is a miracle the fibreglass paddle hadn't simply dropped off, though that would have been an easier fault to detect!

For supper John cooked curry again; it was tasty, but curry on alternate days is becoming pretty monotonous.

'How's the curry Andy?'

'Hmm, okay' I replied.

'Christ Andy do you ever give any praise?' shouted John. He smashed his fist onto the table with such force, that afterwards, I suspected the shock wave had probably started the keel bolts leaking. I began to reply, thought better of it and pretended nothing had happened. Out of the corner of one eye I watched his fist clenched around a fork. I hoped it wasn't about to come my way. We finished the meal in silence.

John — Day 142, Thursday January 19

(Day's run 167 nm)

Wind rising all day from SW until its a steady force 9 with a big sea. We changed to the No 2 yankee poled-out to port, and No 2 staysail. Good speed until after supper . . . too cocky (and seasick). We were pooped by a big sea over the port quarter, the next wave broached us to port. The No 2 yankee supersail went aback on its pole, then massive floggings had the boat heaving and stretching. CRASH. The pole breaks the heel track off the mast and the pole heel zips over the starboard rail. No 2 yankee supersail is burst along the foot at the clew. The spinnaker pole heel-track hoist on the mast is broken at the pole end, and the track fitting is left on the pole-end. The mizzen staysail halyard whizzes around with its snap-shackle, looking for a head to smash. Feeling a bit threadbare.

Andy — Day 142

Near disaster this evening, while running downwind with No 2 staysail up and No 2 yankee poled-out.

Accidents do happen but most are avoidable, we were pushing too hard again. It is always the same, if we try to sail just a little faster, something breaks. After supper we debated changing down to No 3 yankee.

Outside a full gale and more was laughing and shrieking, challenging us to a game of dare. There was no moon, clouds were scudding low overhead, the night was as dark as the inside of a tar barrel with the lid on. The 'speedo' needle twitched excitedly between 9 and 10 knots, peaking at 12 when the waves got their timing right. We rubbed our chins and fidgeted, neither wanted to be the first to give in.

As the wind eased perceptibly, our knuckles regained their colour, but we didn't notice the wind's change in tactics as it sneaked round a little more south.

The Aries realigned our course, taking the waves over the opposite quarter. I was sitting at the chart table, John was braced against the boot rack, and we chatted quietly about nothing in particular. As I got up to go to bed, there was a low rumble — there couldn't be a ship out there so what could it be? In a second the rumble of an old wheelbarrow became an avalanche.

We lurched, began to slide into a broach, then we were swamped under tons of water. A second onslaught caught the stern, slewing us sideways until the boat tripped over her keel. I thought a roll was inevitable. *English Rose* also thought about it, but then, deciding not to show off, she returned to an even keel in slow motion.

We tried to regain our composure then realised something was very wrong on deck. From the noise it sounded as though Neptune, disgusted at having failed to knock us for six, had leapt aboard to beat us to death with a sledgehammer.

We donned our armour, taking special care with the harness, and John scrambled aft to check the Aries while I crawled forwards. Neptune had leapt overboard leaving the spinnaker pole to continue his demented tattoo.

I flicked the yankee halyard off its winch, then John was alongside to help claw down the sail. We bundled it away half-noticing that the foot now resembled the tassled edge of the bedspread. 'Never mind, don't worry' was John's only comment.

We were shaken so much that we didn't bother to raise any more sail, preferring to see the rest of the night through at a paltry five knots. In our haste, neither of us had noticed the mizzen halyard swinging wildly, the heavy snap shackle at its end looking for an eye or skull. Miraculously the Aries was undamaged.

John — Day 143, Friday January 20

(Day's run 150 nm)

Out to put up the No 3 yankee at three in the morning. The solitary No 2 staysail is unable to push the boat at more than 4 knots. A huge lumpy sea throws me all over the place, adding to the physical and mental shock of the damage last night. I feel clumsy, weak, and incredibly ineffectual.

The voyage has reached an interesting stage, 143 days is far and away longer than any two people have sailed continuously before, the nearest singlehander would be back around Hobart now. We find it hard to concentrate for long. The statistics are a numb jumble.

Andy says we had gale-force winds on some part of every day in the preceding 13 before Cape Horn, and since then it has been a succession of gales.

Given a few hours sleep, a hot drink and a good wash, we are back in business as before. But are we? The passage of the days, weeks, months, spills into a blank wall of fog. How many times has that No 3 yankee been dragged up onto the foredeck?

Morale is the key. Keeping clean, sleeping well and feeding, are vital to the mental outlook which is in itself the index of efficiency. Slamming sails slowly induce headaches: so unwind the reel. Sunshine and smooth seas, with 7 knots of headway, smooth the knotted brow: so reel in again.

The above paragraph is pertinent to the future on land. There is no point taking on more than can be managed. There is more to be gained by a cheerful relaxed countenance than an impression of a busy fool. REMEMBER.

Andy — Day 143

I carefully surveyed last evening's damage and began planning the repair work. Straightening the mast track may be a problem, but fortunately only a couple of feet has pulled off. The two pole-end sliders were repaired this afternoon. The sliders are hauled up and down the track by a rope that runs inside the mast. Needless to say the rope snapped and pulled out making the replacement a tricky job. Lastly the sail needs repairing — about 5 feet of the foot has disappeared and the clew reinforcement is shattered. Being such heavy material the sewing machine is useless, meaning hours of hand stitching.

The breakage put both of us into minor shock. Until lunchtime we didn't feel like doing anything.

John — Day 144, Saturday January 21

(Day's run 166 nm)

'Are you awake John? It's two o'clock (in the morning!) the kettle's just boiled. I've just gybed. We're on 070 degrees. The glass has fallen one point.'

'Oh' (trying to sound keen and alert).

'Well then, I'll see you later.' Andy cowled in Damart hood, hunches his gangling and now ultra-thin 6 foot 3 inch frame, as he moves forward a couple of paces, and disappears into his sleeping area, a place which, as the forward sleeping area, usually accommodates six. Now, four of the five spare bunks are filled with red sail bags, sacks of onions, or other provisions. The fifth has been removed so that when Andy sits up with a start, in the middle of the night, he won't bang his head — and he does a fair bit of sitting up with a start. There have been 20 days so far this year, and gales on some part of 17 of them.

It's dark. I sleep on the port side of the saloon. There are 12 bunks, two of them double, on this boat, but I choose to sleep on a padded long seat, with a canvas lee-cloth on the open side, and my feet jam inside a cupboard against the main bulkhead. It's silly. Turning my head now, I can see the glow of the ring on the Shipmate paraffin stove. The fumes are in my throat. I will get up, really I will.

The boat seems to be sailing OK. The Aquair stern generator is screaming away in stops and starts. Somewhere outside, its extra-leaded, extra-long line, skitters from wave to wave. 'John?'

'John?'

'Yes' (brightly). Eyes unglaze.

'I just wondered if you're awake.'

Oh yes — very much awake' (wryly).

There follows a short discussion about the boat, proving to both parties that I am awake. There have been a lot of discussions about the boat in the past 140 days. Sometimes I wonder just how interested I am in sailing, certainly not as interested as Andy. He's asleep now. He won't be so keen either, when I wake him at five o'clock.

I never can find my socks in the dark. Off with the flannel nightshirt, and on with the moleskin shirt which I've been nursing in the bunk for the past three hours. Not so cold is it? Not as cold as Kerguelen. Stand up between the saloon table and the bunk seat, adjusting the polar wear duvet jacket, Damart hood. Slide the feet into the slippers, rigid with the coils of masking tape round them.

Totter to the companionway. The Aries self-steering vane slants from side to side, beyond the mizzen mast. It isn't all that dark. No sign of a ship.

Back down the steps. Flick 'waypoint 1' on the satnav. The pale green digitrs read 'W1 RL Brg 267M', then change with headaching swiftness to 'W1 RL 98.6nm'. I straighten up, leaving the pool of yellow light over the chart table, I drop down a step past the boot rack and the swaying oilskins, and come to a halt, gripping the hand-holds either side of the cooker. 'Isn't it warm? What's 180 from 267? What's 14 into 98.6? Pretty slow speed, we'll be lucky to make 150 miles by noon.'

This cup of tea idea is a new one. A reward for using only one ring of the three on the cooker for 144 days (AND never fitting the cabin heater at all!). We have used only 15 of the 55 gallons of paraffin. If only the local Customs officer had brought meths instead of white spirit at the start, all those months ago, back at Ardmore. It's more than 20,000 miles back now . . . Where was I? Oh, Yes well, if he'd brought the meths, we could have had all three rings burning. Ah, well mind you, that's about all we didn't bring though (positive thinking!)

Back to the chart table with the cup of tea, it's not the same out of a seven-hour-old flask.

Now I can get on with the three-hour watch. How many times does 14 go into 98.6? The Tamaya calculator will know.

My mind is wandering all the time: am I really as old as 45? Surely there won't be any sail-changing? We're getting well north of the Falklands — why don't they answer on 2182?

Marie Christine won't forget I didn't call her on her birthday. Well, I haven't called her since before Christmas; we were near

New Zealand then — no, well out towards Cape Horn.

Well, I'd better get the oilskins on and pump out the aft bilge. Can the position really be 43 degrees 37 minutes S, 43 degrees 37 minutes W?

Andy — Day 144

Now we are leaving the Southern Ocean I have started to calculate a few statistics to see how rough the Roaring Forties have been. The log shows the wind reached gale force 8 or above at some point on 40 days including 13 consecutive days prior to Cape Horn and 17 of the first 20 days of January. No wonder we are haggard and jaded.

This afternoon I spent a while up the mast trying to straighten the buckled track. The aluminium proved tougher than expected, so I sawed off the damaged section. Feeding a new rope down the mast was easier than expected.

* * *

The damaged track was eventually replaced at Ardmore, five months after our return. Trying to straighten the old piece was a waste of time, even in a workshop full of tools. The buckled section simply could not be straightened sufficiently accurately to allow the slides to run freely. We were fortunate that the two foot section wasn't vital. If a length of track for the mainsail slides had pulled off, we would have been stuck. I made a mental note to include a spare length of track on any future voyage.

John — Day 145, Sunday January 22

(Day's run 150 nm)

Felt rough these past couple of days. Some sort of chill. Fine sailing but sinus headache takes the edge off it. All I can do is keep trying to sleep it off. It'll pass . . . always does. Always does.

Not much to say, not keen to write.

Andy — Day 145

This afternoon's near gale was remarkable for its warmth; standing on deck with my shirt sleeves rolled up I felt no chill at all. John thinks it may have been a 'Pampero'.

John seems a little under the weather at present suffering from a sort of chill. I hope it isn't a bug on the lookout for another healthy body to inhabit.

* * *

Pampero's are violent thermal winds originating on the baking plains of South America. Several hundred miles offshore we were skirting the fringes of the shaded Pampero areas shown in *Along the Clipper Way*, so undoubtedly our warm wind was a Pampero.

Prior to Cape Horn I occupied a while tracing several maps of the Atlantic — one to show the routes taken by Chichester, Knox-Johnston and Naomi James, another one showing the traditional sailing ship route and a third to show the prevailing winds and surface currents. The various maps were uncluttered and easy to examine at a glance. By overlaying the sheets of tracing paper all the information appeared as though drawn on one sheet, allowing us to decide which route looked most promising. The books written by the singlehanders mentioned, as well as others, were read and notes made of significant points. We hoped to avoid all, or most of the pitfalls encountered by our predecessors.

Ice was eventually our overriding concern. The clipper route takes ships across a thousand miles of sea within the pecked ice-limit lines shown on the chart. It is the area where tabular bergs up to 200 miles long may be encountered. Such floating islands are not abundant, nor do they occur every year, but an encounter with one even a hundredth of that size was a dangerous possibility.

We held to the west. Our track through the Le Maire Straits and to the west of the Falklands had not been followed by anyone except the Whitbread competitors who stop at Rio or Mar del Plata. Their experience showed the winds inshore were likely to be light, further north a strong south-going current makes an offshore route prudent. We therefore planned a route along the fringe of the ice zone, barely touching the area of Pamperoes and rejoining the clipper route at about 30 degrees S.

13

A holiday at last

John — Day 146, Monday January 23
(Day's run 204 nm)

Goodbye to Southern Ocean. Second biggest run of the whole voyage at 204 miles. A good current with us. We did average 156 miles per day for 87 days. On and on!

I had a haircut, shampoo, wash and shave and changed into summer gear. Still feel low though, what a hell of a long trip this is, no way out, just keep on pounding away.

Andy — Day 146

Our second highest run took us out of the Southern Ocean early this morning. To celebrate I opened a can of ginger beer specially saved for the occasion since Christmas.

* * *

Chichester remarks after leaving the Southern Ocean, 'I think that anyone who sails a yacht in the Forties is a fool'. I felt a sense of fulfilment and pride, but it took second place to simply being happy. I aimed to enjoy each individual day, rather than gritting my teeth and counting the days till the end. My passion for sailing was rewarding, but not enough. Nature provided the support to my morale. I loved to watch albatrosses, and the clouds of icebirds, and I longed to swim with the dolphins. I fell in love with everything around me, even the gales that piled the sea into snowy mountains. The sky above became my crystal ball. Revealing all that had gone before, and all that was to come.

Not every day had been enjoyable, boredom had thankfully been rare but affairs of the heart had caused distress. I was sorry to be leaving the Forties and understood why John had returned.

Within hours we came across oil and floating rubbish. There had been no trace of man in the Southern Ocean. We were returning to a busy world.

John — Day 147, Tuesday January 24

(Day's run 144 nm)

A sunny day. Crisp and dry, for the first time in three months. A good spring-clean lifts things a bit; it seems forever, since things were really dry in the boat, funny how it can happen so suddenly. Now we are both hoping for a good wind to lift us through the Variables and into the South-East Trades. It'll be a close run thing for the 200 days.

Andy — Day 147

I gave the engine a quick look over this morning, tightening the alternator belts and checking for loose bolts. I also checked the water tanks: one is full, the other virtually empty. After lunch I continued work on the yankee.

John — Day 148, Wednesday January 25

(Day's run 82 nm)

Suddenly it is HOT — and calm. Sunstroke and prickly heat become the new enemies. Becalmed for much of the day, we got her chuckling along at 5 knots by nightfall, under the mainsail, heavy genoa and mizzen.

Great triumph of the day was Andy's discovery of the big boy [sail] as a ghoster in really light airs. The old morale recovers again, after a big anti-climax after Cape Horn. Man can be destroyed — never defeated.

21,000 miles out and all's well. Better not talk of it too much though . . .

Andy — Day 148

The few flies that have hitched a ride over the last past months, have taken the warm weather as a signal to multiply alarmingly. Fly spray is something I must add to my list of forgotten items to carry on another trip. To ease the insect invasion, we heaved a sack of onions, a pile of potatoes, and several cooking apples overboard. We are left with ten pounds of potatoes and a couple of dozen onions. The waste is annoying though not unexpected. Many of the vegetables were sprouting and due for consigning to the birds anyway. If necessary we can manage with Smash and dried onion.

Later I sorted through my gear, cleaning the mould out of the lockers. My clothes are dry, thanks to the plastic bags, but in need of an airing to clear the mustiness. I laid a couple of jerseys out in the cockpit as a start. My Exacta camera, an antiquity of only sentimental value, is damp. The Rollei is better cared for and continually in use, so it is intact.

While rummaging around I came across a brown paper parcel full of red kidney beans. Unfortunately they no longer resembled overgrown baked beans. The damp had reduced the package to a squiggy lump reeking of everything unmentionable. No wonder John's nose has always twitched when he comes to wake me. We had both assumed my socks were the guilty article. A thorough scrub with Jif has cleared the air.

For most of last night we lay becalmed with the sails slatting annoyingly, and knocking out the slightest whisper of a breeze. We lack a large ultra-light sail like a ghoster, which is sufficiently light to the unaffected by rolling in light airs. Even the light genoa is too heavy to remain filled at times. This morning I tried an idea that has lingered in my mind for some time. In place of the conventional headsails I raised the big boy. Nothing much happened until the limp mainsail was dropped to give an uninterrupted airflow. The garish triangle unfolded, wobbled a bit after its long rest, then remembered how to please us. We trickled forwards at half a knot.

When I woke John the sun was playing on the sail, filtering down to the cabin in a spray of colour. He looked at me quizzically, sighed and raised his eyebrows muttering, 'Andy what next', signifiying resignation to my latest unusual idea. After supper we dropped the big boy and raised the genoa, main and mizzen to catch a steady northerly breeze.

* * *

We began to use the genoas more frequently on the last leg. When coming down the Atlantic we had several times frightened ourselves by leaving the giant sail up for too long. The ensuing battle to keep it inboard when dropped in a rising wind had made us reluctant to use it often. Now back in the Atlantic we were well practiced in shorthanded sailing, handling the genoas was no longer a daunting prospect. Our method with all the headsails was simple. Alter course to a broad reach or downwind, ease the sheet a bit and drop the sail. Running off the wind reduces the apparent wind speed lessening the force on the sail. Running straight downwind will blanket the headsail behind the main, further easing the job, though risking an accidental gybe. Once the sail is on deck the original course can be resumed to avoid losing miles downwind. It was an idea I had not come across until John suggested it. Not only does the sail come down easily, the foredeck crew are saved a soaking when thrashing to windward. At no time on the voyage did John or I have to change into dry clothes after working on deck.

Another useful idea on the foredeck was the placement of lengths of shockcord lashed at their middle to the toerail. One end was finished with a plastic bobble slightly smaller than a golf ball, the other end had a loop stitched in, just big enough for the bobble to pass through. When a sail was dropped the elastic ties could quickly be whipped around it to stop it blowing over the rail. Because the elastic ties were attached to the rail the bother of trying to thread loose ties under the sail and around an immovable object was avoided.

John — Day 149, Thursday January 26

(Day's run 94 nm)

Pretty calm all day. Makes a nice change. Nonetheless, we are both restless to push on.

Unwind — reel-in. So it goes on. No success at all on the radio, what can we do? Maybe Portishead will come on when we get north a bit.

Finding it hard to concentrate for long on anything — as this log will show.

Andy — Day 149

All signs of the Southern Ocean swell have disappeared, tonight we are becalmed on a mirror-like glassy sea, even the stars are clearly reflected.

* * *

The wind was remaining light and variable and we seemed to be crawling when in similar conditions at home *English Rose* would easily slip forwards at 5 or 6 knots. We began to suspect the gooseneck barnacles under the quarter didn't stop at the waterline. A few days before, the hull log impellor had stopped, and we discovered a 4-inch long barnacle had made the plastic fitting its home. I am somewhat squeamish and found holding the slimy appendage so I could pull it off, a distasteful job making me cringe.

Years ago I read of Joshua Slocum's voyage in *Spray*, the first solo circumnavigation. One aspect of his voyage in particular still fascinated me — how he managed to navigate without a chronometer. His time piece was an old alarm clock boiled in oil! I scanned our navigation books for a clue but without success. Eventually a method was found in of all places, *Along the Clipper Way*! That book was a veritable mine of information.

Chichester recommended taking a noon sight as usual to find the latitude. The morning or afternoon sight needs to be a simultaneous sight of the sun and moon. Alternatively if the moon is not visible, two stars may be used at twilight. Since accurate GMT is not known, the first sight is given an assumed time. The interval between the sights will be short enough to count the seconds aloud if no stop watch is available. The second sight is given a time equal to the assumed plus the interval. The position for the assumed time can now be easily calculated and plotted. Now for the clever bit. Half an hour is added to the assumed time and a second position calculated and plotted. The actual position is then somewhere along the line connecting the two plotted positions. If that line cuts the noon latitude then 'bingo' a position is obtained without a chronometer. The position is of course slightly in error due to the sun not moving in a straight line. This error is small if the two positions calculated differ by half an hour or less, and straddle the noon latitude.

Apart from an occasional sight to check the satnav, my sextant had remained in its box for quite a while. I decided my brain was in need of a little activity so I hauled out my sextant when the sun and moon were visible. After one and a half hours of calculations I came up with a position only a few miles in error, using Chichester's method. I also calculated a correction for the chronometer by the same method. The mental stimulation was satisfying. I felt released from the constraints of time signals and quartz crystals. I could sail anywhere without them.

John — Day 150, Friday January 27

(Day's run 54 nm)

A calm so intense that going on deck at 02.30 was like walking into a hall of mirrors. No horizon, and the sky seemed a mirror too.

I got her sailing again as the sun came up at 05.00 Smooth sea, blue sky, warm sun. As I turned in, Andy went over onto the starboard tack, and we headed north. The shadow from the ripples, dappled the white paintwork over the saloon windows above me.

When I awoke after such a steady motion, it was 08.45. Andy had seen a 10-foot hammerhead shark from the bow, and an 18-inch fish by the self-steering gear. He climbed the mast to check the rigging, and found two of the eight rivets missing from the port lower spreader root plate on the mast; it was probably damaged when the spinnaker pole tore off its track on January 19. Andy spent the morning up the mast, lashing the reaching strut horizontally to both lower spreaders. Another worry . . . 'Toujours gai, archy, toujours gai . . .' as the Mehitabel cat said.

We're both lashing on the sun cream now. My prickly heat has started up on the calf muscles.

Andy — Day 150

John woke me at 5.00 am as he has on 150 previous occasions. Often I am already half awake but this morning I was sound asleep, tired after staying up for too long in the calmer weather. 'Come on, out of your pit', John's authoritive barrack square voice brought a dream of Marie to an abrupt end.

After breakfast I greased the engine control lever in the cockpit, gave the Aries a squirt of oil then sat in the pulpit to finish my dream about Marie. The bow is a wonderful perch, we sit with our legs dangling over the water, watching the bow wave curving away in a white speckled crescent. I sat gazing down, counting the tiny Portuguese men'o'war. As I watched a long brown shape drifted past, giving me a start. I rapidly leapt inboard realising a large hammerhead shark was nosing around. With a flick of its tail it disappeared to haunt someone else. Perhaps I wil give swimming a miss over the coming weeks.

I was itching for something to occupy me, stitching the yankee day after day was becoming a bore. The mast caught my attention, 'why not climb to the top for a bit of exercise?' someone was shouting from within me. I climbed and stayed at the masthead for a while gazing over the 280 square miles of ocean I could see surrounding us. There was not a thing in sight.

On the way down I stopped abruptly at the lower speaders. Two rivets were missing from the portside root fitting and several more looked on the point of falling out. It was a sickening discovery — would it mean stopping in South America or carrying on at the risk of losing the entire mast? I sat on deck thinking about it, wondering whether to tell John, I knew he would find the news depressing. Sooner or later he would discover the missing rivets himself, so of course I had to tell him.

I climbed up again to check whether it was really serious. Pushing against the spreader it moved appreciably, causing the root fitting to flex alarmingly. A few hundred more flexes would undoubtedly see the remaining rivets popping out like air gun pellets. The stainless steel fitting had slid down a couple of millimetres chopping the rivets like a guillotine. Replacing the rivets was impossible without slackening the rigging and lifting the spreaders to realign the holes. 'Well', I said to myself, 'I'll tell John but not until I can give him the good news that I can repair it.'

Some sort of bracing strut across the front of the mast seemed the obvious solution to stop the movement. I considered a wooden pole, then I noticed the aluminium reaching-strut strapped to the deck. The strut is used with a reaching spinnaker, to hold the guy clear of the shrouds. My tape showed it to be exactly the same length as the distance between the spreader ends. Also the light aluminium pole had a number of metal eyes riveted on, useful for tying it in place. John was awake by the time I went below, he took the news quietly, and shortly came on deck to see what I was up to.

I spent a couple of hours up the mast putting on numerous lashings, and padding the pole ends to protect the sails. This evening we are back to crashing along closehauled, and up aloft all looks well.

* * *

We were back into shorts, soaking up the sub-tropical sun to restore our faded tans.

Working on the yankee occupied many hours spread over a week. John offered to help several times but I refused his assistance preferring the pleasure of achieving something alone. I have a great belief in self-reliance. Some days I sat below listening to Dudley Moore and Peter Cook or some other tape. At other times I sat outside. Eventually the repair was completed. Our supersail was not quite as good as new, but nearly so!

John — Day 151, Saturday January 28

(Day's run 122 nm)

Last night was really rotten, we came head-on to a NE near-gale. Bumping and crashing into head seas all night long, the 'speedo' impellor kept being driven up into the hull, so it was out of action for most of the night. There was quite a bit of sail-changing as we had to come down from full main and No 1 yankee and working staysail, through to No 2 yankee and No 2 staysail and the trisail.

I felt very sick making a spicy beef supper at 02.30 in the morning. The fresh air has left us now, and it will be stale tropical mugginess for some thousands of miles. Eeh, Gum!

Windward all day, and self-steering tube No 6 breaks (six left).

At lunch, Andy said he was determined to reach Ardmore without stopping. If we failed, he would set out and try again, probably single-handed. Only about 6,000 miles to sail. Pretty threadbare, easily tired, back-ache as usual.

Andy — Day 151

I felt headachy and tired all day, having a disturbed night and morning sail changing and beating to windward.

The infamous 'tube' on the Aries snapped unexpectedly this afternoon. It struck another blow to our confidence, conditions didn't appear extreme. Perhaps the servo rudder hit a floating object?

Steady rain all afternoon induced me, despite feeling rough, to stand outside for an all over wash. It was freezing, I returned below hoping to find a brass welder!

John — Day 152, Sunday January 29
(Day's run 154 nm)

Unpleasant night. I find it hard — and frightening — changing down a reef in the mainsail on my own at night, in the pitch dark. My 23.00–02.00 sleep was ragged with rainstorms and lightning. We sailed beautifully on course all day at 7.5 knots.

I'm frightened most of the time — have I always been a coward? A coward is just a sort of species, nothing I can do about it. Always trying to overcome it, never succeeding. An endless game. Andy is not. He is young and doesn't waste time thinking about it.

Andy — Day 152

A heavy shower this morning enabled me to collect six gallons of rainwater in a little over 20 minutes. The main had one reef tied in so water running down the sail collected in the fold of sail along the boom, then poured out at the gooseneck end, into my waiting bucket. The deluge came in the middle of preparing a batch of dough. I nipped out to hang up the bucket, then returned to the galley to continue kneading, still dressed in dripping oilskins because I needed to empty the bucket into a jerry-can every few minutes.

Considering we are supposed to be in the Variables, the wind remains remarkably steady. On deck there is a little too much spray to sit out, though it has been cloudy with no sun so there is little advantage being out.

John — Day 153, Monday January 30
(Day's run 184 nm)

Out there in the dark, reefing the first and later the second reef in the main. My back hurts and it is absolutely black. After all these years, I've grown accustomed to 'getting someone else to do it' for me. When I can't get the tack-cringle ring on the hook on the inner end of the boom, I sulk — but there's only me to do it — and of course I can. I think about Rebecca at school, and hope she learns the same lesson early on. 'There's nothing good or bad, but thinking makes it so.'

Saw the first curtain of small flying fish today. Very hot in the saloon. Airless. 184 miles was grand progress towards the South-East Trades. Only 47 days left if we are to beat 200 days — it'll be a close run thing.

Andy — Day 153

47 days remain if we are to be safely home within our target of 200

days. Averaging 130 miles a day the mooring chain will be aboard with a few hours to spare. In the Forties we notched up a satisfying average of 156 miles a day. Unfortunately with two areas of Variables and the Doldrums to contend with in the near future our speed is likely to take a turn for the worse. 200 days was a purely hypothetical target, a nice round number.

Arriving home unharmed, still talking to each other, and with the boat seaworthy is the real aim. Nevertheless I will be disappointed to exceed that round number.

We saw a flying fish today the first for three months. The heat and humidity are becoming intolerable, oh for the coolness further south!

John — Day 154, Tuesday January 31

(Day's run 143 nm)

Magnificent day. Milky blue sea, closehauled under blue skies, in NNW force 3. How many others had such a lovely day? Cold at home, MC would love this.

The first realisation that the voyage is coming to a close. Fewer than 50 days left quite probably. Both begin to wonder if we'll get everything done in time.

We passed a couple of pink plastic floating buoys, similar to those at home — they probably came from Africa. I heard 'Cameroun News' on the radio last night, the first African station. We're coming HOME!! The next big event will be entering the HOME Hemisphere (N). Morale picks up again — it *always* does. Man can be destroyed — but never defeated.

Andy — Day 154

My back feels raw tonight, I spent three hours working on the Aries this morning, shirtless and without suncream. The sun hardly showed itself, we will have to watch out for sunstroke when the sun bears down all day. Several parts on the Aries had worn badly, hence the long overhaul. The spares box is almost empty of new parts, slightly worrying, although the old pieces were saved and can be rejuvenated to last a few thousand miles if necessary. All is not lost.

The lack of spray this afternoon finally allowed me to dry the mass of clothes I washed several days ago. Three months backlog of underwear, socks, trousers and shirts adorned every available inch of guardrail turning our graceful sleek ship into a multi-coloured washing line.

We dined in style at suppertime, baked ham with pineapple, baked potatoes and sweetcorn. Rounded off with Angel Delight and Mandarin oranges. A trifle more enticing than the corned beef hash and beans which I made regularly on the days between John's curries in the Forties.

John — Day 155, Wednesday February 1

(Day's run 92 nm)

Five months at sea. Cape Finisterre, Gran Canaria, Cape Horn, is all the land we've seen.

A hot muggy day, creeping remorselessly to windward through the Variables and towards the South-East Trades, which should carry us to the Equator. Andy and I did a lot of photography of daily routine in the morning. We've got to do it.

I'm enjoying the Sony Walkman again: Joan Armitrading, Don Maclean, Skye, Super Tramp, Vangelis.

At supper of pork and cranberry sauce (with my vinegar, lemon juice, two apples, sultanas, garlic, two onions, and peas and rice) we were discussing the radio problem. Then, before doing the washing-up, I switched the set on and for the first time the 8 MHZ had Portishead loud and clear. I told the operator I'd been trying for 30 days, but we were fading: he phoned Ardmore and gave them 'Position 26 degrees S 20 degrees W. All well.' He told me they were very happy to get it!

Andy — Day 155

A cheery card from home marked '1st Feb' got the day off to a good start. Mum left a pile of envelopes with various dates scribbled on, today's was the last. Obviously we are expected home before long.

* * *

My back had burned more badly than I first imagined and trying to sleep was agony. The coarse woollen blanket wrapped around the foam mattress scraped and tore at the blistering skin with each roll. After a hard night I begged a sheet from John's supply and the soft cotton gently massaged the pain away. Within a couple of days I was eager to be sunning myself again.

A lingering headache had taken the edge off my enthusiasm for several days. I suspected it was due to the stuffy atmosphere below and the unpleasant motion beating to windward. It wasn't crippling, forcing me to lie down, so I did my utmost to 'work it off'. There was the usual string of minor sail repairs including four more broken piston hanks and a couple of slides off the mainsail.

I also began to concentrate more on my writing. I had purposefully bought several thick pads of paper in Glasgow, thinking the voyage would be an opportune time to write about building *Kinnego* and my subsequent adventures as a novice singlehander. Trying to capture for the future the memories that could not be relived. I liked to write with a pencil, there being numerous mistakes to correct, not to mention at least three or four revisions before anything became coherent and readable. With the increase in literary activity the chart table pencils began to shrink rapidly. John noticed and accused me of eating them! I retorted, 'The lead is broken, whenever I sharpen them I have to keep sharpening and sharpening!' A feeble excuse but it avoided having to admit to my efforts to write.

My secretive nature was curious, like a schoolboy hunched over his desk with an arm hiding the work that his neighbour will eventually see anyway. I only wrote while John slept off-watch, if he woke unexpectedly the papers were shuffled away, I pretended to be working on the designs for *Kinnego*.

John — Day 156, Thursday February 2

(Day's run 77 nm)

Classic Variables. Black clouds with blue skies round them, and a breeze in and out from all directions. Very hot sun, and I fear I've got burnt.

We are so pleased with the radio contact home. Tonight we got Portishead again on 8MHZ but were unworkable for the phone.

John — Day 157, Friday February 3

(Day's run 54 nm)

Another day of tacking round the black clouds. I got a good shower and hair wash before lunch, off the end of the boom on the mizzen mast. Very refreshing.

Our day's run was a lot further than the distance made good, this was due to all the tacking.

I can get through to Portishead now at sunset, but by the time our turn comes up, they have faded again.

John — Day 158, Saturday February 4

(Day's run 79 nm)

Still in the Variables, no real change. Perhaps a slightly clearer sky. No birds, no flying fish, just calm seas. Slow going, to the Trades. Full mainsail and light genoa.

Got through to Ardmore for a 12 minute call to MC and Rebecca, at 19.30. Absolutely thrilled to speak to them. Bec fine at Gordonstoun. Jennie and Malcolm Sandals in good form. Keith Longney just arrived for the new season as chief instructor. Bookings good. New Land Rover due soon. Hurricane winds have demolished one of the buildings, and some roofing taken off our house — the usual. MC in good form.

Andy — Day 158

Becalmed yet again, these Variables are tiresome. Twice we have imagined the clouds ahead look like the Trades, each day the rain showers have returned. The showers bring a moderate breeze which backs, veers or boxes the compass. Occasionally we find ourselves sailing round in circles despite our efforts to maintain a reasonable heading.

The regular showers allow us to enjoy at least one, and often two, thorough washes each day. I have developed a passion for collecting rainwater, even the slightest shower beckons me on deck with a bucket. Today I washed the last of my dirty kit, every item of my clothing is now soft and fresh apart from the shorts currenly being worn. I hung out my oilskins to rinse off the salt and washed out the insides of two pairs of boots. Drying them without first flushing out every trace of salt is a waste of time.

The calm weather finally convinced us that the aft bilge was filling up from an undiscovered leak. The aft bilge has always taken in water, especially in rough weather when it floods in through the aft locker hatch. We pumped it as regular as clockwork, looking forward to a break when we returned to calmer waters. Only the break never came. With the floorboards up I discovered a fine jet of water at a seacock, ceaselessly filling the bilge for us to pump out. If only we had looked earlier. Dismantling, greasing and re-assembling was straightforward enough. The only problem was trying to stem the flow from the 1½ inch pipe while the seacock innards were out. I sat on the loo with a big toe pressed over the hole. It worked, leaving both hands free for the messy job of greasing the parts.

'We can't hear you Andy'. 'Well I can hear you fine, so tell me all your news' I shouted down the radio microphone to my parents. 'We still can't hear you Andy' came back their reply. I knew they would never hear me clear enough to have a two way conversation but if only they could realise reception at our end was fine. I was eager for news of home and Marie. I suppose if a voice over the phone is unintelligible, the listener assumes their voice will sound likewise at the other phone. Our radio can only push out a 400 watt signal, the reply from Portishead is sent with several thousand watts, so we can hear better than the recipient. The wasted call isn't worth worrying about, if I had realised the problem before leaving I could have left instructions about how best to use the radio calls.

John had better luck talking to Marie Christine. I admire his perseverance with the radio, every night since Cape Horn he has twiddled the knobs and listened for a reply. No-one answered until three days ago. John has a greater sense of responsibility than me to those at home. He doesn't subscribe to my idea of leaving the radio till we are closer to home.

I often wonder about returning home unannounced, assuming the radio remains silent. Sailing into Ardmore silently and without ceremony, our friends sitting down to breakfast then suddenly seeing us and dashing down the hill. A romantic idea of two 'lost' travellers returning unannounced.

John — Day 159, Sunday February 5

(Day's run 53 nm)

The wind took a holiday, today being the Sabbath. I dived off the bows a couple of times after lunch. Deep blue warm sea, but the boat quickly overtook me. I caught the alloy rope step ladder, and clambered aboard, over the stern. Fearful of sharks! Many gooseneck barnacles under the counter. I hope not elsewhere, beyond the few along the waterline. Becalmed at dusk.

John — Day 160, Monday February 6

(Day's run 72 nm)

After a big shower at dawn (05.00) a steady wind set in from NE and the black clouds made way for the fluffy white ones of the South-East Trades. We are in a NE offshoot, on the western border, but the wind stayed steady and we began to make progress at last. The wind should veer slowly to the east and then south-east, in the coming couple of weeks.

Conditions are idyllic, with the hot sun, blue skies and smooth seas. Slowly, my skin is settling down in this environment. Another six weeks of holiday, a month of running about without clothes. Feel relaxed and the old mind is turning over well.

At 19.30 it all changed. A big shower came through, and after that the wind died altogether, just twirling around every now and then. Ugh! By 21.00 it had settled again from the NE, and we were on our way again.

John — Day 161, Tuesday February 7

(Day's run 142 nm)

Wind veered a little towards ENE and we began to pick up speed north again. Having the forward heads' hatch closed, means it is stifling hot in the saloon. I did no writing heeled over to port, the typewriter has to be wedged up on 'Ocean Passages for the World' to get it level on that side. Andy and I are using all our patience, and just waiting it out.

John — Day 162, Wednesday February 8

(Day's run 142 nm)

Another baking hot day. So hot that it's not possible to do much more than just hang on and wait for the sun to go down. The light wind veered SE in the evening and cooled us a little. 38 days to 200 is not long.

John — Day 163, Thursday February 9

(Day's run 158 nm)

Cooler today as we have more wind on the beam. We are going fast except for the several rain clouds which go by — a few a day — but they do affect the wind, forcing us away to the west at low speed for maybe half an hour.

Eating up the miles to the Equator. Prickly heat not too bad. Will I ever run around without any clothes for a month at a time again I wonder. Seven months away from things is very calming at 45. Keeping the heart up.

Andy — Day 163

A prime concern of mine these days is trying to obtain an even suntan. Afternoons are spent sitting in the cockpit reading, smeared with cream and wearing a straw hat. An occasional light shower provides a refreshing cool wash. As we head north the showers are shorter and less frequent.

* * *

'The choicest sailing in the world'. That is the Admiralty's description of the South-East Trades. I had read the description months previously but was unprepared. After months of gales, a while passed before we were accustomed to the reality that in the Trades, force 4 or 5 was the strongest wind to expect. The anxiety of rough weather, such a burden for so long, shrank into insignificance. In the warmth we shed our clothes, I stopped when I reached my shorts. The rain kept us fresh, moderate winds ticked off the miles. We never sailed at high speed, just a tolerable average, I began to suspect whoever had written, 'The choicest sailing in the world' must, like us have emerged from the Forties. Though we enjoyed the relaxation, the wind to be truthful, was poor. Changing in strength throughout the day, our restful holiday was eventually spoilt by impatience. I found a large area of the South Atlantic 'dead'. The albatrosses were gone, and no other birds took their place for over a thousand miles.

Apart from my occasional headaches and John's back trouble, we remained remarkably healthy. However with the coming season at Ardmore rapidly looming, being just healthy wasn't sufficient. We needed to be fit, our legs in particular needed the cobwebs shaking out. I began by doing ten squats a day holding the shrouds for support, shortly after rounding the Horn. Ten a day increased steadily to 50, then 50 each watch including a few sit-ups on the cabin roof when the boat's motion allowed. Press ups were usually impossible and anyway of a bit of vigorous winching every day had kept our arms like iron.

John — Day 164, Friday February 10

(Day's run 139 nm)

A cooler day but very little wind, ESE in afternoon but its a very pale trade wind; maybe we haven't reached it yet?

We had a cold supper — making this the first day of the whole trip, without one hot meal in the day.

There were a few Portuguese man o' war jellyfish about, and dolphins at sunset.

John — Day 165, Saturday February 11

(Day's run 114 nm)

Another day of pale winds. We seem to have arrived when the South-East Trades are at their weakest. How different from July 1968, when they threatened to bring the mast down on the damaged *English Rose IV*.

It's hot and the radio won't get through to Portishead. Infuriating. Twinge of sciatica in left leg makes it painful to sit at the chart table. Always something.

Andy — Day 165

Nothing new today, the same heat, sunbathing, reading and writing. It was John's turn to prepare supper. Corned beef, delicately sliced, and garnished it with potato salad, coleslaw, sweet corn, peas, sauerkraut and pickled gherkins. All this was from tins and bottles, and it saved him a roasting down in the galley in this weather.

* * *

'Potato salad and coleslaw: do you really think we'll eat two dozen tins of each?' I was going through the stores list with Marie Christine, six weeks before leaving Ardmore. Several of the items seemed to me more appropriate to a vicar's garden party than a gruelling voyage.

'Well, take them, if you bring them back we'll use them up here. Oh, and while I remember, how much flour do you want?'

'You mean for baking? Hmm, well I can't bake bread and I don't suppose John can, so do we need any at all?'

'Who knows what cooking you'll try?' she replied with a twinkle in her eye, 'just to be on the safe side, I'll order a hundredweight of flour and three dozen instant cake mixes.'

'Yes MC'.

'Then of course you need yeast, baking powder, cornflour, custard powder . . .'

Marie Christine was a genius, even down to the smallest details of poppy seed to decorate our loaves, and a slim volume explaining the mysteries of kneading and proving the dough.

I read, then experimented, then re-read the instructions after each failure, and eventually devised a recipe which an expert might frown on:

3.25 cups plain flour (white or brown).
2 teaspoons salt.
2 teaspoons sugar.
1 cup drinking water.
1 oz cooking oil (guessed).
Dried yeast (equivalent to 0.5 oz fresh yeast).

I used a red plastic washing-up bowl for mixing and frequently doubled the above quantities to produce two good sized loaves. Heat is the key to successful bread-making: too much in the proving stage will kill the yeast, not enough, and it goes to sleep. By lighting the oven half an hour prior to mixing the ingredients, the hob would be sufficiently warm for proving when needed. The baking tins were left on the hob during this time. In exceptionally cold weather, one of the top burners would be lit to speed the initial warm-up, and then turned off during the proving.

Dried yeast is used in a variety of ways, depending on the make. Sometimes it is mixed in with the ingredients and then warmed water added. Another way is to add a little warm water to sugar and yeast in a cup, this will bring it to life over a period of 10 or 15 minutes. I favour the latter method, since only a small quantity of water is added directly to the yeast, and the remainder can be brought to the boil and poured onto the flour. As the yeast is not already mixed-in, the excessive heat does it no damage, and the flour is warmed to perfection. Cooking oil is used in place of fat, and on one occasion I used peanut butter but this was unsuccessful.

This is my method:

Mix the yeast, sugar and warm water in a cup, then put it to one side. Measure out the flour, salt and sugar carefully, then mix. Grease the baking tins, and dust with flour.

Sprinkle flour over the surface you are going to knead on.

When the yeast concoction is ready: pour the measured amount of boiling water (less what is in with the yeast) and the cooking oil, into the flour, then stir well with a wooden spoon and finally add the yeast.

Stir again, before finally turning out the mixture onto the

floured surface. At this stage there is a fair amount of flour about, so keep the windows closed to avoid a blizzard.

Don't be downhearted by the mess before you! The kneading will bind the ingredients, but it is hard work and requires a simple technique: start with a ball of dough, flatten it with the palm of your hand, fold the circle in half, and revolve the semi-circle a quarter turn. Continue flattening, folding and turning for about ten minutes, keeping your hands and the work surface floured to prevent sticking.

There are other techniques for kneading, but I found the above method successful whether becalmed in the Doldrums or beating into a gale in the Southern Ocean.

When the dough is to your satisfaction (assume ten minutes until experience dictates otherwise), divide it into rolls or press it into bread tins. Remember the dough doubles in size during the proving, and then increases a little more again in the oven, so don't overfill the tins. Proving is done on the hob, and traditionally the tins are covered with dry (clean!) teatowels. I favour sealing the tins in plastic bags to prevent draughts.

Now the next stage: determining when the dough has risen sufficiently, does require experience. So how does the first-timer manage? Fortunately the yeast is alive, and will say 'yes, I've finished' or vice versa, in reply to a nudge. Gently, make an indentation with a knuckle, and watch carefully. If the dent remains, then the dough is ready for the oven; it will have approximately doubled in size, and taken about half an hour to do so in a normal temperature. More time is needed in the Antarctic, and less in the Tropics.

Before putting the loaves in the oven, peel away the plastic, and paint them with milk or egg and sprinkle on a few poppy seeds if you are so inclined. We stopped using these tiny ball-bearings because they refused to stick, rolling into every inaccessible corner. Finally bake in the oven, preheated to 450 deg F, for half to three-quarters of an hour. The loaves are cooked if they sound hollow when tapped.

I found brown bread never rose well, leaving the loaves heavy and uninteresting, possibly due to our oven not being hot enough. Unfortunately the two jerry-cans of white flour wasn't sufficient to provide two loaves every four or five days. The solution was to occasionally use half white and half brown flour mixed together. Producing a tasty variation and using our supplies to best advantage. The bother of bread making was never grudged, we eagerly awaited baking day when the bread was usually still warm at lunchtime.

John — Day 166, Sunday February 12

(Day's run 134 nm)

23,000 miles out from Ardmore. Sciatica in left thigh to ankle so acute I did my two night watches in my bunk — stretched out. I kept awake by listening to a tape of *Kidnapped* by Robert Louis Stevenson.

Andy called me on deck while I was trying to get the radio to contact Portishead; it was 08.30 and he'd seen a school of whales. He first saw one shadowing us, under the end of the boom, out on the port side. Then he noticed the others, lolling about on the surface on the starboard side. Would the fellow under the boom end have attacked us, if we had been heading for the others? Was this a bull patrolling his harem?

A hot day with a steady E to ESE wind, but it's very light; will the belt of Doldrums be wider than usual?

My back improved after a couple of 'clicks' and some Distalgaesic tablets to relieve the spasm. On we go. Frustrated by lack of radio communications: unreel then reel-in, that's the way.

Andy — Day 166

'John, there's a whale alongside about 15 feet away!' I was startled by the mammal's appearance while doing a few sit-ups on the coach-roof. The creature must have seen me dive below to tell John and grab my camera, and then thought we weren't interested because it wandered off.

John — Day 167, Monday February 13

(Day's run 149 nm)

Hot again. We went off the wind a bit to make 22 degrees W at the Equator, and immediately noticed the loss of the breeze. These are the South-East Trades alright, but a very light version only.

The day passes with thinking and reading Bernard Ferguson's *Trumpet in the Hall*, which I'd first read when it was published some years ago.

I'm looking forward to the end of the voyage now alright. Still no luck with the radio.

14

Nearer home than Horn

John — Day 168, Tuesday February 14

(Day's run 153 nm)

Nearer Cape Wrath than Cape Horn — at last! Hot and humid, but still edging north, not far to the Doldrums now, maybe. The white cotton-wool clouds of the Trade winds are like sloping shell-bursts, they're so different from the towering black rain-clouds of the Variables with their skirt-like skeins of rain. And different again from the racing ragged-topped black demons of Cape Horn.

There is still the very occasional stormy petrel around, and we had the biggest flying fish of the trip so far, land on the deck during the night.

Andy — Day 168

The heat is interminable. My left wrist feels as though it is being attacked by prickly heat. We overtook the sun on it's northward journey five days ago, leaving it behind will surely see us into cooler climes soon.

The North Atlantic, our 'own ocean' is less than 150 miles away. Rain and gales fringed by the wastes of Greenland and the Arctic. Sometimes I wish the warm and cold areas of the world could share out their extremes of temperature to give a uniform temperature climate. But sameness is boring, nature has the right idea.

A giant flying fish crashed aboard last night, dying a noisy death in the cockpit. I stayed below till it had quietened down.

Star-gazing is my latest nightly pastime, initiated a week ago by the reappearance of the familiar Plough. Each night I look out, searching in vain for the Pole star. It should be visible, peeping over the horizon, but refuses to show itself. The Southern Cross no longer holds itself high, sulking after it's failure to draw us further south.

I did a little maintenance today, the batteries were topped up and the log impellers renewed. The manufacturers recommend replacing the tiny propellers every 5,000 miles, but ours lasted five times that distance and still appeared intact. Good old Brookes and Gatehouse. Of greater importance, I repaired the makeshift seal on the forehatch with another application of Life-calk. Since emerging from the Forties, hauling the genoa out repeatedly had pulled off most of the original sealant.

John — Day 169, Wednesday February 15

(Day's run 148 nm)

Writing this four miles south of the Equator under a full moon, between black thunderheads in the Doldrums. We have kept up a good speed all day, with very few calm patches, if any, after we'd both had a good shower off the mizzen boom at 8.30 in the morning.

The thunder and rain brought out the birds, a whale (seen only by Andy) and a school of dolphins, but it's muggy heat and we long for home. Still no luck with the radio.

John — Day 170, Thursday February 16

(Day's run 149 nm)

Moving well until 15.00 when the wind suddenly changed from SE to NE, very light then calm.

We had a 30-foot finback (?) whale round the boat at 09.30, which was fun. Some gulls, fawn above and white below, were darting down onto the surface, and there was the odd single tern and petrel as well as a few dolphins at night.

John — Day 171, Friday February 17

(Day's run 78 nm)

Blazing hot day of near-Doldrums calm. Bad lightning last night kept me away from the likely areas of strike: rigging, mast, chart-table, wheel.

Andy got the dinghy out and took some photos of the boat from a hundred yards out to starboard. In the afternoon we both had a swim with the snorkel and flippers, I pulled a number of gooseneck barnacles off the hull, by hand; they are up to 5 inches long and they'll slow us in light winds. There's a tiny pilot fish by our bow.

While diving I found a 5-foot scrape down the anti-fouling, along the port side of the top of the keel. We must have hit something quite hard. Was it the mess of seaweed, with something inside it, which we hit in the Southern Ocean on Christmas Eve?

Otherwise the old ship is in good shape, bless her cotton socks.

Maybe the biggest thunderstorm I've ever sailed in, after supper. Grand shampoo for the hair, from water off the boom, and massive lightning. There were 20+ flashes per minute for more than two hours. Is it related to the full moon?

Andy — Day 171

Another day in the Doldrums. At first light I washed a few clothes including my thick Faroese sweater. The final thousand miles will be unpleasant enough without the discomfort of dirty clothes which lose heat.

The last fortnight has been relaxing, I feel rested, almost to the point of boredom. Revitalised and ready to start again. I like to think of this last leg, from the Equator two days ago to home as a separate voyage.

After the washing I inflated the dinghy to take a photo of the yacht becalmed. As I rowed out I gazed back at our home with affection. The flawless sleek white hull gently rising and falling in the moderate swell, breathing and alive. She is the first thing I have seen for months apart from a lump of granite and a few seabirds.

Safely back aboard I promptly dived over the pulpit for a swim. A school of tuna fish were leaping well clear of the water nearby making me think a shark was prowling around. It is a strange sensation swimming in mid-ocean with the seabed a thousand fathoms down. Staying at the surface seems a greater effort than in shallow water. I felt the imaginary shark watching the strange tentacled creature that was me. Without wasting any time I quickly hauled myself aboard again.

After lunch I had another short swim to inspect the hull. I was wearing flippers, goggles, and had a divers knife strapped to my shin for protection. The knife gave little sense of security, a couple of minutes was all my imagination could stand. John was braver and stayed over the side for half an hour, cleaning off some of our ample growth of barnacles.

The main disadvantage to swimming (apart from being eaten!) is being left covered with salt afterwards. Luckily this evening we sailed into a heavy rain-shower. I had nearly finished rinsing off the shampoo and soap suds, when a clap of thunder sent me scuttling for cover. I thought the world had ended as the boat shivered and my ear drums went numb. The bang signalled the start of a spectacular electric storm. The rigging answered the storm by buzzing tunefully like a child with a comb covered in tissue paper.

* * *

Maintenance was beginning to occupy my time again, checking the Aries and stowage. All the navigation lights had failed, and the Aquair spinner looked on the point of disintegrating. The mast lights had failed months previously — we assumed the plastic conduit inside the mast had fallen down, chopping through the wires. Instead it was the main fuse! After that discovery we had the deck light again, but unfortunately the tricolour masthead light continued to blow the fuse if turned on. Lifting the floorboards around the mast to inspect the wires and connections, I discovered that all were soaking wet. The VHF co-axial cable connector needed a thorough clean and dry, the other wiring was dried as well as possible but that was all I could do. At the masthead the tricolour light fitting was too tightly screwed together to undo it for a look inside. We resigned ourselves to sailing without lights.

John — Day 172, Saturday February 18

(Day's run 82 nm)

Clawing our way out of the Doldrums. A pale north wind allows us NW or NE, and we tried both during the day. A couple of Stugeron put me to sleep after banishing queasiness. I slept from 13.30–17.00, and it was the first good sleep in the afternoon for some time. I could do with a good night's sleep after 171 wakings at two in the morning!! I have trouble keeping awake in the 02.00–05.00 watch.

This voyage up from the Horn to the Doldrums in a month has somehow given me a feeling of mortality and an understanding of the Earth's shape: 40 degrees S, Variables, Trades, Doldrums, Trades, Variables, Home.

Andy saw a couple of 18-inch tuna jumping while I slept, and one of the hooks of the treble-hook on Chichester's spoon has been bent; maybe we had something on?

During the night I saw a tanker on the horizon, it was lying stationary, cleaning its tanks I think. Strange to see the presence of other humans.

Andy — Day 172

Two jumping tuna-fish persuaded me to troll our lines again this afternoon. When reeled in this evening one of the hooks had straightened. Had I caught a fish or a lump of wood? For supper I opened a tin of tuna instead of the real thing. But I did make a pint of real lemonade.

* * *

We carried the lemons for months without ever using one, stockpiling them as a medicine to suppress the dreaded scurvy, should we be struck down. Several were beginning to mould, some were lost altogether so I decided now that home was in sight we could do with a treat. My Penguin cookery book recommended peeling the lemons thinly then adding one pint of boiling water and a quarter of a cup of sugar to the rind of two lemons. When cool the rind is removed and the juice from the lemons squeezed out and added to the sugary water. The recipe concludes with the recommendation 'serve with ice', but even without it we found the tangy drink very refreshing.

John — Day 173, Sunday February 19

(Day's run 82 nm)

Gliding imperceptibly north-east, almost close enough to Africa to cross our outward track last September. We would prefer to be heading NW — or maybe we should be tacking N. The daily mileage is so small, and there is no sign of the North-East Trades.

Many smallish fish, about a foot long, are jumping around for most of the day, but we couldn't catch them with our spinners. One followed under our stern, in the shade of the counter, but I couldn't interest him in a hook wrapped in silver paper, dibbled from a broom stick.

The twelve hours of darkness is oppressive now.

Andy — Day 173

This evening I started the salad sprouter.

* * *

Numerous useful gifts found their way aboard — the sprouter was a present from one of John's friends. We didn't use it earlier, fearing it might consume gallons of precious freshwater. The clear plastic trays stack vertically to make a column the size of a large can of paint. A few seeds (we carried beansprouts) were sprinkled into each tray then a mug of water is poured in twice a day. After two days the seeds had sprouted sufficiently for harvesting. They found their way into sandwiches or were cooked in fried rice and curries. Like the bread and lemonade the freshly cultivated beansprouts were a delicious addition to our basic diet of tinned foods tainted by monosodium glutamate. To our surprise the sprouter didn't use vast quantities of water when at last we got around to using it.

John — Day 174, Monday February 20

(Day's run 70 nm)

Meandering N by E in a vacuum off the African coast. We made a tactical error, coming east instead of west, a couple of days ago. Pilot charts shows 0.5 knot current going SE and dead winds around and ahead. We tacked to head W in NW wind at noon; eventually we should find the wind veers NE?

It's very hazy, and the rigging is coated with red Sahara dust — I thought I'd seen the last of that. We came too far east! Push on, will we ever make it in a month?

Burns' Supper — Equatorial Supper — Circumnavigation Supper — Hope for North-East Trades Supper. Andy's haggis with bashed carrots and mashed potatoes. Plus two glasses of Marueen Lawrie's Chinon wine (the only alcohol we have on the voyage).

Andy — Day 174

We ate a multi-celebrational dinner this evening: Haggis, mashed potato and carrots. It was supposed to be a Burns' Supper but neither of us knows the correct date for that particular night so we included crossing the Equator and a host of other events in our party. John opened our solitary bottle of wine, and after two glasses my head was reeling as I drifted off to bed in a happy mood.

An alarming noise of grating gear-wheels coming from the genoa halyard winch made me think it needed stripping down again for re-greasing and oiling. Unfortunately it needs more than a smear of lubricant this time, one gear-wheel is cracked right across. The genoa halyard carries a greater load than the main so after a consultation with John I swapped the two winches. The damaged part may hold together — if not, we will have to think again.

John — Day 175, Tuesday February 21

(Day's run 107 nm)

Idyllic sailing: warm sun and smooth sea. But there is red Sahara dust everywhere, and we aren't getting very far. Still trying to get west and pick up the North-East trades. Oh, well.

John — Day 176, Wednesday February 22

(Day's run 103 nm)

We are in a desert! The red Sahara dust lies on everything. Africa is being blown away. We have spent nearly a week groping around in this haze. WHERE ARE THE NORTH-EAST TRADES?

For all that, it is mighty pleasant on a smooth sea with balmy days, and time to while away on reading a good book stretched out on a sail on the foredeck. At the moment the book is *The Walkabouts*. Usually there is no time for reading in my life.

Worried that we still have no radio contact. We are having some electrical problems: masthead light and steaming light failed, VHF a little doubtful, chart table light suddenly temperamental, and of course the big HF radio weak.

John — Day 177, Thursday February 23

(Day's run 121 nm)

Still we glide on, over a still featureless sea, seeming to get nowhere, just waiting, waiting, waiting, for an ENE wind to blow us home. I feel stiff all over with tension. Patience is everything.

Managed to get through to Portishead at last, and they passed a mesage, 'All well, transmitter failed. Position 8 degrees N 26 degress W.'

Andy — Day 177

As part of our spring-cleaning campaign the bosun's locker came up for inspection this afternoon. Like several areas of the boat the painted fibreglass has an endless desire to grow a coat of mould. No amount of scrubbing and washing with disinfectant inhibits the fungus.

Our latest spell of radio silence is over, I spoke to Portishead this evening. The operator complained about our transmitter over-modulating, whatever that means. However the polite chap had his wits about him, he noted the Ardmore number and a message 'All well, transmitter failing' to which the infernal machine responded by doing just that.

John — Day 178, Friday February 24

(Day's run 113 nm)

Called at 02.00 by Andy: big ship crossing to SE ahead. It disappeared safely. At 03.30 the Belgian bulk carrier *Federal Maas* bound with coal from Argentina for Denmark, passed across our bows. She sent a cable to Ardmore for us via Portishead, and I kept in touch with her until 16.55, when she was 149 miles away on 053 degrees T and still hearing us strength 3 of 5 on VHF channel 16 and 14 on high power. It had been at 09.00 when she'd first come up clear on 2182 MF for a test.

I sit at the chart table on a folded sheet to keep off the sweaty plastic, and in the evening I put on a 'T' shirt, but I find I don't like wearing clothes anymore!

We are in the North-East Trades now, but they are nice and moderate NE4, and we make 6 knots on 350 degrees T pretty hard on the wind. I feel a bit queasy so I took a Stugeron tablet at 18.30, just after changing the heavy genoa down to the No 1 yankee.

John — Day 179, Saturday February 25

(Day's run 155 nm)

Boat heeled umcomfortably. Long nights now. Wind howling in

rigging again. Some pounding. Stugeron. It'll be a rough go from here to Ardmore. Thick haze of Sahara dust continues.

John — Day 180, Sunday February 26

(Day's run 168 nm)

Crashing and banging towards the Azores. Both taking a few Stugeron, and hoping the boat holds together. Nothing to do now but hold on.

180 days is the equivalent of six years' worth of classroom lessons, according to Andy. I wonder if I've learned anything more than a few verses and a bit of extra patience.

Andy — Day 180

Our present situation, thumping to windward up the North-East Trades is reminiscent of the South-East Trades five months ago. Except this time I am avoiding seasickness with Stugeron, and the knowledge of home just over the horizon is keeping my morale up.

The low haze of Sahara dust which has obscured the horizon for some days has suddenly thinned, allowing me to pick out the Pole Star at last. My angled bunk is a great success.

* * *

The angled bunk was a delightfully simple idea that I regretted not trying earlier. By sliding a length of wood under one edge of the bunk boards the cushion could be angled to bring it approximately level. As we crashed along I slept in relative comfort.

John — Day 181, Monday February 27

(Day's run 172 nm)

Andy changed down to the No 2 yankee soon after midnight. Bumpy. Log is out of action for most of the time, as pounding forces the impellor up into the hull. We came out of the sand haze in the early hours and the glass shot up from 1,014 to 1,017 in four hours. Too cold to sit out for long, even though we are enough off the wind to make it an easier motion. Roll on.

Andy — Day 181

As we approach home I wonder what will become of my future civil engineer, yachtsman, unemployed? John is back to cooking curries again.

* * *

The sunny holiday was coming to an end, so too was the voyage. the temperature had fallen, requiring us to wear 'T' shirts and we turned over in our minds a piece of sober news grimly passed to us from a tanker. The south-west approaches to the English Channel had already experience 16 days of gales during February. Six days is the monthly average. Did that mean we were to expect a hammering or would the excessive bad weather clear for a lengthy spell of calm?

John — Day 182, Tuesday February 28

(Day's run 170 nm)

Wind fell away a bit during the day, and we increased sail to full main, mizzen, No 1 yankee, and working staysail. I threw away 132 pints of Long Life milk which has blown. It had done well, we had consumed 170 pints of the total before it began going off.

Slowly, slowly, must catchee monkey? Got the musty duvet out and aired the polar wear. Easier winds allow me to have my little sing-song on the after deck once again.

Andy — Day 182

The universal turning block, the only irreplaceable part of the Aries is failing. This block, through which the steering lines pass, is screwed to the cockpit coming alongside the wheel. The centre holes of its plastic pulley wheels have enlarged, allowing the wheels to catch on the block casing. With no replacement at hand the repair is crude. I simply filed the edges off the wheels reducing the diameter until they can rotate without catching.

* * *

The North-East Trades ran out of puff at this stage, two days sooner than expected. The weather was continuing its battle to defeat us, 200 days now seemed an impossible target.

John — Day 183, Wednesday February 29

(Day's run 89 nm)

Wind fell flat at midnight — bye-bye North-East Trades! A new wind, first from the north then from NW by W, strengthened during the day, over smooth seas with a long low northerly swell.

Days are passing. We only averaged 116 miles per day in the month of February (the next worst was September, 126 miles per day). Let's just hope we have a fair passage from here on. Sunny days — but we must get on home.

Andy — Day 183

We have definitely left the Trades, the wind swinging round to the north and north-west pushing us onto the other tack. The tack meant re-arranging my bunk to angle it the other way, thank heavens John didn't put *English Rose* about while I was asleep.

The calmer weather drew me out of my books and writing, to tackle a bit of maintenance. Several days ago I rewired the bow light but sailing to windward has caused it to fall again. I peeled off the black sticky tape around a connector to find it blackened from a

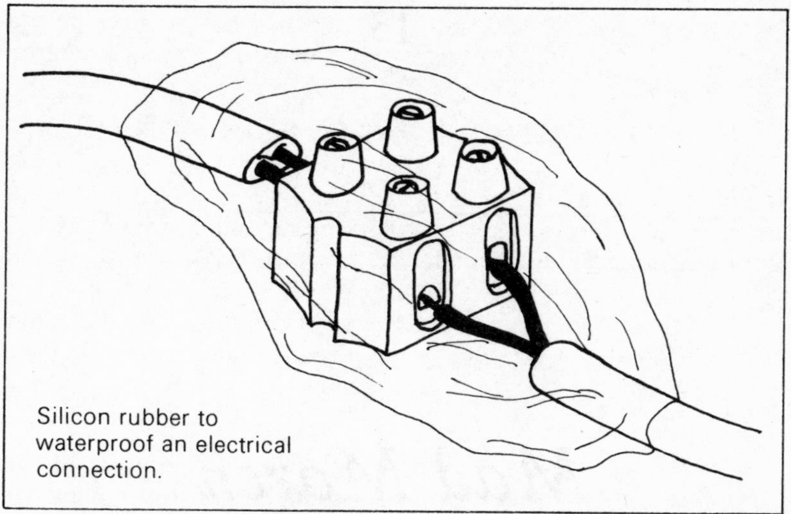

Silicon rubber to waterproof an electrical connection.

short circuit. Not surprisingly water had leaked in. With the connector replaced I liberally smeared on silicone rubber forming a ball, hopefully it is more watertight than tape. Checking and greasing the main steering occupied a couple of hours, because to get at it the aft cabin first needed clearing of spare sails, wood, plywood, rope and John's diving tanks.

The greasing was a messy job and I was happy to spend a couple of hours afterwards sorting through our spare rope. Several cardboard reels had reverted to a soggy pulp, spilling the rope into tangled heaps. Does it really need untangling? Home is within sight and none of the running rigging needs replacing. Unfortunately if I don't do it now the list of jobs back at Ardmore in preparation for the coming season will mount up alarmingly.

Sitting outside I thought about my future again. After rounding Cape Horn I decided that to continue earning a living from sailing would take away much of the pleasure. Working in another field, sailing would remain a fulfilling hobby. I realised that rushing back to sea on another voyage, shortly after returning from this one, could never be as fulfilling. Perhaps in five or ten years, when the memories are fading. I think any sooner would emerge as a poor second to rounding the Horn. If not sailing, then how will my bank account stay out of the red?

Civil engineering is the obvious choice. I have the relevant degree and it would provide a steady job. But is it truly what I want to do or do I simply want to conform? There is no point worrying about the question, as my Mother frequently says: 'something will turn up'.

15

Mad March

John — Day 184, Thursday March 1

(Day's run 140 nm)

Rushing through the night with the heavy genoa well eased out, for a westerly wind on the beam. By 05.00 Andy and I were up under the deck floodlight taking down the genoa and putting up the No 1 yankee which is filthy red with the Sahara dust. The wind strengthened all day, and by afternoon it was very squally, up to force 9 or so from the west. By suppertime we were down to No 2 yankee and No 2 staysail alone, and I was taking a Stugeron pill with Andy's Kipper Kedgeree with sweetcorn, peanuts, raisins and rice.

A huge swell is running and the squalls are pushing us north-east.

Andy — Day 184

An increasing wind required a steady reduction of sail, and by the afternoon we had squalls peaking at force 8 or 9. The first squall was quite a shock — it was the Southern Ocean all over again.

I made a batch of fudge this morning. Inadvertently I used twice the quantity of milk, so I had to add extra sugar, thus making an enormous panful of fudge.

John — Day 185, Friday March 2

(Day's run 156 nm)

A bumpy powerful NW wind with a high sea running. Onto the Stugeron again. We're surprised by this wind — it should be North-East Trades, not NW!

Too bumpy to write much. I don't like that howl outside. Rig: No 2 yankee, No 2 staysail, trisail and one reef in the mizzen. We're not sailing the boat as hard as in the Whitbread. I hope she'll keep on going to the end OK. Both in good form.

John — Day 186, Saturday March 3

(Day's run 168 nm)

Wild WNW wind continues at about gale force with a mighty swell. Stugeron: one at breakfast, and one before tea. Nasty taste in the mouth. Reduced sail at 16.30 to No 3 yankee with No 2 staysail and trisail.

Trying to think what it is I've learned from the trip:

1 'Neither good nor bad, but thinking makes it so.'
2 Remember the good things not the bad.
3 Accept the mistakes of the past. What's done is done — live for the future.
4 My little concert on the stern.
5 Seeing the planet on 'the magic carpet'. A better understanding of the rhythm of seasons and mortality. I should take a more relaxed approach to things in the future.

Andy — Day 186

Waiting, listening carefully to be sure a breaking wave isn't about to hit — then I quickly poke my head through the main hatch. When we are down in the troughs, nothing can be seen. A warning splash forces me to retreat, then look out again as soon as it has passed. Finally I strike lucky and we are on top of a swell, no splash, and I take a quick scan round the horizon for ships, then back to chart table for five or ten minutes before repeating the procedure. I wish we had an observation dome — then we could maintain a constant lookout without going outside.

How long can this storm last, and will *English Rose* take the hammering? Remember Tetley's trimaran broke up not far from here — he was rushing. We are carrying the smallest sails, heaving-to is the only way to ease the strain any further. But stopping now, how can we think of such a drastic measure? We know these last miles might prove the toughest. Try not to think about the spreaders, things always turn out alright. Or do they? CRASH — Christ! That one knocked the kettle from the stove into the saloon! John is awake, muttering 'What the hell are you doing Andy? My colourful reply is drowned by the next collision.

John — Day 187, Sunday March 4

(Day's run 170 nm)

Strong WNW gale eased and veered NW during the day. Keeping

on going. Duvet bed cover soaked in one corner in a bumpy night.

Andy — Day 187

A copper-coloured sunset with a tinge of red. According to Reed's Almanac that is a sign of wind. Have we really avoided the Variables? Can it be that 200 days is still within our grasp? What a thought, home in less than a fortnight.

John — Day 188, Monday March 5
(Day's run 159 nm)

NW wind pushing us a bit too far E. Still we are making good runs. 300 miles SW of Pta do Castelo on the Azores at noon.

Andy — Day 188

At lunchtime John refolded the chart. Ardmore now appears in the top corner, we are presently at the bottom. This evening he tuned into Radio 4. We really are close to home.

A Portuguese man 'o' war washed onto the aft hatch this morning. John stood on it! Somehow he touched the slime and has had to put up with an irritating sting since.

John contacted another ship this evening. The weather synopsis they passed on gives the position of the Azores High as just south of Ireland. Just our luck to have it lurking in our path, ready to steal the wind at the last fence.

John — Day 189, Tuesday March 6
(Day's run 166 nm)

26,000 miles out from Ardmore. A beautiful fresh spring day. Much sun and blue sky. Mares' tails too! A pale wind as we nod into the old swell at 3–4 knots. Hurrah! I spoke to MC briefly on radio at 19.30, she is delighted with progress.

Andy — Day 189

An interlude of calm has replaced the strong headwinds, enabling us to gather our thoughts and tidy up. Tonight we are becalmed and slatting.

John — Day 190, Wednesday March 7
(Day's run 88 nm)

Our speed was too good to continue all the way home. Light winds for yesterday, and again today I fear. We have started to clean up the boat, so as to look smart when we get in, and this is good for morale.

Skirted around about 60 miles to the east of Sta Maria. Radar not working. Tropical fruit mix and raisins run out.

Andy — Day 190

A slow day which is not going to help our chances of finishing within 200 days.

John began sorting through his kit — he suddenly realised it is packing to go ashore.

John — Day 191, Thursday March 8

(Day's run 166 nm)

Getting colder. The weather forecast on 'Farming Today' warns of snow in Scotland this weekend. I was woken at 09.30 by something tickling the side of my face, it was a small finch from the Azores which had taken refuge in the cabin. It stayed a while and then flew away.

We are washing down the inside of the boat, but the wind got up during the day, and by nightfall we have only the No 2 yankee and No 2 staysail still up.

Andy — Day 191

I had a shave today, not a total trim, just tidying the edges. I made a second razor yesterday specially for the purpose.

This morning bread-making and cleaning the wet locker occupied a couple of hours. This afternoon I sat on deck stitching a sail and greasing the piston hanks. I enjoyed a brief glimpse of the sun and the chance to escape from the confines of the cabin where I had begun to feel sick. Somewhere overhead a plane passed, but it was too high to see.

John — Day 192, Friday March 9

(Day's run 169 nm)

We increased sail at dawn, adding the mainsail with two reefs to the No 2 yankee and No 2 staysail. A good run makes it seem possible that we might make the shelter of Barra, and so get inside the Outer Hebrides on Friday March 16.

We were bashing into a growing sea all day, but still busily washing out the inside of the boat. I feel so keen to get home and run again. Andy very talkative and excited.

Managed to phone MC again and I'm delighted to learn that the businessmens' courses are all full for the coming year, and that we'll be running another series of courses for YTS. MC seems pleased with things. It looks as if we'll pick up Duff Hart-Davis of the *Sunday Telegraph* somewhere off Barra, he's hoping to fly up from Glasgow in a Sea King helicopter, maybe he'll come down a rope into our Avon dinghy if we tow it on a long line? Also it looks as if we may be talking to the John Dunn radio show as we sail up the coast each day, and ITN will probably be at the finish too.

This is all exciting stuff after 192 days at sea, but we must always remember 'more soldiers are killed returning from patrol than on the way out . . .'

John — Day 193, Saturday March 10

(Day's run 152 nm)

Still holding the course alright, but I'm concerned about the southwesterly movement of the high from Shannon. We may get NE winds as a result, which is just wrong . . . time will tell. A two-handed voyage from here to Barra at this time of year is a formidable task: keep the brain going.

Andy — Day 193

We continued our clearing up and hopefully the boat's interior will be spotless on arrival at Ardmore.

We are crossing the many shipping lanes in and out of the English Channel. Last night I spotted a ship which passed about a mile off our starboard side. The officer on watch replied to my 'All Ships' call on the VHF. We chatted for a while and he passed on several interesting facts. Our white deck light was clearly visible at two miles. The radar reflector gave a bleep on their bridge at a range of six miles. Then he added 'Ships generally switch off their radar on clear nights so you had better keep a good lookout'.

* * *

'Hello, is Marie there.'

'Yes, it's me.'

'Oh, hello, er, um.' After five months without contact or news, I was speaking to Marie. At the best of times trying to speak naturally over the radio is difficult, knowing a thousand other ships are listening. I was tongue-tied but we did manage a conversation of sorts. She wouldn't be coming to Ardmore as my parents were planning to do, so I promised to see her in Glasgow.

'Well, if she really wanted to see you' she'd drop everything and rush up to Ardmore' said John.

'Can't you see she isn't able to take leave from work just at the drop of a hat?' I stomped off to my cabin muttering to myself.

John — Day 194, Sunday March 11

(Day's run 156 nm)

Wind fell away but we kept moving north at 5 knots. Just found that one of the two alternator belts is broken, we only have one spare and that is much smaller than the remaining worn belt. The other spares are the wrong type! Something of a crisis now with radio.

Andy — Day 194

So near and yet so far. The wind has fallen light backing to north-east, right on the nose. We either sail further west or east.

Yesterday one of a pair of alternator belts snapped, the adjusting nut has seized so we will have to rely solely on the remaining belt. If it snaps the single spare can't be fitted without freeing the nut. John is finding the prospect of losing power and hence radio contact an increasing concern.

John — Day 195, Monday March 12

(Day's run 115 nm)

The wind backed to a northerly gale, and we spent the day thudding into a big sea under headsails alone — not a lot of fun I'm afraid.

Got through to MC at 17.00 at Ardmore. No chance of making it there before Sunday noon, and I doubt that too. What a pity we couldn't get there for the weekend, with people coming up to see the finish. All we need now, is a good break with the weather for six days.

Andy — Day 195

Shortly before 02.00 the boat was knocked down. I had been on watch since 23.00 occupying my time as usual with a little reading, writing my diary, and peering out occasionally on the lookout for ships. At 01.40 I went into the cockpit, checked the course and thoroughly scanned the horizon. There were no ships just a clear sky with few clouds. I watched a cloud up ahead — at night they often looked dark and evil. Time was ticking by, another glance astern to check that no ships were creeping up then I quietly nipped below to light the stove. The yellowy blue meths flame subsided, then another match ignited the vapourised paraffin, disturbing the peace with a steady hiss. It reminded me of a trapped serpent. The idea trickled through my mind as we trickled forwards, except that my ideas were going back — somewhere a serpent fitted in. The flashback was quick and in a split second I was at *The Serpent's Coil*, the book I had read months ago describing two Atlantic hurricanes.

A creak disturbed my thoughts, we heeled, then a furious roar from nowhere threw *English Rose* on her side. Then silence... except for a waterfall flooding through the hatch as we rolled upright. My moment of panic, fear of being trapped below, was replaced by action. On with a harness, out into the cockpit, yelling to John to dress fast.

I fumbled my way up the steps and paddled through the flooded cockpits. I grabbed the wheel to turn us downwind, but there wasn't any wind. No sound except for the water sloshing around my feet. I looked up, expecting to see a giant finger poised ready to push us over again. There was nothing. Not even the dark cloud. John appeared at the hatch fully clothed in oilskins still rubbing the sleep from his eyes after the rude awakening. 'Well, that was exciting', I tried to shrug off the fright as a joke but my voice betrayed me.

'Yeah, what do you think Andy?'

'I suppose we could drop the genoa, no point taking chances'.

'Bang goes my 2 o'clock leap into bed' I thought, 'still can't be helped'. We changed to the No 2 yankee and continued on without incident. Within 24 hours the light wind was a howling north-easterly gale.

* * *

The sudden and unexpected knockdown was for me the most terrifying moment of the whole trip.

John — Day 196, Tuesday March 13

(Day's run 139 nm)

Awful gale-force headwinds all day. What a cruel end to the voyage — headwinds all the way from the Equator . . . Reel out, reel in. Patience, patience, patience. Water dripping all over my bunk.

Good radio contact with Portishead, now on a daily schedule at 13.00 hours on 4 MHZ.

Bashing along under No 3 yankee, No 2 staysail and mizzen with a couple of reefs.

Andy — Day 196

Today was Budget day, instead of listening to the Chancellor on Radio 4 I tuned to Radio 1 and 'Steve Wright in the afternoon'.

* * *

Since coming into the range of Radio 4 we had listened to the weather forecasts hoping to glean some information. The land forecast always gave an outlook to cover several days. They promised continuing easterly winds, so our northeasterly gale looked set to remain. The forehatch seal began to leak steadily, filling the bilge. The aft bilge overflowed due to water coming down the aft hatch. It stirred up the bilge cleaner John had poured in several days previously, and the greasy water sloshed over the galley floor. The galley became a skating rink, and as we moved around the oil on our boots from the leaking drum in the aft cabin spread everywhere, leaving the cabin slippery and dangerous. We pumped the bilges hourly and the vigorous exercise pulled a muscle in my right shoulder, leaving the arm weak and painful for several days to come.

John — Day 197, Wednesday March 14

(Day's run 61 nm)

Clash with Andy over the lack of spare alternator belts, should we get Duff to bring one? AB — 'No', JR — 'Yes'. Desperately frustrating time with violent squalls and calm lulls. We are making little or no progress towards Barra, and morale is at its lowest. (Barra 031 degrees T 548 miles). We must just hang on and grit the teeth.

Worries: Keeping people waiting at Ardmore (people who've come a long way for the finish); alternator drive belt (if it breaks we lose contact with the outside world); missing the RV with Duff Hart-Davis (helicopter off Barra); worst of all . . . getting nowhere.

* * *

The alternator belt argument brought our frustration to a head. No progress in light winds, delaying our return to Ardmore, was cutting into the time available for Andy to have a holiday. It was the last straw.

Andy — Day 197

My patience is finally slipping. I suppose I shouldn't be surprised that we find each other's company tiresome after six and a half months together.

* * *

We had our first and only argument of the trip or perhaps more accurately I lost my temper with John. Why was I angry? John had arranged for a reporter to come aboard for our last day at sea. The planned intrusion during the final hours seemed wrong, robbing us of the completeness of circumnavigation alone. Of course he couldn't help with sailing the boat, but he would be a distraction. I told John I was keeping my fingers crossed for a violent storm since rough weather would prevent a pick-up. I couldn't give a damn about the alternator belt, the failure of which would also jeopardise the rendezvous.

My final outburst was a promise to John that I intended taking a fortnight's holiday regardless of when we arrived home. If the holiday interferred with the businessmens' courses, that was too bad, I needed a break. It was the first occasion in eight years that my voice had raised in anger. Normally quiet, and able to ignore a difference of opinion, I found John's continual nagging about the alternator belts too much, and lack of consideration for the girl I loved tipped the balance.

Afterwards I felt slightly ashamed of myself. It was John's boat after all. He paid for everything, except my clothes and waterproofs, so who was I to tell him where to go and who to pick up? After lunch I lifted the saloon floorboards to look at the seized nut on the alternator. An hour later it was free.

John — Day 198, Thursday March 15

(Day's run 41 nm)

All aches and pains with the tension of just getting nowhere, when we are so close to the finish. How cruel – there must be a reason, I wish I could see it and relax. The clash with Andy yesterday hasn't helped, we are both pretty tense with the waiting. The awful run of only 41 miles in the last 24 hours is driving me mad. (Barra: 034 degrees T 524 miles).

BBC 'John Dunn' radio programme, BBC York, and BBC Highlands: all live over the HF radio, on it goes.

Three sets of double sonic booms during the afternoon and evening. We need a break in this awful weather.

Andy — Day 198

The gale has passed and we are under way again, either north or east. The wind remains dead against us.

John — Day 199, Friday March 16

(Day's run 70 nm)

Another frustrating day of light fluky headwinds. At 02.39 (GMT) this morning we were on the latitude of Bishop Rock Lighthouse once more; 192 days have passed since we were logged abeam of the lighthouse by the Keeper on September 5 last year. Some trip.

Andy — Day 199

After lunch I hand-steered for two hours, trying to achieve every possible mile. I did the same yesterday. Although the sun was out I found sitting in the cockpit chilly, requiring numerous layers of polar wear.

I spoke to Marie again but reception was poor and static cut short our conversation.

John — Day 200, Saturday March 17

(Day's run 107 nm)

Moving well just east of north until noon, then away onto the port tack to run in closer to Ireland. The wind is exactly on the nose — from Barra. What can we do but keep calm and make the most of each day? How cruel. This delay is getting to poor Andy.

Andy — Day 200

A pleasant sunny day spoilt only by the usual contrary light wind. The radio suggests a change is approaching, probably equinoctial gales.

* * *

At the outset of the voyage sailing down the Irish Sea, a couple of piston hanks were lost. John suggested using shackles instead and I scoffed at the idea visualising the difficulty of screwing together 20 shackles on a stormy night. The idea lay dormant until the final week of the voyage. I began reading Adlard Coles' *Heavy weather sailing*, he recommended using a shackle at the top and bottom of a storm jib with hanks in between. If shackles were his recommendation then I supposed it must be a good idea. I checked over the storm sails for the last time, cutting the top and bottom hanks off the No 3 yankee, replacing them with large harp shackles.

John — Day 201, Sunday March 18

(Day's run 68 nm)

Blue skies and flat calm. Apart from conversation with Andy, the mewing of a flock of kittiwakes here off the west coast of Ireland is the first sound I have heard from living things on the whole voyage — except for an occasional angry squawk from Cape hens, as we nearly ran them over.

Big patches of oil on the sea, and our bows are black with the stuff, all along the water-line, where it has covered the weed-growth.

Miner's strike versus the police. Capture of McGlinchy, the INLA leader who is wanted for 30 killings and 200 bombings. The Boat Race has been delayed for a day, because Cambridge hit a barge and sank yesterday. Scotland win the Rugby Grand Slam. Just the stuff of home. There are so many other countries where you CAN'T disagree with the government, in the same way as the UK miners do. Andy and I feel we are in a spaceship, we could go on and on.

John — Day 202, Monday March 19

(Day's run 98 nm)

At last the wind fills in from the SE–S and we pick-up to 5 knots.

I spent my watches 19.00–23.00 and 02.00–05.00 out in the cockpit at the wheel, listening to Barbara Streisand, Neil Diamond and Don Maclean belting out their stuff on the Sony Walkman. I wore the full duvet suit and boots, with the Damart hood and a cap, The full moon came up at 02.00, first just a smudge of orange on the horizon, then lifting higher and higher into a golden ball. I'm feeling full of beans, but of course I got a head cold.

Gliding along all day. Spoke with MC on the radio and we are all set for getting in on Thursday mid-morning . . . what larks.

Andy — Day 202

Tomorrow will probably be our last full day alone, we expect to meet Duff early the next morning. In readiness for our passenger I spruced up the forward cabin and prepared a bunk.

Our spring-cleaning is complete and the boat's interior looks immaculate. Early this morning with nothing better to occupy my time I thoroughly cleaned the cooking pots, using steel wool and Jif to scrub off the black carbon. I worked in the cockpit keeping my binoculars handy to study several nearby fishing boats. I wondered if they realised where we had been.

The calm conditions seemed an opportune time to shift the unwieldy 75 lb anchor from the aft cabin to a more accessible home in the forepeak. The move was achieved without unduly chipping the varnish around the companionway.

What else needs doing? We are twiddling our thumbs. Relieved to have avoided a stormy passage up the Irish west coast but time is dragging. We hand-steer. I repaired the bow light for the third time in as many weeks, and we read. The radio is getting hot with frequent use, we were both interviewed by the BBC and there were many calls to Marie Christine, Marie and my parents.

We're eating well, still enjoying curries, spaghetti bolognese, and baked ham with pineapple. The tastes and habits evolved over six months are hard to break.

I've written a lengthy article about the trip, I'll have it typed then photocopied and send it to friends, avoiding numerous lengthy handwritten letters. I sit at the chart table, reading and re-reading it, adding and crossing out sentences in the search for perfection. But I'm impatient to write the last paragraph.

We have re-read 'Nobby' Clarke's letters sent to John from last July and August. 'Nobby' is the administrator of yachting records. We realised that since we hadn't 'tied the knot' — that is, crossed our outward track when homeward bound, the timings at Bishop Rock will be disallowed. 'What happens if we pick Duff up without first "tying the knot"?' John posed the question at lunchtime. We didn't know the answer, and the question preys on our minds. Will our voyage be disallowed altogether? I am sorry we haven't made the trip in 200 days or less, but never mind. So long as we arrive home safely within the next three months we will have made the non-stop trip faster than any other boat has. Though I must remember that that was a singlehander.

John — Day 203, Tuesday March 20

(Day's run 161 nm)

The pace quickens and I'm so excited I can't sleep, so I feel tired and headachy.

Good VHF with Malin Head all day. We slipped across to the east, to 'tie the knot' in our circumnavigation, six miles south of Skerryvore Lighthouse at 19.05 GMT.

Good SE wind with Duff Hart-Davis on VHF in Castlebay on Barra. Busy night on watch with many fishing boats between Tiree and Barra.

Andy — Day 203

Slowly but surely the wind veered to SE then S hardening to a fresh breeze giving us a 24-hour run of 161 miles, the best for ten days. We 'tied the knot' at five minutes past seven this evening.

Skerryvore light, the isolated granite tower off Tiree that we logged abeam at 2.00 pm on our second day at sea was logged abeam for the second time this evening. The light appeared flashing once every ten seconds at 6.00 pm, a perfect landfall after 8,000 miles from Cape Horn. We sailed well past the light, then tacked to recross the outward track a second time leaving not a shadow of a doubt that we had finally 'tied the knot'. We had sailed well off our route to Barra but felt the extra miles were worthwhile if the 'knot' satisfied 'Nobby'.

The fresh southerly has become another gale, promising a bit of fun at the rendezvous with Duff in the morning.

John — Day 204, Wednesday March 21

(Day's run 125 nm)

Marie Christine and I were married 20 years ago today. I'll miss the anniversary by one day.

Andy — Day 204

'Andy, I've just had a call from Duff on the VHF, they say they can see us' I had nipped below for a few minutes warmth after spending most of my 05.00 till-dawn watch on deck, keeping a lookout to avoid the steady procession of fishing vessels leaving Castlebay. The weather was foul: full gale and rain. I leapt into the cockpit expecting to see several smiling faces alongside, but there was nobody. Muldoanich Island was close ahead. I shouted down to John 'I'll disconnect the self-steering and take us under the lee of the island', a second later I continued 'I can see the boat John, they're here'. He looked through the hatch then disappeared to find his oilskins, before joining me in the cockpit.

The tiny Castlebay ferry motored round in circles guiding us to the island like a worried sheepdog. We waved frantically then felt a little foolish and began shouting, which proved useless in the wind. John slipped below, to describe over the VHF our plan for getting Duff aboard.

Our dinghy was inflated, thrown over the side and towed astern. A gust of wind promptly blew it back aboard snapping the Aries' plywood wind vane. Once under the lee of the island we found shelter and the waves diminished altogether.

John

John Alan Mcleod the lifeboat coxswain brought Duff out to board us in his Euroworker at 06.30. It was a cold stormy morning, and we hove-to on the north side of the island, letting the Avon dinghy drift down on a line to the Euroworker. Duff clambered into the dinghy and we hauled him towards us. He was cold and soon very sick as we headed NNE towards Neist Point on Skye. Andy slept while I managed the boat.

Soon we had a rough southerly gale behind us. I spoke on VHF to a 70-foot prawn boat, the *Prevail* of Gardenstoun, whose crew had read four of my books. Rather childishly this lifted by morale no end. It was so exciting to be involved with people again.

At 11.30 a BBC Television News camera team over-flew us in a blue and white monoplane. They filmed us for half an hour in dramatic conditions to the north of Neist Point.

I slept after a lunch of fresh rolls, cheese and tomatoes, washed down with wine brought aboard by Duff.

Andy

Over lunch I chatted with Duff, forming an agreeable opinion of him, which cleared my prior feelings of resentment at having to take him aboard.

While John rested after lunch I guided *English Rose* past Eilean Trodday and Ant Iasgair, names familiar from our pasage 200 days previously. Thoroughly enjoyed the intricate pilotage and grand scenery of Skye disappearing astern at a rate of knots. Once into clearer water I concentrated on our supper. Duff had brought steaks, wine, fruit, vegetables and bread to name only a few of the items in his box of goodies. I wanted our final meal to be a meal to remember, a meal to impress Duff and make him realise that we were used to living well.

The gale pushed us north at a high speed and we became concerned about overshooting Ardmore or returning too early, so we hove-to after supper.

John

Duff had recovered enough by supper to consume his portion of fried steak, fresh onions, potatoes and cabbage and a little more wine, this too, was all fresh stuff from Duff.

He and I talked through the 19.00–23.00 watch as we lay hove-to several miles off Ullapool. He turned in at 21.30, leaving me free to reflect on this last night of the voyage.

Andy

At midnight we were becalmed, and I began to worry about arriving late rather than too early. Marie Christine would not thank us for upsetting the elaborate welcome home we suspect she's planning.

John — Day 205, Thursday March 22 1984

Started tacking into Laxford early, to rendezvous with our fishing boat *Ardmore Rose* at 10.30. It was loaded with press people and Grampian TV were in a helicopter, filming for ITN. Sinclair's speedboat came up the loch too.

As we picked up the mooring there was a 21-gun salute from shotguns and a cannon on the shore. Schoolchildren and lots of people on the shore. We tied up under sail at 11.30 at our second attempt. Customs aboard. Lovely to see Marie Christine and Rebecca again. HURRAY! Champagne lunch. Grand dinner for 25 in the Wooden House. What a finish.

Andy — Day 205

By 2.00 am we were making steady progress. I handed over to John though I didn't expect to sleep.

* * *

The darkness paled into grey, then thinned steadily to reveal the coastline. The snow covered peaks of Stack, Arkle and Foinavon glowed prominently, above Ardmore. They guided us home. The wind had fallen light again, requiring more sail as we turned to tack up Loch Laxford. The Aries was disconnected and I took the wheel, easily handling the boat under small sails, while John attended to the radio. We waited until the message came over the radio that all was ready. Strangely, I didn't feel in a rush to sail in, in fact I could have waited for several hours. The sun was out, we were safely in Loch Laxford, and all the tension was gone.

Half an hour later the silence was shattered. A helicopter buzzed overhead, and Malcolm appeared in the fishing boat accompanied by a dozen press reporters. We tacked back and forth while the cameras clicked. There was another wait while the media men returned to Ardmore. The radio crackled again, everyone was ready. John took the wheel for the final run into Ardmore. Paddy's Isle slipped past to port, then the wind became fluky off the hills, forcing us into shallow water close inshore.

Our luck held and we skirted the rocks. I spotted Mum in the crowd, and I shouted and waved to her, then we were past and heading straight for the mooring. We hoped to pick it up under sail. On the first run in we stopped short, and drifted towards the salmon farm cages, before gaining sufficient momentum again for a second try. Another tack and gybe took us round in a circle. I reached forwards with the boat hook, thinking 'too fast this time John, but never mind'. Ten feet, five, I caught the buoy and flicked a turn round the cleat. Ashore a salute of cannons, shotguns and flares boomed across the loch. John dropped the sails then helped me with the mooring. The chain loop appeared over the bow roller and slipped around the cleat. That was the end of our voyage.

We smiled at each other, shook hands and were silent. A thousand memories passed before us. Then we realised we were no longer alone.

* * *

'Come on Andy, the trip's over', my father was trying to coax me down into the waiting longboat. I stood on the aft deck gazing at the badly-furled mainsail and the clutter below in the cabin. Then I sighed, climbed down to the boat and sat facing forwards as we motored ashore.

I had often imagined stepping ashore, being greeted by Marie Christine, Malcolm and Jennie. I'd enjoy a good night's sleep, pack a few belongings then hitch-hike to Glasgow. I couldn't afford the train fare and didn't believe anyone would rush to a remote corner of Scotland to greet us.

Instead, Ardmore was alive with people, all cheering and waving. Had they really come to see me as well as John? The trip had obviously given pleasure to others not only ourselves. The noisy welcome helped to ease my conscience of selfishness. Another cheer broke out as the keel grated on the beach. I leapt ashore first, scrambling up the grassy slope to where my mother stood. I didn't stumble or stagger, my legs felt fine apart from trembling slightly with excitement.

We talked and I looked around, enjoying the tickling smell of fresh creosote and hearing the familiar jangle of sheep bells. The school looked immaculate. Malcolm had obviously been working hard in our absence.

Our aim to make the fastest non-stop circumnvigation had been achieved. I was delighted with our time of 203 days, 3 hours, 20 minutes.

A buffet lunch followed and then I retreated to the fresh air outside to talk with my parents, and to say goodbye to Duff. The afternoon and evening disappeared in a whirl of tidying the boat, packing my belongings and talking. There wasn't time for reflection.

Next morning I woke early in my sleeping bag on the floor in Malcom's sitting room. My parents occupied the spare beds. Kicking the habit of waking at 05.00 took several days. Nobody else was up so I wandered along the shore, enjoying the little sounds we'd missed for so long. *English Rose* lay quietly in the middle of the loch. I looked at her with affection.

Had I benefitted from the solitude? Was I changed? I thought of the three principles John strives to develop in the people who come to his school. Self-reliance, positive thinking and leaving things and people better than you found them. My university years as a singlehanded sailor had developed these things otherwise I wouldn't have survived those early adventures, nor would John have chosen a crewman unable to take care of himself. I hadn't become aggressive or introverted, I realised with relief that my character had changed little in most respects.

These introspective thoughts were replaced by memories: the Sahara dust clouds, washing in the rain, the day at Cape Horn. Someone shouted, 'breakfast is ready', jolting me back to the present. In the morning sun I climbed the steep grassy hill to Malcolm's croft house. I was happy to be home.

After breakfast my parents and I said goodbye to Malcolm and Jennie. Nothing was ever too much for this generous couple. Whether it was beds for the night, varnishing tins, anti-fouling or tying down buildings in a storm, they always smiled. Their efforts had not only helped to make the trip a success, but also ensured the school was ready for the new season, now only a week away!

On the journey to Glasgow my thoughts were all of Marie. I recalled a saying she often quoted, 'If one is put on a pedestal, falling off is almost inevitable!' 'Yes', I said to myself, 'Remember you are still Andy Briggs. A little wiser now but basically the same quiet chap who left Ardmore in September. So keep your feet firmly on the ground'.

It was early evening when we arrived in Glasgow and found Marie's new address. I wandered around corridors and staircases clutching a dozen red roses. When I found her she looked just as I remembered her. And she could still smile at me.

John — December 1984

Nine months have passed since we landed. I found the McConnell rice much harder to cook on electricity than on gas: I don't seem to be able to get the electricity to go to a low heat fast enough. Andy's Mum says he has changed, is much more self-confident. I don't feel more confidence myself, but I do feel much more relaxed, up to now at least. I look back on the trip as perhaps the best I have ever made. Perhaps the most tangible result has been being re-united with my parents: this would never have happened without those long watches in the Southern Ocean.

English Rose VI was back to work for the school within a few days of our return. The boat is at her moorings under the wood, waiting, on the edge of the 'magic carpet'.

Appendix 1

Damage report

Andy

English Rose rested quietly at the mooring, only the dirty waterline, and the jury spreader betrayed that she had not been there all winter. The gooseneck barnacles were soon scraped off, and the hull polished until it gleamed. The galley, main cabin and decks were painted. The weight of spares was removed and replaced with the necessary gear for the coming season.

Whereas a racing boat might finish each leg of the Whitbread Race with a long list of expensive repairs *English Rose* needed only superficial maintenance after her 28,000-mile non-stop voyage.

The aluminium toerail had been worn by the shackles securing the headsail sheet blocks (see sketch). On our return, stainless steel plates were bolted inside the toerail, and a hole for the shackle pin was drilled through the plate. Simple and effective.

Two weeks into the season a strand of the 8 mm '1 x 19' stainless

Aluminium rail worn by the shackle securing the headsail sheet blocks.

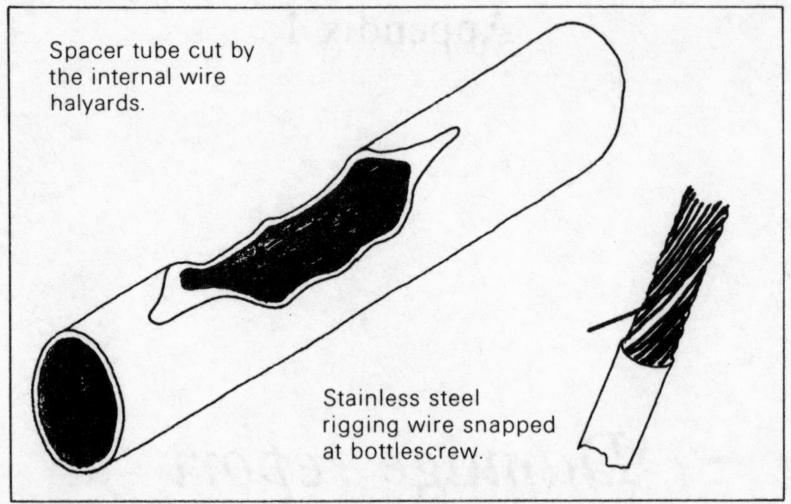

steel wire inner forestay snapped at the bottlescrew (see sketch). But it had survived 100,000 miles and it is the only rigging wire to have failed.

The mainmast had to be re-wired because the insulation on the wiring for the Brookes and Gatehouse wind instruments, the masthead light, and the VHF was worn through in places. The chafe could have been avoided by using rubber grommets on the mast conduit or by parcelling the wires with insulation tape at the conduit entry and exit holes. Unfortunately the conduit is 2 inches in diameter and so is too large to fit through a hole in the mast wall without unduly weakening the mast.

The spreader root fittings required new rivets. The two spacer tubes through the mast surrounding the bolts which secure the lower and intermediate shrouds, were replaced. These aluminium tubes were badly cut by the internal wire halyards (see sketch). The new tubes cost nothing, not even postage, and were fitted in one day.

Within two months the 'new' mainsail and the old No 2 yankee were torn. But the 'new' mainsail was not new when we left Ardmore on September 1. It had already clocked up 25,000 miles over the previous five seasons. But nothing was irreparable and I soon had the boat up to scratch with some help from Malcolm and the new instructors.

'Make do and mend!' That is the key to successful and affordable ocean voyaging. Whether the voyage is around the world or across the Atlantic. The wind really is free, and if you don't race, don't over do it and avoid the menace of chafe, your damage report will be as short as this one.

Appendix 2

Consumable stores

Andy

Marie Christine ordered all of our food, the following lists show the variety and quantity.

Although we carried 95 x 16 oz tins of baked beans and numerous tins of spaghetti we rarely ate these simple meals. The Stevens Lefield meals and tinned meats formed the basis of our evening meals. This was expensive but our voyage was not a two week cruise. The extra cost ensured the variety of good hot food which helped so much to maintain our morale. Some of the varnished tins showed traces of rust after seven months but we never found a 'blown' can.

The potatoes and onions lasted well, provided we sorted and threw away anything doubtful every three or four weeks. Most of the remaining potatoes and onions were thrown overboard after five months. But this was because they were sprouting, and spawning a plague of small black flies, not because they were rotting.

The waxed 10lb red Cheddar cheeses were a failure but the Long Life milk more than made up for the loss. We consumed 160 pints before the remaining 140 pints had to be thrown overboard after five months.

Fresh bread was delicious, we would have eaten many more slices than our self-imposed ration of four a day if we had taken more flour. But we hadn't expected to be baking bread.

We ate well throughout the 203 days and felt no ill effects from the lack of fresh food. At the end of the trip there was sufficient food still aboard to go round the world again!, and with our knowledge of catching rainwater, to supplement the freshwater remaining in the main tanks, we wouldn't have gone thirsty.

The excess of food and water possibly added several days to the voyage. With less weight we could have sailed faster in light airs. But, But, But... we did make it.

'Fresh' Foods

2 40 lb boxes, Golden Delicious apples
1 box oranges (88)
1 box grapefruit (50)
18 lemons (individually wrapped in foil)
4 cabbages
1 string of garlic
1 cwt box of potatoes
1 56lb bag of small onions
1 28lb bag of shallots (lasted well)
10 dozen eggs (mostly thrown away)
6 large white sliced loaves
300 1 pint cartons of Long Life milk

Stevens Lefield

20 beef goulash
20 beef casserole
20 spicy beef
3 mince and onion
20 chilli con carne
20 lamb casserole
20 lamb curry
20 turkey marengo
19 liver and onion
18 pork and cranberry
3 haggis
20 chicken supreme
20 coq-au-vin
18 boeuf bourgignon
20 lamb biriani
20 chicken biriani
3 turkey, sausage and beans
3 rice pudding and apricots
3 fruit salad
5 rice
5 noodles
3 beef casserole (two helpings)
3 chicken casserole (two helpings)
12 chicken curry

Tinned food

16 oz tins:
95 baked beans
12 ham

15 oz tins:
24 peach slices
24 vegetable salad
24 spaghetti
24 ravioli
24 potato salad
24 steak and kidney pie
24 steak and gravy
24 minced beef
48 Devon custard
46 creamed rice
36 raspberries
48 tomatoes

12 oz tins:
48 corned beef

11 oz tins:
48 sweet corn
48 Mandarin orange segments

10 oz tins:
48 garden peas

24 green beans
24 whole carrots
24 broad beans
48 new potatoes
24 grapefruit segments

8 oz tins:
24 mushrooms
12 strawberries
24 fruit cocktail
24 sliced pineapple

7 oz tins:
24 tuna fish
24 coleslaw
12 kipper fillets

6 oz tins:
24 Nestlés' thick cream
12 Tip-Top cream
144 Carnation evaporated milk
12 ham
48 bacon grill
12 chicken in white sauce

4 oz tins:
48 hot dog sausages
12 chicken breast
12 sardines

Tinned sponge puddings:
12 mixed fruit
12 raspberry
12 treacle
12 chocolate
12 strawberry

Drinks
960 tea-bags
15 boxes of herbal tea
24 4 oz jars coffee
40 beef and tomato Cup-a-soup
40 chicken Cup-a-soup
40 vegetable Cup-a-soup
40 tomato Cup-a-soup
192 hot chocolate sachets
12 750 ml bottles of ribena
48 1 pint sachets Rise and Shine
162 1 litre fruit juice

Sandwich fillings
24 4 oz jars, liver paté
24 4 oz jars, ham paté
12 10 oz jars, sandwich spread
12 8 oz jars, cheese spread

John McConnell rice recipe

1 Four persons (two if Andy and John) = 10 fluid ounces long grain rice.
2 Melt walnut-size butter in saucepan and get hot.
3 Add rice and stir until rice is coated with molten butter and get hot.
4 Add 12 fluid ounces of cold water to sizzle.
5 Add one level teaspoonful of salt and one bay leaf. Stir.
6 Bring back just to boiling.
7 Fit tight-fitting lid to prevent steam from escaping.
8 Cook on lowest gas for 20 minutes.
9 Do not remove lid during 20 minutes.
10 Remove from flame and leave to stand without removing lid for five minutes, and then serve.
11 Be precise in all this!

12 4 oz tubes, cheese spread
3 10 lb cheddar cheese (waxed)
24 16 oz jars, marmalade
12 12 oz jars, blackcurrant jam
12 12 oz jars, raspberry jam
12 12 oz jars, blackberry jam
12 jars, Nutella
4 7 lb tubs, honey
4 7 lb tubs, peanut butter
6 16 oz jars, Marmite
60 1 lb tins, Danish tinned butter
3 1 lb packets, margarine
12 3.5 oz tins, chicken in jelly

Dry Stores

12 cheese sauce mix
12 parsley sauce mix
12 white sauce mix
12 caramelle pudding
12 trifle
48 Angel Delight
5 1 lb icing sugar
24 sponge mix
10 chocolate sponge mix
1 7 lb custard powder
6 15 oz dried apple flakes
24 surprise peas (Large)
24 Green Beans (Large)
10 onion slices
2 2 lb kidney beans
1 large box egg powder
1 7 kg Cornflakes
20 375 g All Bran
48 Ryvita
24 bran crispbread
24 drums, oatcakes
24 150 g Hovis crackers
24 250 g Digestive biscuits
1 5 gallon drum sugar
24 11 oz Five Pints
3.5 2 kg Millac
12 750 g salt
3 1.5 kg porridge oats
1 3 kg currants
1 3 kg raisins
1 large box tropical mix
2 5 gallon drums muesli
1 small box cornflour
1 small tin baking powder
1 5 gallon drum brown flour
2 5 gallon drums plain flour
1 5 gallon drum self-raising flour
1 1.7 kg dried yeast
2 5 gallon drums long grain rice
18 12 oz Uncle Ben's rice
24 boil-in-the-bag rice
24 savoury rice
24 savoury curried rice
24 500 g spaghetti
36 4-minute noodles
72 medium smash
1 2 lb chicken bouillon
1 2 lb beef bouillon
96 packets dry roasted peanuts
3 tins biscuits for cheese

Extras

6 500 g cooking oil
1 5 lbs cooking fat
2 bottles, Lee and Perrins' sauce
1 bottle Tabasco sauce
2 bottles Soy sauce
1 half pint, lemon juice
12 half pints, vinegar
12 small jars, pickle
12 small jars, mayonnaise
24 12 oz tomato ketchup
24 5 oz tubes, tomato puree
1 half tube, mustard
12 4 oz Andrews' Liver Salts
1 selection of jars of curry powder
24 3 lb fruit cakes
herbs and spices

Miscellaneous

72 Camping Gaz cylinders
55 gallons of Paraffin (19 gallons used)
3 gallons of Methelayted Spirits (two gallons used)
180 gallons of diesel oil
400 gallons of drinking water (220 gallons used)
10 large bottles of washing-up liquid
24 pan scrubs
1 Gross matches
24 dish-clothes
6 bottles of Jif cleaner
2 tins of Brasso
60 rolls of kitchen paper
24 large boxes of tissues
72 toilet rolls

Appendix 3

English Rose VI: technical specifications

English Rose VI
Designed by Holman & Pye
Built 1975

Sectional view
F fuel (180-gallon tank)
FW freshwater (2 x 180-gallon tanks)
B batteries

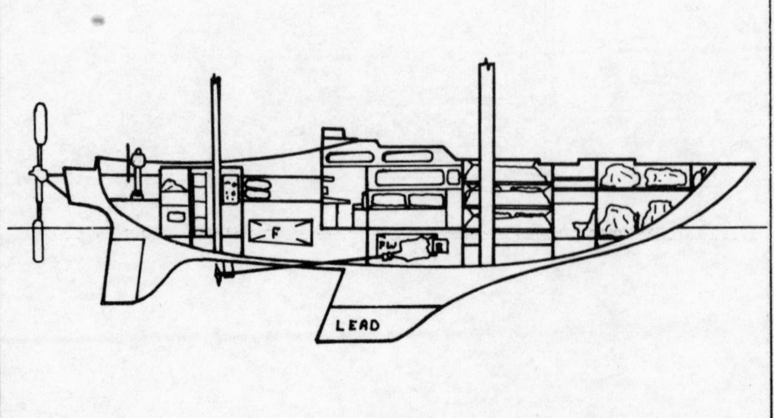

LOA *57 feet*
LWL *47 feet 6 inches*
Beam *14 feet 6 inches*
Draft *8 feet 4 inches*
Headroom *6 feet 6 inches*
Sail area *1,314 square feet*
Displacement *42,000 lbs*
Ballast (lead) *17,151 lbs*
Engine *80 hp Mercedes*

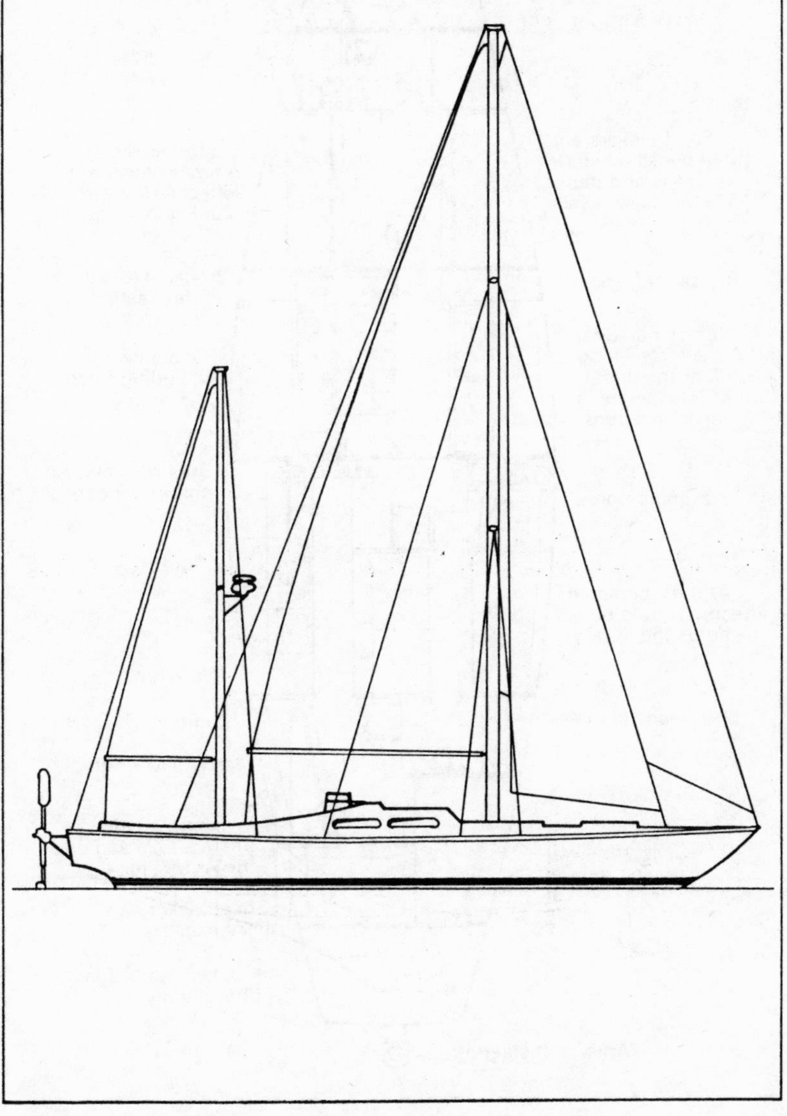

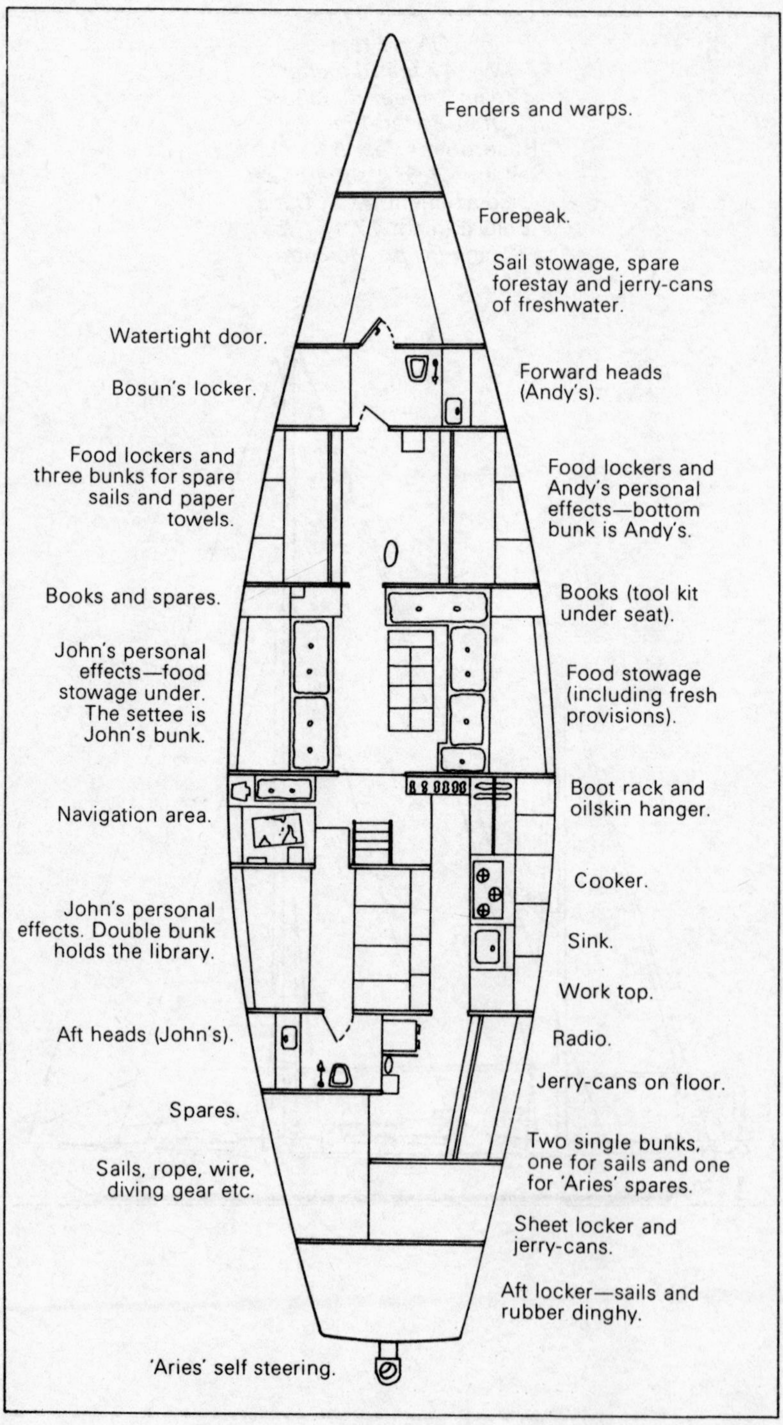
Fenders and warps.
Forepeak.
Sail stowage, spare forestay and jerry-cans of freshwater.
Watertight door.
Bosun's locker.
Forward heads (Andy's).
Food lockers and three bunks for spare sails and paper towels.
Food lockers and Andy's personal effects—bottom bunk is Andy's.
Books and spares.
Books (tool kit under seat).
John's personal effects—food stowage under. The settee is John's bunk.
Food stowage (including fresh provisions).
Boot rack and oilskin hanger.
Navigation area.
Cooker.
John's personal effects. Double bunk holds the library.
Sink.
Work top.
Aft heads (John's).
Radio.
Jerry-cans on floor.
Spares.
Two single bunks, one for sails and one for 'Aries' spares.
Sails, rope, wire, diving gear etc.
Sheet locker and jerry-cans.
Aft locker—sails and rubber dinghy.
'Aries' self steering.